VOICES OF CONSCIENCE

D1379299

Voices of Conscience

Essays on Medieval and Modern
French Literature in Memory of
James D. Powell
and
Rosemary Hodgins

Edited by
Raymond J. Cormier

Fairleigh Dickinson
University Library

Teaneck, New Jersey

Temple University Press
Philadelphia

Temple University Press, Philadelphia 19122

© 1977 by Temple University. All rights reserved

Published 1977

Printed in the United States of America

International Standard Book Number: 0-87722-090-5

Library of Congress Catalog Card Number: 76-15343

PQ
153
.V6

CONTENTS

v

EDITORIAL BOARD

It is the editor's happy duty to record his deepest thanks
to the following unselfish scholars who read and evaluated
the articles submitted for consideration.
John R. Allen (University of Manitoba); Anna Balakian
(New York University); Louis A. Brownstein (LaSalle College);
Douglas R. Butturff (Queen's College-CUNY); James J. Duggan
(University of California, Berkeley); M. Luisa Caputo-Mayr
(Temple University); Normand R. Cartier (Boston College);
Janet H. Caulkins (University of Wisconsin, Madison); Angel
L. Cilvetti (University of Rochester); Alan J. Clayton
(Tufts University); Giles Constable (Harvard University);
Joseph Danos (Northeast Louisiana University); Peter F.
Dembowski (University of Chicago); Anthony A. Francis
(University of Tulsa); †Jean Frappier (University of Paris-
Sorbonne); Frederick Goldin (Queen's College and Graduate
Center-CUNY); William L. Hendrickson (Arizona State Univer-
sity); George R. Humphrey (Temple University); Hugh T.
Keenan (Georgia State University); Douglas Kelly (University
of Wisconsin, Madison); Charlotte Costa Kleis (Temple
University); Frederic Koenig (SUNY-Buffalo); Norris J. Lacy
(University of Kansas, Lawrence); Raimundo Lida (Harvard
University); Marthe LaVallée-Williams (Temple University).
Also, Philippe Ménard (University of Toulouse); Diana
T. Mériz (University of Pittsburgh); Edward D. Montgomery
(University of North Carolina, Chapel Hill); Daniel Moors
(Princeton University); Stephen G. Nichols (Dartmouth
College); W. F. H. Nicolaisen (SUNY-Binghamton); Susan J.
Noakes (University of Chicago); D. D. R. Owen (St. Andrews
University, Fife); Jean Charles Payen (University of Caen);
Anthony Rizzuto (SUNY-Stony Brook); Barbara Nelson Sargent

(University of Pittsburgh); Howard Scherry (Hamilton
College); Eric Sellin (Temple University); Albert Sicroff
(Queen's College-CUNY); Nathaniel B. Smith (University of
Georgia); Louis F. Solano (Harvard University); Roger J.
Steiner (University of Delaware); Sara Sturm (University
of Massachusetts, Amherst); Marcelle Thiébaux (St. John's
University); Ruth Thomas (Temple University); and James J.
Wilhelm (Rutgers University).

It takes more than a love of words these days. Among the
academic advantages at Temple University is a realistic
attitude toward scholarly research and publication. I was
impressed to learn during my campus interview-visit in
1972 that the Dean of the College of Liberal Arts had most
generously recommended a subsidy for the publication by
Temple University Press of a memorial volume for James
Powell. Later, my predecessor as department chairman related his wish to hand down the editorship of the proposed
Festschrift, given the accord between my areas of speciali-
zation and those of his mentor, Jim Powell. I agreed; but
in the intervening months, we lost our colleague Rosemary
Hodgins, so that it then seemed most fitting to conjoin the
dedication of this book in remembrance of both losses.

In autumn, 1973, a call for articles was sent to a
number of friends, former students, teachers and colleagues,
as well as to many other leading specialists in medieval and
modern French literature. The response was impressive; the
numerous essays that reached us ranged broadly over topics
in medieval and modern French and Spanish language and
literature.

Of the fifty-odd submissions, I have selected only
eighteen studies; faced with the triple problem of balancing
quantity and quality, appropriateness to the volume's com-
memorative aims and my own personal inclinations, I suspect
that the choices will doubtless appear arbitrary to someone.
The readers' reports, what I had absorbed about Jim and
Rosemary's lives of academic abnegation and a certain concern for coherence and marketability were my guides.

I cannot deny myself the pleasure of thanking publicly
Dean George W. Johnson for encouraging me--not by words
alone--to inherit the stewardship over this undertaking;
the Editorial Board for their indispensable role; Professors
William Calin of the University of Oregon and especially
Larry Crist of Vanderbilt University for a critical reading
of the manuscript; and, finally, Mr. Michael Schwager for
his skillful organizational assistance and Ms. Gloria J.
Basmajian for a superb typing job.

Nor can I improve upon the two following biographical
eulogies, originally read before the College of Liberal Arts
Faculty at Temple University, spring 1972 and fall 1973.
They will serve as timely testimony for two lives whose
voices of conscience, I hope, are echoed in this volume.

Raymond J. Cormier

Philadelphia

JAMES D. POWELL (1910-1972)

Dr. James D. Powell died of a heart attack on March 18,
1972. In 1971, he had been inducted into the Temple University Twenty-Five Year Club.

James Powell was born in Pittsburgh on July 28, 1910.
He received his B.A. from Oberlin College in 1932 and his
M.A. and Ph.D. from the University of Chicago in 1933 and
1939, respectively. He served as Chairman of the Department of Foreign Languages and as Assistant Dean of Kemper
Military School in Booneville, Missouri, from 1934-42.
During World War II he was a special agent for the F.B.I.
as well as an officer in the United States Navy in which
he remained on Reserve Status until he retired in 1970 at
the rank of Commander.

Jim Powell came to Temple in 1946 as an Instructor of
Romance Languages. In 1956 he became Professor and Chairman
of the Department of Foreign Languages. He was chairman of
the Department until 1968 when it was split into five separate entities, after which he continued as Chairman of the
Department of French and Italian until 1970. Dr. Powell was
a member of the International Arthurian Society, the Modern
Language Association of American, and the American Association of Teachers of French. He was a past president of the
Pennsylvania chapter of the American Association of Teachers
of Spanish and Portuguese, and of the Middle States Association of Modern Languages.

The subjects he taught and loved were Medieval French
and Spanish literature, Phonology and Morphology, Syntax
and Phonetics.

The skeletal sketch of a life, as revealed by dates of
employment, associations of which one is a member, and the

like, is hardly adequate representation of this figure who
was so extraordinary a man in the quick. I can, without
rhapsodizing, say that James D. Powell was one of the most
intelligent men I have ever met. Anyone who tried to joust
verbally with him soon learned how quick-witted and knowledgeable he was. It was always wise to avoid making dogmatic
statements in his presence--although he himself loved to
goad his interlocutors with tantalizing cultural one-liners--
for he was an almost infinite storage bank of facts,
especially in the areas of religion, hagiography, and mon-
archical genealogy. The fact that this extraordinary
intellect was not dehumanized or alienated from the mundane
life is borne out by the pedagogical emphasis of Jim
Powell's career and by the devotion he inspired in so many
who studied or worked with him. In order to go beyond the
above-mentioned skeletal sketch, I should like to pass along
two personal accounts which bear witness to the vintage and
intensity of this man's humanity.

After the funeral there was a small buffet for close
friends and relatives who had attended the ceremony. It was
a ritual in which people were brought together for a moment
by the force which that man had exerted on their lives. It
was a harmonious moment that helped to alleviate the chill-
ing finality of the interment, for inevitably the strangers
brought together in the Powell home began to talk to one
another of the role Jim had played in their lives and it
was quickly manifest that he would live on in a real and
not merely sentimental manner.

A cousin told us that he had been raised by Jim's
parents. He said that it was not always easy being raised
in the same house with the brightest pupil in the city. He
said that his new parents were concerned when he was having
some apparent difficulty in mastering some material at
school. They decided that he must have hearing trouble and
took him to the ear specialist who pronounced him healthy.
They then took him to the eye specialist who said that his
eyesight was normal and that he had no trouble reading.

They were not satisfied and took the cousin to the family
doctor for a full physical and mental examination. After a
cursory examination, the doctor called the parents in and
said: "This boy is quite normal in every respect; your
problem is that you first raised that other boy, Jim, who
is so brilliant that by comparison you thought the normal
boy must be retarded or handicapped."

        People had journeyed from far and wide to attend the
funeral. One gentleman--a career officer in the Army--had
been one of Jim Powell's first students at Kemper. He spoke
warmly of the long friendship that had brought them together
from time to time. He told of how Jim coached him for his
language reading examinations when he had returned to graduate study. He further related how, when he was to sit for
an examination to be integrated into the regular army, Jim
took him under his wing. Jim gave him a reading list. He
said that Jim told him that he did not approve of the books--
which were of the College Outline Series variety--but that,
in light of the imminence of the examination they would have
to suffice. Jim coached his friend for a month or two with
the result that the latter did extraordinarily well in the
examination, placing among the top handful of candidates.
The only problem, the officer asserted, was that many people
asked him why he had been hiding his good mind under a
bushel basket all the previous years; in addition to which
he claimed that, ever since, his colleagues have felt that
he has failed to live up to his magnificent potential. As
he put it, modestly, "I owe it to Jim's tutoring that I
scored as well as I did, but unfortunately he did much too
good a job for me to maintain credibility."

        I could tell similar anecdotes about the role this man
played in my life, as could most who were close to him. He
could express anger and righteousness as well as any man,
but when he believed in someone and trusted him, his expression of that trust was unbounded and it was inspirational to
the recipient. He was like both a father and friend to many
and it was significant that the six pall bearers were all

young. There was no generation gap, save perhaps that sort of gap contrived by respect; and a paradoxical sense of filial amity grew on all of us who were fortunate enough to have the opportunity to work under and gradually to know well this man.

James D. Powell is survived by his wife, the former Virginia Salisbury.

Eric Sellin

ROSEMARY HODGINS (1925-1973)

It is with a degree of numbness that I eulogize Rosemary
Hodgins, for mingled with the usual sadness at the loss
of an esteemed and able colleague are a mindless anger and
many unanswered questions.

The passing of a ninety-year-old in peaceful sleep is
sad and leaves a void for those close to him or her, but
it is not tragic; however, the unexpected arbitrary designation of a woman in her prime is inconsolably tragic, on
a personal level or in the abstract.

Rosemary Hodgins was born in Kansas City in 1925. She
received her B.A. from Northwestern University in 1946 and
her M.A. from the University of Kansas in 1957. During
these years she had also worked as a translator. She joined
the Department of Foreign Languages and Literatures at Temple
University as an Instructor of French in 1966. She received
her Ph.D. from the University of Kansas in 1967 and was
advanced to the rank of assistant professor. She also became assistant to the Chairman of the Department of Foreign
Languages, virtually running many segments of the Department. In 1968, the Department was split into five separate
entities and Dr. Hodgins became assistant chairman of the
Department of French and Italian, a position she filled
along with her teaching duties until 1970. During these
years she also assumed the directorship of Temple University's summer program at the Sorbonne in Paris and forged
it into the excellent program it now is. Her conscientious
teaching, her acute mind, and her enormous service to the
Department and the University in the above-mentioned
capacities earned her tenure in 1972. She had begun to
resume her research on three versions of the late medieval

play La Pacience de Job which she had only been able to get
to in fits and starts during the years of administrative
responsibility, but late in the fall of 1972, Rosemary com-
plained of difficulty with her voice and of a general lassitude. By Christmas she was sufficiently ill to decide she
could not teach and she requested a medical leave of absence.
She still thought it was merely a severe recurrence of the
asthma from which she had suffered for several years. However, she so rapidly weakened that she entered Temple
University Hospital and then the Hospital of the University
of Pennsylvania for a full examination in February, 1973.
After several weeks of testing came the shocking diagnosis:
amyotrophic lateral sclerosis and six months to live.

As this cruel illness slowly but surely reduced
Rosemary to a shadow of herself physically, those of us who
visited her admired the way in which she maintained her will
to live, her humor, and her courage. Rosemary had always
been an exacting and even stubborn teacher; and her character
remained intact to the very end. An old friend who took care
of her during her illness said that Rosemary categorically
refused to stay in bed, even when she weighed only seventy
pounds and was unable to ingest food. She insisted on being
placed upright in a chair by the window. Rosemary Hodgins
died on August 11, 1973, six months after the diagnosis.
She is survived by her father, Mr. Harvey Hodgins.

Rosemary took her Ph.D. in medieval French literature,
but she also loved nineteenth-century literature, especially
Balzac on whom she had written her Masters thesis. She
regularly taught courses in later medieval literature, the
nineteenth-century novel, French civilization, composition,
and explication de textes. Intelligent and mercurial,
Rosemary was an uncompromising perfectionist. These qualities attracted to her a certain highly-devoted student
following and served her well in the double thrust of her
assistant chairmanship and Sorbonne directorship. She was
one of the three faculty members who created the original
draft of the program proposal for a Ph.D. in French at Temple

University and her wisdom and high academic standards were
useful guides in assuring a stable basis for the program.

But how does one gracefully bury those who die early?
We seek in vain some clue in the network of fate, some
rationale behind this sudden individual devastation, some
abstract dimension to warrant this tragedy. But catharsis
is the property of fiction and hubris that of ancient kings.
There is no ready answer; nor has destiny ever been reputed
to be fair, but rather aloof, imperious, without clemency.
In the face of the cold facts, a stopped pendulum and the
onward roll of the earth, how can we not feel pettiness and
anger? And please forgive me if I have been unable gracefully to eulogize or bury one who died early.

                                    Eric Sellin

Part I

Text/Context

STUDIES IN OLD FRENCH ETYMOLOGY, SYNTAX, AND PROSODY

ENCORE UNE AUTRE ETYMOLOGIE SUGGEREE POUR LE SUBSTANTIF FEMININ BAUME/BALMA = "GROTTE"

Willa B. Folch-Pi

Devant la quantité énorme d'études érudites sur l'étymologie du mot baume = "grotte," et ses variantes, on peut bien se demander s'il existe dans les langues romanes un autre mot qui ait provoqué autant de recherches que celui-ci.[1] Néanmoins, il y a lieu pour une suggestion de plus sur l'étymologie de ce mot.

W. Meyer-Lübke décrit le substantif féminin *balma (REW, 912 [1968]) de la façon suivante:

> *balma (ligur. oder kelt.) "Höhle". Lomb. balma. gen., piem., südostfrz. barma, gen. arma,[2] prov., afrz. baume. Das Wort reicht westlich bis in die Gaskogne und nach Valencia, nördlich bis nach Belgien. Bedeutet auch "überhängender Fels", "natürliche Grotte", südfrz. "Wasserreservoir", wallon.] "Kanichenhöhle", "Maulwurfshügel", "horizontale galerie an einem Berge, um eine Kohlenader auszuschöpfen." Ablt.: wallon. bomé "ein Loch graben". -- Zanardelli, App. less. top. 2,3; M.-L., GRM. 1, 645; Scheuermeier 16; Skok, R. 20, 199; Wartburg.[3]

Dans le Dictionnaire étymologique de la langue française (1968), O. Bloch et W. von Wartburg présentent le mot comme baume:

> BAUME, "grotte." En fr. n'est usité qu'en parlant de la Sainte-Baume (près de Toulon), rare en a. fr., mais fréquent au XVIe s. Empr. de gaulois balma, attesté au VIIIe s. au sens de "grotte habitée par des ermites";[4] cf. a. pr. balma, de même sens; répandu comme nom de lieu sur le territoire qui a été habité par les Celtes: Gaule, Catalogne, Nord de l'Italie et régions germaniques de l'Ouest.

Comme dit P. Skok ("Notes d'étymologie romane," Rom, 50 [1924], 200):

3

La question posée par M. Meyer-Lübke . . . relativement
à l'origine ligure ou celtique du mot *balma "grotte,
caverne", n'est pas tranchée définitivement par
Scheuermeyer [sic]. . . . Ce qui résulte de ses
recherches . . . c'est que l'origine rhétique doit
être écartée. . . Nos connaissances sur ce mot sont
aujourd' hui assez précises. Nous en savons les nuances
sémantiques et l'étendue géographique. . . . Mais ce
qui nous fait encore défaut, c'est la connaissance de
la parenté de ce mot.

Skok conclut que l'origine est ligure.

A l'autre côté, Johannes Hubschmid, dans son étude:
Alpenwörter, romanischen und vorromanischen Ursprungs (Bern,
A. Francke, 1951) dit du mot (15-16):

Überhängende Felsen, sog. Balmen, finden sich vor allem
in Alpengebiet. Sie boten, nach Ausweis der Funde,
schon in prähistorischen Zeit Hirten und Jägern Schutz
vor den Unbilden der Witterung. Es ist deshalb nicht
erstaunlich, dass sich für diesen Begriff in den romanischen und schweizerdeutschen Alpenmundarten, vom
Gotthard und dem Comersee westlich bis nach Ligurien
und der Provence, ein sicher vorromanisches vielleicht
sogar vorindogermanisches Wort erhalten hat: rom.
balma. Doch ist dieses Wort nicht auf die Alpen
beschränkt.

Il cite aussi ce que lui paraît être une variante: balwa.
"In den bayerischen Mundarten der Ostalpen hat sich diese
Variante bis heute behalten" (16).   Cependant, dans un autre
article écrit plus tôt ("Zeugen für das späte Aussterben
des Gallischen," VR, 3 [1938], 121), Hubschmid dit:

*balmā > *balva
Für 'Höhle", 'geschützer Raum unter einem vorspringen-
den Felsen' u. ä. sind (oder waren) von den Pyrenäen
und dem östlichen Katalonien an bis nach der Normandie,
Belgien und dem Alpengebiet bis zum Gotthard Formen
üblich, die auf balma (seit 721 bezeugt) zurückgehen.
. . . Nach der Verbreitung muss das Wort gallisch
gewesen sein.

Walther von Wartburg (FEW, t. I [1928] 223-4) déclare
que ce mot est d'origine celte:

BALMA ist ein ablt. des kelt. stammes BAL- vermittelst
des häufigen suffixes -MA. Der stamm BAL findet sich,
als appeletivem und in ortsnamen in bret. irischen und
korn., und zwar in bedeutungen, die genau den galloro-
manischen entsprechen: mine, schacht; gruppe von
wohnungen (wohl ürsprunglich höhlenwohnungen); senk-
rechte felswand. Innerhalb des gallorom. ist BALMA
zuerst belegt in 8 jh. als name von höhlen, die von
eremiten und heiligen männern bewohnt waren. Ortsnamen
und appellative zeigen das wort verbreitet über das
ganze gallorom. gebiet, Katalonien, Piemont, Ligurien,
den westlichen teil des lombardischen Alpen, die
deutsche Schweiz, das Elsass, Allgau, Oberbayern und
Deutschtirol.

Paul Zinsli, dans son oeuvre Grund und Grat, Die Bergwelt
im Spiegel der schweizerdeutschen Alpenmundarten (Bern, A.
Francke, s.d. [c. 1946]), s'accorde avec cette dérivation
(311). Cependant, Alfred Holder, dans son Alt-celtischer
Sprachschatz (Leipzig, 1891), présente le mot comme
d'origine romane au point de vue géographique: "bal-ma
f. oberital. balma, nprov. baumo, südostfranz. barme, afr.
balme die felsgrotte, franz. baume, raetisch. palva, bair.
b(p)alfen." Après un examen de la littérature au sujet de
la dérivation du mot balma, J. Pokorny ("Zur keltischen
Namenkunde und Etymologie," VR, 10, [1948], 226-27) déclare
que le mot vient du gallo-roman et ajoute: ". . . für eine
germ. Grundform *balba eintritt, die im Galloroman. durch
Dissimulation zu balma geworden sei."

Plus récemment, Giandomenico Serra, avec un argument
raisonné mais compliqé, rattache le mot balma au nom
toponymique Valva (Corfinio) venant du L. valvae ("portes
à battants."[5]) Il présente l'étymologie suivante:

Documentata la relativa frequenza di casi d'alternanaz
[sic] fra v (b) ed m nelle lingue arioeuropee dal
rilievo di particolari tendenze vivaci nello sviluppo
di relative forme dialettali, accertata l'origine delle
voci Balfen, Palfen, Palven bavaresi, come delle altre
voci Balm e Balve della Germania meridionale e della
Svizzera tedesca da una forma base balba, attestata in
balba sulle carte del IX secolo, a quest'ultima, alla
antica fase grafica Balba di tali nomi si aggiunga ora
il riscontro dei nomi locali italiani qui sotto docu-
mentati nella loro storia grafica e risalenti alla

variante balbae per "valvae", rilevata dal grammatico
latino Adamantius Martyrius, nel suo commentario "de b
muta et v vocali" e dichiarato con il riscontro di
berbex per "vervex."[6]

Serra continue plus loin (55): Valva è la forma primi-
tiva e originaria di tutti le varianti su indicate: di
balma e Balma, Balba, Balve, Balfen, Palfen, Palve, in
quanto che tale forma continua la voce latina valva nel
suo significato speciale di "cavitas, lumen januae aut
fenestrae . . . ."

Il faut souligner ici que le latin utilise le mot valva

seulement au f. pl., c.-à-d. dans les formes valvae, -arum.

En tout cas, Hubschmid, dans la même publication,

dispute cette attribution:

> Ma non posso seguire il Serra quando spiega la voce
> balma dal lat. valva. . . . La presunta etimologia
> latina di balma suppone una evoluzione di -lv- a -lm-
> nel latino volgare. Si potrebbe pensare a una dissi-
> milazione di valva in balba e poi in balma. Ma c'è
> una difficoltà che mi pare insormontabile: il passaggio
> generale di v- a b-. Non esistono altre forme latine
> con v- in b- conservate nel territorio galloromanzo del
> sud-est e del nord. . . . Dobbiamo dunque partire, per
> balma, non da un lat. valva, ma da una base prelat.
> *balma, con una variante *balva.[7]

En revenant à P. Skok (Rom, 50, 201), on voit qu'il a examiné

la plupart des dérivations possibles, y compris la suivante:

"L'évolution sémantique de balma en roman: 'grotte, caverne'

> 'rocher saillant qui peut servir d'abri aux pâtres' >

'rocher' en général > 'lieu escarpé', nous permet cependant

de rattacher au serbo-croate *dolma le roum. dâlma, fem.

'colline', dâlmos adj.:   'montueux, mamelonné'."[8]

Nous nous trouvons ici en plein littoral dalmate.

Nous terminons ici nos citations de la grande quantité

d'études érudites[9] sur le s. f. baume/balma = "grotte" avec

quelques remarques de Jakob Jud dans son article, "Probleme

der Altromanischen Wörtergeographie" (ZRP, 38 [1917], 4-5):

> Den deutschen wie den romanischen Formen liegt eine
> Basis balma zugrunde, die, seit dem 6. Jahrh. belegt,
> sicher nicht lateinisch ist, sondern einer vorromanis-

chen Sprache angehört. Die immer wiederholte Beobach-
tung, dass gerade die Ortsnamen häufig alte, in der
Gemeinsprache bereits ausgestorbene Wörter bewahren,
lassen die Vermutung aufkommen, es handle sich bei
dtsch. balm weniger um ein Lehnwort, als vielmehr um
ein Relikt, das die zurückflutenden Romanen den nach-
drängenden Alemannen überlassen haben.

La conclusion à tirer de toutes ces descriptions contradic-
toires du mot baume/balma = "grotte," c'est que l'étymologie du mot reste obscure. On peut s'accorder avec Skok
que "ce que nous fait encore défaut, c'est la connaissance
de la parenté de ce mot."

Hubschmid, dans l'article cité ci-dessus (n. 7), fait
quelques observations sur la méthode philologique pour
rechercher la dérivation d'un mot (45-46):

> Ma non si deve esagerare l'importanza del sostrato
> mediterraneo e vedere in voci toponimiche relitti
> preindoeuropei, quando queste voci si possono spiegare
> facilmente da un elemento preceltico indoeuropeo o dal
> latino. . . . L'interpretazione dei fatti linguistici
> si deve fare con la massima obiettività e senza pre-
> giudizi. Nuove possibilità di spiegazioni non si
> devono rifiutare senza l'esame dettagliato di tutto
> il problema.

Si l'on se limite à une consideration nette du s. f.
baume/balma = "grotte," il y a peut-être encore une autre
étymologie à suggérer. De ce mot, Scheuermeier cite deux
attestations du VIIIe siècle (de l'abbé du monastère de
Flavigny en 721 et dans l'année 739[10]), au même temps qu'il
remarque:

> Bis in die Zeit des aufblühenden Katholischen Christen-
> tums zurück führen uns die berühmten, südfranzösischen
> Namen der Sainte-Baume [1] und der Baume de St-Honorat,
> [2] d. h. ihr sachlich-historischer Ihhalt; denn diese
> Namen selbst sprachlich für jene frühe Zeit zu belegen,
> ist mir nicht gelingen.[11]

Néanmoins, peut-être peut-on démontrer que cette
datation est non seulement soutenable au point de vue

philologique mais qu'en fait cette attribution est
antérieure au huitième siècle.

Il existe en français un substantif masculin baume
signifiant "médicament employé comme calmant" (Larousse).
Le Grand Dictionnaire Universel de XIXe siècle (Paris,
Larousse, 1867) dit: "Le nom baume était donné autrefois
à des compositions onguentaires auxquelles on attribuait
des merveilleuses propriétés." The New Oxford Dictionary,
t. I (Oxford, Clarendon Press, 1933), cite trois exemples
de ce mot:

> [a] Balm (bām), sb. Forms: basme, bame (balsme),
> bawm(e, baume, baum, bavme, bawlme, baulme, balme,
> baulm, balm. [M.E. basme, bame, a. OF. basme, later
> bâme (= Pr. basme, It. balsamo): -L balsamum: see
> BALSAM, -UM. . . .] 1. An aromatic substance, con-
> sisting of resin mixed with volatile oils, exuding
> naturally from various trees of the genus Balsamo-
> dendron, and much prized for its fragrance and medi-
> cinal properties, . . . c. 1220 Hali Meid.13 Swotes
> smirles . . . [th] at is icleopet basme. . . .
> [b] Balsam (bō·lsam) sb. Forms: Balsam, balzam, bal-
> zama; balsome, -um, -ame, -om, balsam [ad. L. balsam-
> um . . . Found already in OE. as balsam, balzam (neut.)
> and balzamam wk . . .] 2. An aromatic oily or
> resinous medicinal preparation, usually for external
> application, for healing wounds or soothing pain.
> [c] Ba·lsamum Obs. [a. L. balsamum, a. Gr. βαλσαμογ
> the balsam tree and its resin (pro. f. Semitic: cf.
> Heb. besem, bāsām,^{12} 'spice'; though the LXX never
> render this word by βαλσαμογ, nor the Vulg. by balsamum,
> words which do not appear in these versions. 1. An
> aromatic resinous vegetable juice. . . .

On trouve ici une autre sous-couche méditerranéenne:
l'hébreu, et la définition donnée par Reuben Alcalay dans
son Complete Hebrew Dictionary (Jerusalem, Masada, 1963)
est "perfume, scent, spice, balm, balsamic."

Dans la version Vulgate de la Bible, on trouve pour ce
mot: resina, oleum, et une fois balsamum (Ez. XXVII, 17:
"Juda et terra Israel ipsi institores tui in frumento primo;
balsamum, et mel, et oleum, et resinam proposuerunt in
nundinis tuis.")^{13}

En grec le mot fait son début dans l'oeuvre du médecin
grec Dioscoride (De materia medica, c. A.D. 50): "BALSAMUM
arbor albae violae, lycij, sive pyrancanthae magnitudine
conspicitur. Foliú rautae proximum, longè candidius,
perpetuò virens. In Iudaea solùm quadam valle & Aegypto
nascitur. . . ."[14]

Par extension, ce mot, selon Du Cange (Glossarium
Mediae et Infimae Latinitatis [1937]), signifie "Sacrum
chrisma, seu oleum sacrum." Du Cange présente deux significations de balsamiticus: "Balsaminus, ex: balsamo" et
"Bonus odoribus refertus." Il donne deux exemples: "Bal-
samiticum consecrevat chrisma," et le suivant, tiré de la
"Translatio S. Augustini, tom. 6 maii pg. 414, 'Quo magis
haec Balsamitica apotheca reserebatur, eo profusis odor
coelestis jaculabatur.'" Le Grand Dictionnaire Universel
s'accorde avec Du Cange: "Saint baume, baume que l'évêque
mêle à l'huile, pour la composition du saint chrême. . . ."
Salvatore Battaglia (Grande dizionario della lingua
italiana [1961]) s'accorde avec les deux: Balsamo . . . la
voce si diffuse anche per tramite della Chiesa (che del
balsamo fa un impiego liturgico, unito all'olio santo per
il crisma: a simboleggiare l'odore delle buone azioni)."

La Curne de Sainte-Palaye (Dictionnaire historique de
l'ancien françois [1875]) fait un pas en avant en donnant
au s. m. baume la signification (comme l'hébreu); "parfum,
chose excellente." Donc on trouve une liaison étroite
entre la Terre Sainte, l'idée de l'onguent, l'idée de
l'huile sacrée et même l'odeur de saintéte.

*
*   *

Depuis le haut moyen âge, il y avait une légende hagio-
graphique très répandue en Europe, surtout au Midi de la
France, qui porte sur ce problème. C'est la légende de la
retraite pénitentielle de Sainte Marie-Madeleine au désert
dans la grotte de la "Sainte Baume," qui se trouve aussi
près de Marseille que de Toulon. Selon la légende, c'est
la Madeleine, commençant son apostolat à Marseille, qui a
converti toute la Provincia Romana à la chrétienté.[15] La

notion d'un onguent sacré est intimement liée avec la
Madeleine légendaire.[16] Ce qui est plus intéressant, c'est
que l'étendue de la légende et de l'usage du s. f. baume/
balma = "grotte" sont d'un accord frappant. Pour en voir
la coincidence, on n'a qu'à comparer les cartes des sanc-
tuaires et des lieux où se trouvait au moyen âge les cultes
dediés à la sainte (présentées par Victor Saxer);[17] avec la
carte préparée par Scheuermeier (à la suite de la p. 132);
avec l'Atlas linguistique de la France (Gilliéron et Edmont
[Paris, 1902] 204); avec l'Atlas lingüistic de Catalunya
(A. Griera, [Barcelona, 1933] v. II, Mapa 208); avec, pour
la Suisse, le Rhätisches Namenbuch de Robert v. Planta et
Andrea Schorta;[18] ou même avec les cartes touristiques de
la France. Surtout il faut faire comparaison avec les
cartes présentées par J. Jud pour l'étendue du parler roman
au quatrième siècle.[19]

Comme exemples on peut citer les cas suivants:
1) en archéologie on nomme l'ère magdalénienne d'après
la "grotte de la Madeleine" qui se trouve près des
Eyzies de Tayac (Dordogne--à quelques kilomètres de la
Grotte de Lascaux); aux cartes de Scheuermeier, il
souligne que l'on a utilisé, dans le même voisinage, la
baume "in Ortsnamen und Dokumenten des Mittelalters;"
2) At. ling.: 204, 873 "Eyguières," Saxer: carte "LE
XIe SIECLE, Eyguières;" 3) At. ling.: 204, 889 "Barcelonette," Guide Vert Michelin, Alpes-Savoie-Dauphiné
(54) "Barcelonette . . . . La Route des Grandes Alpes
y recoupe la voie transalpine par le col de la Madeleine;" 4) aux environs d'Aubenas, At. ling.: 204,
824 "Burzet," 833 "Vogué," Guide Rouge Michelin: "La
Madeleine, Belvédère de (Ardèche), la Grotte de la
Madeleine;" 5) aux environs des Saintes-Maries-de-la-
Mer (dont l'une est sainte Marie-Madeleine): At. ling.:
204, 759 "Les Matelles," 841 "Alais," 852 "Uzès," 864
"Vaucluse," carte de Scheuermeier: "BALMA nach dem
Atl. lg., Gloss., Id. und eignen Aufnahmen." l'étendue
du mot en Catalogne est aussi digne d'être soulignée.
Sa limite sud correspond à la province de Tarragone:
"Valls" (A. Griera, Atlas lingüistic de Catalunya, v.
II Mapa 208). Le manque d'espace ici ne permet ni la
reproduction des cartes même superposées ni des cita-
tions supplémentaires, mais on peut bien démontrer la
concordance des lieux où se trouve le culte dédié à
Marie Madeleine, et des lieux où se trouve l'utilisation
du s. f. baume/balma = "grotte."

Même la date s'accorde. L'image complexe de la
Madeleine légendaire, citée au VIIIe siècle dans "La
Sainte Baume" de Scheuermeier, est attestée au
même siècle par Grégoire le Grand.[20] Cependant, la
légende remonte à une date plus ancienne. Comme
Eggert[21] l'a souligné, la Patrologia Latina de Migne
(t. 13, 155-6) donne une citation d'un clerc espagnol
de Barcelonne, Lucius Flavius Dexter (A.D. 368-430)
qui décrit comment Lazare, Marie-Madeleine, Marthe,
Marcelle, Maximin et Joseph d'Arimathie ont été expulsés
de la Terre Sainte dans une barque sans voiles, rames,
ni gouvernail. La description termine par la phrase:
"Qui per varium mare divinitus delati ad Massiliensem
portum incolumnes appellunt."[22]

Devant cette évidence, peut-être vaut-il la peine de
faire une comparaison des variantes du s. m. baume/balme =
"onguent" avec les formes du s. f. baume/balma = "grotte."
On se souvient ici de la carte de J. Jud qui démontre
l'étendue du parler roman au IVe siècle.

On trouve pour le s. m. baume les variantes suivantes: M.-L., REW, 918, balsamum "Balsam" Ital.
balsimo, frz. baume, prov. balme, basme, baime, sp. pg.
balsamo, asp. blaime;[23] Du Cange (Gloss. Lat.):
Balsamum, balsamiticus, Balsamus "pro Balsamum in
versibus relatis ad voces: Agnus Dei"; W. von Wartburg,
FEW, 226 balsamum, balsam. Afr. ba(1)sme, apr. balme,
basme, mfr. ba(s)me, nfr. baume, St-Pol bom, bmanc.
baom, Châten. bâme, Montbél. bame, npr. baume "id.
soulagement," pr. baime "baume, pâte de senteur",
aveyr. baume "Baume", bearn. basme. . . . Mistral
(Lou tresor dou Félibrige [1879]): baume, balme (1.),
baime, embaime (rh.) (rom. balme, cat, balsam, esp.
port. balsamo, lat. balsamum); P. Robert (Dictionnaire
alphabétique et analogique de la langue française
[1951]): baume, basme, bausme; La Curne de Sainte-
Palaye (Dict. hist.): Basme, baume, Balme (E.
Deschamps), Blasme (corruption Basme, G. Machaut),
Balsismes (S. Bernard, Sermon); Antoni Alcover (Diccionari Català-Valencià-Balear [1935]): bàlsam, bàlsem
(de llat. balsamu); Pompeu Fabra (Diccionari general de
la llengua catalana [cinquena edició, 1968]): bàlsam;
Pal.las (Diccionari català il.lustrat [s.d.]): Bàlsam.
Juan Corominas cite un exemple d'usage dans la vie d'un
saint: "Los arbres d'Engadi, los quals leven lo basme,
florien et fruyt feseren e la licor donaren del basme--
quant aná Josep en Beslem ab Santa Maria, que era
preyn, .I. bou ad si amená - / - en aquela ora los
pastors sobre lur bestiar veytlaven -. . . ."[24] Emil
Levy (Petit dictionnaire provençal-français [1961])
donne: balme, basme, baime (PSW ne donne rien); S.

Battaglia (Gr. Diz.): balsamo, balsimo "Lat. balsamum
dal gr. βαλσαμογ, forse di origine semitica)." A
toutes ces variantes, il faut au moins en ajouter
deux qui se trouvent dans les anciens textes français:
du Roman de la Rose, v.2767 (ed. Lecoy, CFMA, t. I),
basme; et d'une "Edition d'un sermon anonyme de la
Magdalaine" (Charlotte Platz, Bulletin des Jeunes
Romanistes (Strasbourg), 13 [1966], 18): bausme.

Comme variantes du s. f. baume/balma = "grotte,"
on trouve les suivantes: M.-L., REW, 912 (voy. le
commencement de cet article); Du Cange: baume, basme,
bame, baxme, barme [aux pages 540-541], baulme [à la
p. 609]; von Wartburg, FEW, t. I 223-24; Apr. balma,
mfr. baume, ard. balme, Châten., Montbél. bame, Mièges
bamo, Vaudioux bàma, Bourn. bam, bern. id., schweiz.
bauma, waadtl. Vionn. barma. Vd'Ill. barma. bagn.
Herem. Vd'Ann. aost Valtourn. H^te-Sav., Sav. barma.
St-Lupicien barma, dauph. balma, baume, Ch. Gren.
barma, Die baumo, Usseglio barma, Pral. balmo, Prage-
lato, palme, Queyr. balmo; Mistral (L. t. d. F.):
baumo, balmo, barmo, boumo (rom. cat. bauma, balma,
b. lat. balma); Robert (Dic. alpha. et anal.): baume,
balme, balma; Sainte-Palaye (Dict. hist.) Baume, balme,
basme (Sire de Joinville), baumo, "si l'on en croit
A. Thierry, baou serait un mot ligurien"; Alcover (Dic.
Cat.-Val.-Bal.): Balma, baume; Fabra (Dic. gen.):
balma; Pal.las (Dic. cat. il.): balma; A. Griera
(T. d. l. ll.): Balma; Levy (P. dic. pro.-fr.): balma
s. f. "grotte, caverne," (PSW ne donne rien); Battaglia
(Gr. diz.): Balma s. f. "Rocca sporgente, grotta (che
nelle alpi costituisce un ricovero naturale). . . .
Voce che si suole riconnettere a un sostrato ligure
(assai frequente nella toponomastica alpina)."

Il est bien évident qu'il y a une similarité marquée
entre les variantes de ces deux mots--une similarité qui
suggère une étymologie alternative. Puisque dans les repré-
sentations artistiques de Marie-Madeleine au moyen âge
(l'une d'elles à la façade de la basilique de Saint-Maximin-
de-la-Sainte-Baume dans la vallée au nord de la montagne où
se trouve la Sainte Baume même), son attribut est un vase
d'onguent, il est bien possible que la grotte, "La Sainte-
Baume," où la Madeleine a demeuré trente ans "dans le
désert," fût nommée d'après l'onguent, c.-à-d. d'après "le
baume" même.

C'est un fait linguistique bien connu[25] que les sub-
stantifs latins neutres de terminaison -um sont devenus
masculins au singulier en français. Pourtant, les sub-

stantifs latins neutres pluriels de cette déclinaison sont
devenus des féminins singuliers par analogie à la terminaison latine féminine singulière -a. Si l'on accepte la
dérivation qui suit ci-dessous pour le s. m. baume =
"onguent," l'on pourrait suggérer une dérivation pareille
pour le s. f. baume/balma = "grotte," d'autant plus que
Madeleine a oint le Sauveur au moins deux fois et était
prête à l'oindre pour "l'embaumer," autre dérivation, comme
nous avons déjà vu, du s. m. baume = "onguent." Donc, le
mot dérive du pluriel balsama.

1) étymologie du s. m. baume = "onguent": gr.
βαλσαμοy, lat. balsamum > *BALS'MU > afr., apro. baume,
balme, baulme, basme, baime (i < s), bausme > fr. baume,
pro. baume, rom. balme, basme.

2) étymologie suggérée du s. f. baume/balma =
"grotte": gr. βαλσαμα > lat. balsama > *BALS'MA > afr.,
apro. balme, baulme, balma, bauma (Voy. les variantes
citées ci-dessus), basme > fr. baume, rom. cat. bauma,
balma, pro. baumo, barmo (r < l), bòumo (Mistral).

Notes

1. Voir Giandomenico Serra, "Del Mito e delle origini
della voce 'balma'," Rendiconti dei lavore della Terza
Giornata in Carrara (Carrara, Convegno di studi Apuani,
juin, 1956; cité ci-dessous comme Rendi conti . . .) 47:

La voce balma, straniata dalle sue origini latine
dal suo significato primitivo, di grotta eremitica,
sin dal primo schiudersi di un orizzonte di studi
comparativi sulle lingue neolatine, dal Monte (a.
1856) allo Steub e al Diez, dal Körting all'Holder,
dallo Zanardelli allo Jud e allo Scheuermeier, dal
Gröhler, Skok, Vincent Dauzat al Meyer-Lübke, dal
Gamillscheg al v. Wartburg, dal Bertoldi al Battisti
e al Bolelli, dall'Hubschmid e dal Rostaing al Pokorny
e al Vhathmough [sic], brilla tuttora regina. . . .

L'auteur veut bien ici remercier M. Félix Lecoy qui
a signalé cette citation parmi d'autres. Elle veut aussi
exprimer sa reconnaissance au Professeur Louis F. Solano, à
Mme. Diana Mériz et à M. Barry Hennessey pour leurs suggestions provocantes, et surtout à M. Juan Corominas pour ses
conseils très utiles au sujet des difficultés de l'étude
de l'origine du mot baume/balma = "grotte."

2. Cette variante est aussi attestée par J. Hubschmid dans son article publié dans Rendiconti . . ., "Osservazioni su elementi prelatini indoeuropei, e latini o presunto latini e di altre regioni," 45.

3. Cependant, dans l'édition de 1911 de M.-L. REW, 912, on trouve: "*balma 'Höhle,' 'Grotte'. . . . Wohl ligur. oder gall? . . . (*BASSIMA von BASSUS ZRPH. XIX, 57 ist nach Form und Bedeutung gleich unmöglich)."

4. Bloch et von Wartburg ne disent pas où se trouve cette attestation; voy. ci-dessous n. 11.

5. A. Gabriel, Dictionnaire latin-français (Paris, Hatier, 1960), s.v..

6. Serra, Rendiconti . . . , 52-53.

7. Hubschmid, Rendiconti . . . , 44-45.

8. Peut-on attribuer ainsi la signification donnée par M.-L., "Kaninchenöhle," à une dégéneration du sens du mot?

9. Voy. la n. 1.

10. Paul Scheuremeier, "Einige Bezeichnungen für den Begriff Höhle in den Romanischen Alpendialekten (*Balma, *Spelunca, *Crypta, *Tana, *Cubulum)," ZRP, 69 (1920), 7.

11. Voici les notes 1 et 2 de ce passage de Scheuermeier: "1. Die Santa Balma, ein noch heute bis nach Katalonien unter diesem Namen bekannter Wallfahrtsort, ist ein Höhle in der Montagne de la Ste-Baume nördlich Toulon in Dep. Var, in der die heilige Magdalena 30 Jahre lang Busse getan haben soll." "2. Im Jahre 375 gründete der heilige Honoratus auf den Lerinen, einer Cannes vorgelagerten Inselgruppe, eine Mönchskolonie, aus der später bedeutende Schriftsteller der katholischen Kirche hervorgingen. Nach dem Zeugnis von Du Cange soll der 'specus divi Honorati prope Lerinensem insulam" den Namen Balma getragen haben.'" Il ne cite pas de date pour la Sainte-Baume.

12. Pour les caractères hébreux, voy. la citation originale.

13. Biblia Sacra juxta Vulgatam Clementinam . . . (Rome, Desclée, 1956).

14. [Dioscoride]: P. A. Matthioli, Commentarii denuo aucti in libros sex Pedacii Dioscoridis (Lyon, Gabriel Coter, 1562) 51. Pour le texte grec, voy. l'édition définitive: Max Wellman, Pedanii Dioscuridis Anazarbai de Materia Medica (Berlin, Weidmann, 1907) c. 19, 24.

15. Marie-Madeleine est encore la Sainte-Patronne de Provence. Serra (op. cit., p. 45) prétend qu'il y avait un culte de "Matres della grotta che poi si è chiamata Sainte-Baume e che il culto di questa grotta è di origine precristiana." Il est assez difficule de vérifier les légendes médiévales sans soulever les problèmes du folklore préchrétien.

16. Selon la légende, Sainte Marie-Madeleine est une image complexe, composée, en partie, de la pécheresse qui a oint les pieds du Sauveur chez Simon le Pharisien (Luc VII, 36-50), de Marie de Béthanie, qui a oint les pieds et la tête du Sauveur une deuxième fois (Jean XXII, 1-8, Math. XXVI, 6-12, Marc XIV, 3-9), et de la femme qui était prête à oindre son cadavre (Math. XXVIII, 1-10, Marc XVI, 1-8, Luc XXIV, 1-10, Jean XX, 1-10); voy. Victor Saxer, Le culte de Marie Madeleine en occident des origines à la fin du moyen âge (Paris, Clavreuil, 1959) 2.

17. Saxer, Le culte de Marie Madeleine . . .; les cartes suivent la page 182.

18. Romanica Helvetica 8 (1939).

19. Les cartes de J. Jud suivent son texte (ZRP, 38, 4-5).

20. Saxer, Le culte de Marie Madeleine . . ., 3.

21. Carl Edgar Eggert, The Middle Low German Version of the Legend of Mary Magdalene (Bloomington, The Journal of Germanic Philology Press, IV, 1902) 133.

22. PL (t. 13, 155-6 "Flavii Lucii Dextri, Barcinonensis, Chronicon Omnimodae Historiae") donne: "Qui per vastum mare. . . ."

23. L'édition de 1911 de M.-L., REW, 918, donne: balsamum "Balsam" Ital. balsimo, frz. baume, prov. balme, basme, span. portg. balsamo aspan. blasmo, pikard. bām "Minze."

24. Joan Coromines, "'Vides de Sants' Roselloneses, De San Tomàs Apostol," Lleures i converses d'un filòleg (Barcelona, Club Editor, 1971) 341, une traduction en catalan de: Juan Corominas, "Las Vidas de Santos Rosellonesas," Anales del Instituto de Lingüística de la Universidad de Cuyo (Mendoza, 1945). Il est à noter la location de l'arbre.

25. Edouard Bourciez, Eléments de linguistique romane (Paris, Klincksieck, 1956) 88-90.

O.F. DITES ME TOST/DITES MOI TOST

Diana Teresa Mériz

It is common knowledge that the types dites me tost and dites moi tost are indigenous to different areas of langue d'oïl, the former occurring in the northern and eastern regions, the latter throughout the remainder of northern France.[1] However, dites moi tost occurs not infrequently in northern and eastern texts beside the indigenous dites me tost. Likewise, in those areas to which dites moi tost is proper, dites me tost also occurs--the two, on occasion, in the same text, as in the following from the Queste del Saint Graal:[2]

Et il estoit tres devant lui, si li respont: 'Damoisele, veez me ci.'
(p. 12, 26-27)

Mes atendez moi ci, et vos avrez ce que vos querez.
(p. 47, 24-25)

Whereas the occurrence of dites moi tost is commonly ascribed to Francian influence, few scholars have ventured to explain the occurrence of dites me tost in the dites moi tost area.

In his masterful article "L'accent tonique et l'ordre des mots: formes faibles du pronom personnel après le verbe" (Rom, 50 [1924], 54-93), Lucien Foulet appeals to Picard influence to explain the occurrence in non-Picard texts of the type fait se Renart, "qu'on rencontre parfois . . . à côté de la tournure normale fait soi Renart" (p. 63). As he justly observes (p. 69), "les dialectes du XIIIe siècle, et surtout ceux qui ont servi à composer les oeuvres littéraires, se sont influencés réciproquement." Might not one, then, appeal to a similar Picard influence to account for the anomalous dites me tost? A most tempting explanation, were it not for one very disturbing fact: in the

16

dites moi tost area the atonic form of the pronoun occurs
exclusively before a monosyllabic adverb, but in the
northern and eastern regions such a restriction does not
apply. Whereas dites me tost is common to all of langue
d'oïl, dites me erramment is exclusive to the North and
East. Given this, it is clear that Picard influence cannot explain the presence of dites me tost in the dites
moi tost area, since such an influence cannot account for
the nonoccurrence of dites me erramment.

H. Ramsden begins his study of weak-pronoun position
in the Romance languages[3] with a critical review of the
principal theories in the field, placing special emphasis
on Meyer-Lübke's well-known "Zur Stellung der tonlosen
Objektspronomina" (ZRP, 21 [1897], 313-34). In this
connection, Ramsden touches on the problem that concerns
us. "The Old French affirmative imperatives Vei me (ci)!
and Fai le!" he states, "give Vois-moi! and Fais-le! in the
modern language (and not Me vois!, Le fais!), that is, there
has been a shift of stress but without any change in the
order of words" (pp. 11-12).

This statement, modified to fit the syntactic facts of
Old French as we know them, could be taken to indicate that
vei me ci (or dites me tost) represents a vestige of an
earlier stress or rhythmic pattern no longer prevalent in
the Old French period. This would certainly account for the
paucity of examples showing the atonic form of the pronoun.
In our research, for example, we found that only slightly
more than one-fifth of the fifty-five examples of me/moi +
monosyllabic adverb we gathered from approximately one
hundred texts shows the atonic form of the object pronoun.

Nevertheless, attractive as it may be, this view,
though accounting plausibly for vei me / moi ci (as well
as for vei moi ici), cannot account for the nonoccurrence
of vei me ici (or dites me erramment) in texts not of the
northern and eastern regions. And so our problem continues
to remain unsolved.

In his study of the personal pronoun in French, Gérard
Moignet offers an explanation already suggested by several

scholars, among them J. Melander.[4] Having pointed out that
tonic moi and toi are usual after an imperative initial in
the sentence, he states the following with regard to the
type dites me tost: "Notons qu'on peut trouver la forme
atone après le verbe quand il existe un lien étroit entre
le verbe et ce qui suit."[5] Unfortunately, as he does not
specify further, one cannot but be puzzled by the nature of
his "lien étroit." Surely it cannot be a semantic tie, for
it would be difficult at best to posit degrees of semantic
closeness on the basis of the monosyllabic or plurisyllabic
nature of the adverb. Still less could one explain by
appealing to semantic criteria that a given monosyllabic
adverb can, as in the following example, be preceded in
similar contexts by either the tonic or the atonic form of
the object pronoun:

> "Mostrés moi Karle, le rice roi poissant.
> Jo nel conois; por ce le vos demant."
> Li rois respont haltement, en oiant:
> "Veés moi chi, ne m'alés plus querant."
> La Chanson d'Aspremont, vv. 7820-23[6]

> Et ele dresce la teste et dit: "Ou est li chevaliers?"
> Et Mador saut avant et dit: "Veez me ci."
> La Mort le roi Artu, p. 85, 92-93[7]

Is the "lien étroit," then, a syntactic one? If we
turn to the section on pronominal syntax in Moignet's
Grammaire de l'ancien français,[8] where the identical view
is presented, though with different wording, we find that
such is indeed the case. In listing the conditions in which
the atonic pronoun occurs, he states the following (p. 132):
"On note encore le fait quand ce qui suit le pronom est
étroitement associé au verbe; ainsi, un infinitif . . . ou
divers compléments. . . ." Among the examples of the latter
are two monosyllabic adverbs.

Certainly the close association between at least certain adverbs and verbs is a point with which scholars of all
persuasions would agree. However, there is no apparent
reason why the monosyllabic or plurisyllabic nature of the

adverb should at all enter into the matter. Yet it does,
in our view, and in a quite fascinating way.

Even a cursory examination of the data available on
dites me/moi tost reveals no apparent distribution patterns,
if not that the tonic form of the pronoun is greatly pre-
ferred. It cannot be said that one option is more frequent
in certain environments than in others; rather, the tonic/
atonic choice appears to be a free one, with preference
given, as has been stated, to the tonic pronoun. Such
examples as the following confirm this observation:

>   Amie, duce creature,
>   Estes vus ceo? dites mei veir.
>   Marie de France, Guigemar, vv. 816-17[9]
>
>   . . . Oncles, dites me voir:
>   a vos mandé nule novele
>   ma dame ne ma damoizele?
>   Jean Renart, Guillaume de Dole, vv. 3802-3804[10]
>
>   Fermez me tost les portes, que ne soient overtes.
>   Doon de la Roche, v. 1329[11]
>
>   Rendez moi tost Aymeri lo poissant.
>   La Mort Aymeri de Narbonne, v. 4082[12]
>
>   "Mahon," fet il, "a vos me comant gié.
>   Gardez me ci, le col n'aie brisié!"
>   Guibert d'Andrenas, vv. 2281-82[13]
>
>   Mes atendez moi ci, et vos avrez ce que vos querez.
>   La Queste del Saint Graal
>   (ed. Pauphilet), p. 47, 24-25

In contradiction with the pattern generally obtaining
not only with monosyllabic but also with plurisyllabic
adverbs, the type dites me tost was fated to disappear from
the language. Yet it remains an interesting, though abortive, experiment.

Quite simply, the type dites me tost represents, in our
view, an attempt to find expression for the "lien étroit"
existing between adverb and verb by including the adverb in
the same stress group as imperative + object pronoun. This
innovation, however, was made to conform in one very crucial

respect to the norm represented by the imperative + object
pronoun group: since any object pronoun occurring in this
group was a monosyllable, only monosyllabic adverbs were
admitted to the new grouping.

The resultant obligatory occurrence of the tonic form
with a plurisyllabic adverb could not but reinforce its
occurrence elsewhere. Thus <u>dites</u> <u>me</u> <u>tost</u>, an innovation
that could not spread, was doomed to fall into disuse.

Though a convenient stylistic variant, its survival, as
far as we have been able to ascertain, does not extend
beyond the Old French period.

Notes

1. Except, of course, in those areas characterized by
reduction of the diphthong <u>ei</u>.

2. <u>La Queste del Saint Graal</u>, ed. Alfred Pauphilet,
(Paris: Honoré Champion, 1965).

3. H. Ramsden, <u>Weak-Pronoun Position in the Early
Romance Languages</u> (Manchester: Manchester Univ. Press,
1963).

4. J. Melander, <u>Etude sur l'ancienne abréviation
des pronoms personnels régimes dans les langues romanes</u>
(Uppsala: Almqvist & Wiksells, 1928), p. 102.

5. Gérard Moignet, <u>Le Pronom personnel français:
Essai de psycho-systématique historique</u> (Paris: Klincksieck, 1965), p. 68.

6. <u>La Chanson d'Aspremont</u>, ed. Louis Brandin. 2nd ed.
(Paris: Honoré Champion, 1924).

7. <u>La Mort le roi Artu</u>, ed. Jean Frappier. 2nd ed.
(Geneva: Droz; Paris: Minard, 1956).

8. Gérard Moignet, <u>Grammaire de l'ancien français:
morphologie-syntaxe</u> (Paris: Klincksieck, 1973).

9. <u>Les Lais de Marie de France</u>, ed. Jean Rychner,
CFMA (Paris: Honoré Champion, 1966).

10. Jean Renart, <u>Le Roman de la rose ou de Guillaume
de Dole</u>, ed. Félix Lecoy, CFMA (Paris: Honoré Champion,
1963).

11. <u>Doon de la Roche</u>, ed. Paul Meyer and Gédéon Huet
(Paris: Edouard Champion, 1921).

12. <u>La Mort Aymeri de Narbonne</u>, ed. J. Couraye du
Parc (Paris: Firmin Didot, 1884).

13. <u>Guibert d'Andrenas</u>, ed. J. Melander (Paris:
Honoré Champion, 1922).

OLD FRENCH CONTENANCE AND CONTENANT

Glyn S. Burgess

In his monumental study of the terms denoting the face in
the Romance languages, Jean Renson includes a short section
on the French words contenance, contenement and contenant.[1]
He points out that the word contenance occurs in the Chanson
de Roland and that Foulet and the FEW have attributed to it
the meaning "face." Renson considers that such a meaning is
doubtful: "Nous pensons qu'il est plus prudent de refuser à
contenance cette acception et de lui attribuer, dans ce cas,
celle de 'allure générale'."[2] After a discussion of the
terms contenement and contenant Renson adds: "La conclusion
est qu'il faut, par prudence, refuser à ces trois termes le
sens de 'expression du visage' et, à plus forte raison,
celui de 'visage'."[3] Renson's view of the word contenance
is shared by Old French lexicographers. Godefroy, Tobler-
Lommatzsch and Greimas do not recognize the meaning "face"
or "expression." Grandsaignes d'Hauterive does not include
contenance. Godefroy and Greimas offer for contenant the
meaning "expression, appearance" ("mine, maintien," Greimas;
"mine, apparence, façon d'être," Godefroy), whereas Tobler-
Lommatzsch ("Haltung, Gebaren") and Grandsaignes d'Hauterive
("maintien, contenance"), restrict its meaning to "demeanor,
bearing." There is general agreement in the dictionaries
that the word contenement means "bearing, conduct, attitude"
(e.g., "contenance, maintien, conduite, manière d'être,"
Godefroy).

The first examples of the term contenance in French
occur in the Chanson de Roland, which presents three clear
cases.

Suz sun mantel en fait la cuntenance.   (830)

Quant Carles veit si beles cuntenances,
Sin apelat Jozeran de Provence.   (3006-3007)

Cors unt gaillarz e fieres cuntenances.   (3086)[4]

The example in 1. 830 has given rise to a number of
different interpretations which I shall discuss later. The
second example, in 1. 3006, is translated by Bédier as:
"Quand Charles voit leur contenance si belle." Other editors
and translators (Gautier, Geddes, Moignet, Mortier, Owen,
Whitehead, etc.) agree that Charles sees the "bearing" of his
troops. Godefroy quotes this example to illustrate the
meaning "manière de se tenir vis-à-vis de qqn." Bertoni
glosses cuntenance here as "persona," but Foulet gives
"visage." Jenkins and Moncrieff are of the opinion that the
term cuntenance refers to the look of the troops, offering
respectively "such splendid looking (troops)" and "the fair
aspect of them." Robertson translates beles cuntenances as
"handsome, noble faces."

For 1. 3086, in which the term cuntenances refers to
the baruns de France forming the tenth squadron, Foulet also
prefers "visage," but Jenkins opts here for "personal bearing." Bédier renders the expression fieres cuntenances as
"leur contenance fière," Moignet as "l'allure fière" and
Owen as "their bearing proud." Gautier and Mortier translate as "contenance" this and every other occurrence of
contenance and contenant. Whitehead again offers "bearing."
Other translators (Bertoni, Hague, Merwin, Moncrieff,
Robertson, etc.) agree with Foulet that it is the faces of
the barons which the poet is describing as fier. Harrison
prefers the term "features."

The text of the Roland also provides one certain and
one doubtful example of the form cuntenant:

Gent ad le cors e le cuntenant fier.   (118)

Gent ad le cors, gaillart e ben seant,
Cler le visage e de bon cuntenant.   (3115-16)

Bédier, Petit de Julleville and Moignet think that in
1. 118 Charles' "maintien" is "fier," whereas Sayers sees
his "countenance" as "severe" and Harrison his "features"
as "proud." For Crosland his "countenance" is "noble" and
for Bertoni his "viso" is "fiero." Whitehead glosses
cuntenant as "bearing" and Jenkins as "bearing, manner, presence." Owen thinks that Charles' "bearing" is "full of
pride." The reading of 1. 118 is the subject of some doubt.
The Oxford MS has Gent ad le cors e la cuntenance fier.
Bédier, for whom this line presents one of the "leçons les
plus controversées," emends cuntenance to cuntenant "pour
obtenir une assonance régulière."[5] Some scholars (e.g.,
Michel, Génin, Gröber, Mortier and Calin) prefer to retain
cuntenance. Stengel rejects the entire line and substitutes
a line from MSS CV[7]: "Cler ot le vis, le cors gent et
plenier." Bertoni adopts the reading cuntenant, but glosses
the example under cuntenance. Foulet also includes 1. 118
under cuntenance, "visage."

The example of the term contenant in 1. 3116 is vari-
ously interpreted. Some scholars take the expression de bon
cuntenant as an adjectival phrase qualifying visage: e.g.,
"Son visage clair et assuré" (Bédier); "Le visage clair et
plein d'assurance" (Moignet); "Le visage clair et de bonne
mine" (G. F. Jones and A. Demaître); "Chiaro il viso e di
nobile aspetto" (Bertoni). Other translators seem to assume
that the verb aveir in 1. 3115 applies not only to the
phrase cler le visage in 1. 3116, but also to de bon
cuntenant, an interpretation which would almost certainly
require the emendation of de to le: "Clair son visage,
et son maintien vaillant" (Petit de Julleville); "His face
is frank, his looks are confident" (Sayers); "His features
clean, his bearing confident" (Harrison). Whitehead ("of
noble mien") and Jenkins ("bearing, manner, presence")
also seem to understand the phrase in this way. Foulet
glosses the example as "mine."

Finally we can note that the Chanson de Roland contains one example of the word contenement:

En mi sa veie ad encuntret Rollant.
Enceis nel vit sil recunut veirement
Al fier visage e al cors qu'il out gent
E al reguart e al contenement.   (1638-41)

Translators are for the most part agreed that contenement
here means "bearing, demeanor." Hilka, however, suggests
that it could mean "bearing" or "expression" ("Haltung,
Ausdruck"). Sayers expands to "bearing and manner."[6]
Do the terms contenance, contenant and contenement
refer to the face, the expression, or the bearing of the
warrior? The adjective fier may help us here. I have shown
elsewhere that this adjective, used in 1. 3086 with cuntenance and in 1. 118 with cuntenant, refers frequently to
the face of the knight and probably indicates "fierceness"
rather than "pride": e.g.,

Cors ad mult gent e le vis fier e cler.   (895)

Al fier visage e al cors qu'il out gent.   (1640)[7]

With the exception of the Gormont fragment all the
early chansons de geste contain similar examples:

El mostier fu li cuens al fier visage.
          (Couronnement de Louis, 378)[8]

"Vez la Guillelme, li marchis au vis fier."
          (Charroi de Nîmes, 399)[9]

Vet s'en Guillelmes le marchis au vis fier.
          (Prise d'Orange, 397)[10]

Desur un pin antif est Carles al vis fer.
          (Pèlerinage de Charlemagne, 780)[11]

Not one of these texts contains an example of fier referring to the body or the bearing of the personage, unless
we take cuntenance or cuntenant in this way.[12]
The Pèlerinage de Charlemagne is of particular interest,
because this text contains eight examples of the adjective
fier, three qualifying cumpainies (111, 639, 649) and four

the term <u>vis</u> or <u>visage</u>, all with reference to Charles (128,
131, 623, 780). In the final example <u>fier</u> qualifies <u>cunte-</u>
<u>nant</u>: "Li reis regardet Carle, veit le cuntenant fer" (303).
Aebischer glosses this example as "démarche, présentation,
aspect" and Favati as "contegno, attegiamento." However,
not only the presence of the adjective <u>fier</u> but the context
itself suggests that <u>cuntenant</u> here means "face" or "expression" (cf. Koschwitz, "Miene, Haltung"). It seems likely
that the king is struck by Charles' stern countenance rather
than by his "maestoso portamento" (Favati's translation).
G. F. Jones has pointed out, quoting <u>Roland</u> 1. 118, etc.,
that "it was fitting for an austere emperor to have a
withering glance, like many chieftains in Germanic literature."[13] As we have seen, Charles' fierce countenance is
referred to elsewhere in the poem and it has already in-
stilled fear into a beholder:

> Karles out fer le vis, si out le chef leve<u>t</u>.
> Uns Judeus i entrat, ki ben l'out esgardet:
> Cum il vit [le rei] Karle cumençat a trembler:
> Tant out fer le visage, ne l'osat esgarder.   (128-31)

Furthermore, in the only other case of <u>contenance</u> or
<u>contenant</u> in the <u>Pèlerinage</u>, the meaning "bearing" seems
even less likely:

> Par la main tent sa fille, ke ad <u>la</u> crine[e] bloie:
> Hu que veit Oliver, volenters i parol[e]t,
> Fait lui contenan<u>t</u>[e] gent e amisté li portet:
> Volenters le baisast, mais pur sun pere n(en) oset.
>   (823-26)

The reading of 1. 825 is far from certain. The MS offers:
<u>Fait</u> <u>lui</u> <u>contenance</u> <u>gente</u> <u>amiste</u> <u>li</u> <u>portet</u>. Michel inter-
prets as: "Fait lui contenance gente, amisté li portet,"
which is metrically improbable. We can thus read: <u>Fait</u> <u>lui</u>
<u>contenance</u>, <u>gente</u> <u>amisté</u> <u>li</u> <u>portet</u>, or following Koschwitz,
Cooper and Aebischer, etc., emend <u>contenance</u> to <u>contenant</u>
and read for the first hemistich either <u>fait</u> <u>lui</u> <u>contenant</u>

gent or **fait** **li** contenant gent. The last of these versions
is probably the most acceptable, but we should perhaps note
that the expression **faire** contenance **gente** is attested elsewhere (e.g., **Floire** **et** **Blancheflor**, MSS ACV; **Ille** **et**
Galeron, Wollaton Hall MS) and, in addition, I have only
found one further example, in the thirteenth-century chanson
de geste **Elie** **de** **saint** **Gille**, of contenant linked to **faire**.[14]
The context seems to suggest that the meaning of the expres-
sion **faire** contenant **gent** **a** **aucun** (or **faire** contenance **a**
aucun, if we read **gente** **amisté**) is "to display one's feelings towards someone, to smile at someone." For contenant
in l. 825 of the **Pèlerinage** Aebischer gives "figure, mine,
accueil." The translation "mine" is perhaps preferable
here, but "faire bon accueil" may well be close to the
meaning of the expression **faire** contenant **gent**.[15]

        In general the term contenant is rare in Old French.
But Grandsaignes d'Hauterive is certainly wrong to confine
it to the eleventh century. It is attested, for example,
in the **Roman** **de** **l'Escoufle**:

> Il nota bien le contenant
> Du vallet, et si parut bien
> K'il ert dolans d'aucune rien.   (6506-6508)[16]

The contenant of the **vallet** has been affected by grief and
tears, which indicates that the meaning "expression" is
appropriate here. But it is difficult to rule out the
meaning "face" for this occurrence of contenant, which
surprisingly does not appear in the editor's glossary. The
meaning "face, facial features" is certainly acceptable for
the following example from the **Chanson** **de** **Guillaume**:

> Reis Deramé giseit en mi le champ,
> Envolupé de sablun e de sanc.
> Quant Willame le veit, sil conuit al contenant.
>   (1889-91)[17]

It seems likely that a man covered in sand and blood would
be recognized by his facial features rather than by his
expression or bearing.

The first example of contenant in the Roland ("Gent ad
le cors e le cuntenant fier," 118) is similar to that in
l. 303 of the Pèlerinage ("Li reis regardet Carle, veit le
cuntenant fer") and both examples probably refer to Charles'
fierce expression or, to use G. F. Jones' phrase, his
"withering glance." No other Roland manuscript retains the
term contenant at this point, but MSS CV[7] make reference to
Charles' face: "Cler ot le vis, le cors grant et plenier."
The poet of the Oxford Roland describes Charles' face as
fier in l. 142 ("Quant se redrecet mult par out fier lu
vis"). Charles looks fierement in l. 745 ("Quant l'ot li
reis, fierement le reguardet") and l. 2984 ("Mult fierement
tute sa gent reguardet"). The second example of contenant,
in l. 3116, is of considerable interest. Unless we modify
the reading to Cler le visage e le bon cuntenant (or bon le
cuntenant), we should probably interpret the phrase de bon
cuntenant with Bédier and others as an adjectival expression
modifying visage. As Charles' face is thus of "good"
cuntenant, the meanings "face" or "bearing" are impossible.
The best translation is without doubt "expression."

But what is the sense of bon in l. 3116? There is no
other example in the Roland in which the adjective bon is
applied to a person's face, expression or even bearing. The
bonté of Charles' cuntenant has been interpreted as beauté
(Gautier, Soufflet), moral goodness ("He has a good man's
bearing," Hague; "Clear was his face and filled with good
intent," Moncrieff), fierceness ("And clear was all his
countenance and fierce he rode to war," Bacon), valiance
("Clair son visage, et son maintien vaillant," Petit de
Julleville), radiance ("Bright is his face and shining with
the light of victory," Way), confidence (Bédier, Harrison,
Moignet, Owen, Sayers), nobility ("His face, noble of mien,
is clear and bright," Robertson), or as a vague notion without much semantic content ("Clair le visage et de bonne
mine," Pauphilet; "Le visage clair et de bonne mine,"
Geddes, Jones-Demaître). Nothing in the immediate context
confirms the notion of confidence, and the adjective bon

does not seem to convey this meaning elsewhere in the text.
The meaning of bon in l. 3116 may perhaps be allied to the
use of bonté in an earlier passage which also refers to
Charles: "Tant nel vos sai ne preiser ne loer / Que plus
n'i ad d'onur e de bontet" (532-33). Ganelon may well be
referring here to Charles' courage or nobility (Whitehead),
rather than to his largesse (Jones-Demaître) or valeur
morale (Foulet). The phrase de bon cuntenant may therefore
mean "of noble expression." Nobility is stressed again when
we are told in l. 3121 that Charles rides "mult gentement."[18]
It is perhaps their fairness of countenance that Charles
admires in his troops in l. 3006: "Quant Carles veit si
beles cuntenances." But cuntenance may mean here "appearance." We note that Charles' reaction to the sight of his
troops is one of confidence: "En tels vassals deit hom aveir
fïance!" (3009) and the feeling that one would be "foolish"
to despair in the presence of such men: "Asez est fols ki
entr'els se dementet" (3010). The beles cuntenances, which
Charles sees, are later described as fieres by the poet,[19]
who tells us that they are allied to strong bodies:

        La disme eschele est des baruns de France.
        Cent milie sunt de noz meillors cataignes;
        Cors unt gaillarz e fieres cuntenances;
        Les chefs fluriz e les barbes unt blanches. (3084-3087)

I should translate the expression fieres cuntenances here
as "fierce countenances."
        When Charles is returning from Spain, leaving behind
him the Twelve Peers and 20,000 men, we are told that: "Suz
sun mantel en fait la cuntenance" (830). Whitehead suggests
that the expression faire la contenance here means "to conceal one's emotion." Jenkins relates the term contenance to
the "act of containing" and thinks that the line may indicate
that "Charles directs his troops clad (not in armour but
only) in his cloak." Mortier and Petit de Julleville translate: "Sous son manteau, il cache sa contenance." Bédier
renders the line as: "Sous son manteau, il cache son

angoisse." But in the Commentaires he suggests a parallel
with the expressions faire la mine and faire la tête and
appears to modify his translation to: "he makes a display
of grief," approving Littré's gloss: ". . . en fait la
contenance [d'homme affligé]." Moignet's translation, "sous
son manteau, il a la contenance de ses sentiments," is difficult to understand, and he is forced to explain in a note
that Charles "a la contenance que lui vaut son inquiétude,
étant donné la situation et les présages qu'il a eus."
Müller emended en fait to enfuit, "buries," as do Génin,
Boehmer (enfoit), Petit de Julleville and Gautier, who translates: "Sous son manteau cache sa contenance." Clédat
reads en fuit and translates "Charlemagne, en se cachant
sous son manteau, se soustrait à la nécessité de faire bonne
contenance," an awkward translation, which has the merit,
nevertheless, of explaining better than other versions why
Charles should hide beneath his cloak.[20]

Mario Roques in a long note on this line in Romania
comes to the conclusion that the best translation is: "A
ce retour, l'empereur se tient, reste sous son manteau."[21]
Roques' remarks were stimulated by a short article published
by Bertoni in 1925, in which he suggested that en fait should
be emended to cutet, "hides," and cuntenance could be translated as "face."[22] However, in his edition Bertoni retains
en fait, translating: "Sotto il suo mantello occulta la sua
cera," and accepting that in the expression faire la cuntenance "è insita l'allusione qualcosa di nascondere, da velare
agli occhi altrui, cioè il turbamento dell'imperatore."[23]

Leo Spitzer agrees with Bertoni and Bédier (i.e.,
Bédier's translation: "il cache son angoisse") that Charles
hides his grief, but adds that the term contenance here is
"psychophysique," referring "ni au corps ni à l'âme séparé-
ment, mais aux deux réunis, intégrés."[24] For Spitzer
contenance indicates simultaneously "le maintien physique"
and "le self-control moral."[25] Similar to this is the
notion expressed by F. Lecoy, that faire la contenance means
"maîtriser la violence de ses sentiments, garder une attitude calme et digne en dépit de la colère, de la confusion

ou de la douleur."[26] But several scholars think that the
term contenance means simply "face" (Bertoni,[27] Calin,
Hague, Harrison, Sayers, Way). Jones-Demaître expand the
meaning to "triste visage" and Owen to "anguished face."
Some editors (e.g., Stengel and Jenkins) think that the
meaning of l. 830 is clearer if we introduce a line from MSS
CV^7TV^4 ("Plore des oeils, tire sa barbe blanche"). But
this is not necessary as we have already been informed in
the preceding laisse of Charles' feelings:

> Sur tuz les altres est Carles anguissus:
> As porz d'Espaigne ad lesset sun nevold.
> Pitet l'en prent, ne poet muer n'en plurt.   (823-25)

Let us see what in this difficult line can be established with some degree of probability. First, Charles'
general state of mind and the remark of Naimes in l. 832
("E dit al rei: 'De quei avez pesance?'") suggest strongly
that the idea expressed in l. 830 is intimately connected
with grief. The reading of MS T helps to confirm this:
"Desoulz son elme en fait sa douliance." But we need not
conclude that there is a "necessaria connotazione dolorosa"
(Segre) for the term cuntenance itself. Secondly, although
Charles is on horseback, making it, as Roques has pointed
out, undesirable for him to hide his face,[28] we have to
admit that the act of covering one's face or head with one's
cloak is well attested in Old French and signifies profound
grief: e.g., Yvain, 3960-61: "En lor mantiax anvelopées /
Vindrent, por lor lermes covrir"; Perceval, First Continuation, MS M 17382, 84: "De son mantel la chiere coevre. . . .
Fu molt penssis et angoisseus."[29] Thirdly, the reading en
fait is found in all the manuscripts containing this line
(CV^7TV^4) with the exception of V^4 ("Soto so mantel el fa la
contenança"), which offers, nevertheless, the verb faire.
Thus the presence of faire in the original text would seem
more likely than that of enfoïr or cuter.
    Any translation of l. 830 must explain satisfactorily
the pronoun en, the article la and the role of the verb

faire. The parallel suggested by Bédier between the expression faire la contenance and faire la tête or faire la mine
has to be viewed with suspicion. There is no evidence that
the locutions faire la tête and faire la mine were in use at
the time of the Chanson de Roland. In addition nothing in
the context suggests that faire la contenance shares the
pejorative meaning of the modern expressions. The article
probably retains in 1. 830 its demonstrative force, as in
the case of 1. 1790 ("Respunt dux Neimes: 'Barun i fait
la peine'"), in which Neimes' reply would mean literally:
"That effort is made by a baron" (cf. Owen: "A baron's
effort, this"). L. 830 occurs in the middle of three
laisses parallèles, which emphasize Charles' grief. The
function of the definite article accompanying contenance
is probably to sum up the general situation, to stress, as
Moignet saw well, that Charles' contenance is imposed on
him by circumstances. The pronoun en may well have a
similar function. Foulet cites a number of cases of en
with the meaning "à la suite de, et comme conséquence de"
(e.g., 1. 139: "Li empereres en tint sun chef enclin";
1. 2373: "Sun destre guant en ad vers Deu tendut").[30]
The function of faire Foulet defines, correctly in my view,
as the "réalisation de l'idée exprimée par le substantif"
(e.g., 1. 3043: "Einz i murat que cuardise i facet";
1. 3898: "Deus facet hoi entre nus dous le dreit"). But
if faire does express the idea contained in the term
cuntenance we cannot translate the verb as "hide" (Bédier,
Bertoni, Calin, Geddes, Harrison, Jones-Demaître, Merwin,
Owen, Pauphilet, Robertson, Sayers, Whitehead, etc.).

I think we must admit that Charles does cover his face
with his cloak and that he does so in order to conceal his
grief, rather than because he is attempting to exercise
control over his feelings (Spitzer, Lecoy) or because of an
overwhelming feeling of lassitude or indisposition (Roques).
I can find no evidence to support the meaning "grief" for
cuntenance itself, but the term does seem to be associated
here and elsewhere with the expression of feelings. In an
interesting passage from Partonopeu de Blois, the locution

faire contenance is used absolutely in conjunction with the
concept of shame:

>   Car ses maris, rois Menelaus,
>   Bons chevaliers, pros et loiaus,
>   Soffrist sa honte sans vengance
>   Et sans faire nis contenance,
>   Si que sol plaindre ne s'osoit
>   Por les Troiens qu'il redotoit
>   Et por le grant chevalerie
>   Qui se tenoit en lor baillie.   (201-208)[31]

On the abduction of his wife the bon chevalier is evidently
expected to faire contenance, even if he does not go as far
as exacting revenge. Faire contenance is clearly to perform
an action less radical than revenge, or less specific than
making a formal complaint (plaindre, 1. 205), but sufficiently active to prevent an accusation of total passivity.
Tobler-Lommatzsch, who do not cite this example, give only
"sich eine Haltung geben" for the expression faire contenance, a meaning too vague to fit the context here. It is
possible that Menelaus did not give full vent to his feelings, did not make it perfectly clear what his reaction was.
Perhaps he did not even cry. Charles stresses in his reply
to Neimes that his grief was such that it was impossible for
him not to display it ("Si grant doel ai ne puis muer nel
pleigne," 834) and the poet tells us specifically that
Charles cried ("Carles li magnes ne poet muer n'en plurt,"
841).

The locution faire (la) contenance in the Roland and
Partonopeu de Blois could perhaps be translated as "to display one's feelings fully," an interpretation which is also
acceptable for the phrase faire contenant (gent) in 1. 825
of the Pèlerinage de Charlemagne. Moreover, it is probably
in one's facial expression that reaction to a situation is
reflected most distinctly. In Chrétien's Yvain we are told
that Harpin de la Montagne's victims will put on a smile in
Yvain's presence and at least look as if they are happy:

> Mes por vos tant con nos poons
> Nos resforçons a la foiee
> De feire contenance liee. (3874-76)[32]

There is an element of self-mastery here but the accent is
on display and it is from this point of view that Roques
is right to link the expression _faire la contenance_ with
the verb _se contenir_. The first occurrence of this verb
is found in the _Vie de saint Alexis_ ("Unc puis cel di nes
contint ledement," 140) and there is one example in the
Roland: "Pur Pinabel se cuntienent plus quei," 3797.[33] I
should translate the verb in these example as "to display,
to show oneself." In _Erec et Enide_, Enide has donned her
best dress in readiness for departure, but she is in doubt
concerning Erec's intentions. Chrétien describes her
reaction to her situation as follows:

> Molt s'est Enyde merveilliee
> Que ses sires ot an corage,
> Mes de ce fist ele que sage
> Car plus lieemant se contint
> Qu'ele pot, quant devant lui vint. (2676-80)[34]

This passage is well translated by Comfort: "But she very
wisely showed herself with as cheerful a countenance as
possible, when she appeared before him." Enide does not
behave joyfully, she assumes a cheerful expression.

In general I am inclined to render two cases of
cuntenance in the _Roland_ as "face, expression" or possibly
"appearance" (3006, 3086) and l. 830 as "beneath his cloak
he gives expression to his feelings." _Cuntenant_ I should
translate as "face" or "expression" in l. 118 and as "expression" in l. 3116. It could be noted that the term _cors_
appears twice in the same line as our terms (118, 3086)
and once in the preceding line (3116). The linking of a
reference to the body with one to the face is a well a
attested device in the _Roland_:

> Cors ad mult gent e le vis fier e cler. (895)

Cors ad mult gent, le vis cler e riant.   (1159)

Cors ad gaillard, el vis gente color.   (3763)

Heingre out le cors e graisle e eschewid,
Neirs les chevels e alques bruns le vis.   (3820-21)

Vairs out les oilz e mult fier lu visage;
Gent out le cors e les costez out larges.   (283-84)

Bédier may be right to translate contenement in l. 1641 as
"allure," but one cannot rule out the meaning "appearance"
here or for the MS P variant for l. 3116 ("Cler a le vis
et bel contenement"). When Philippe de Thaün speaks of
the lion, possessed of a "fier cuntenement" and "fier
vengement" (Bestiaire, 53-54), he may also have in mind
the lion's fierce appearance.[35]

A general survey of other examples of contenance in Old
French produces no definite conclusions. It is possible to
find examples in which contenance is glossed, probably
correctly, as "face, expression" or "appearance": e.g.,

Et Gauvains a mout regardé
Sa contenance et sa figure.
          (La Mule sans frein, 520-21)[36]

Quant Cesar vit lor contenance
Bien sot que par desesparance
Se voudront a la mort livrer.
          (Robert de Blois, L'Enseignement
               des princes, 1377-79)[37]

Quanque je voy me desplaist et ennuye,
Et n'en ose contenance moustrer.
          (Charles d'Orléans, Ballades, X, 9-10)[38]

In other cases the meaning is certainly "conduct, bearing":
e.g.,

Uns chevaliers preuz et vaillanz,
Et si ert biaus et avenanz
Et de mout sage contenance.
          (Guillaume de Dole, 663-64)[39]

De sa biauté, de sa semblance
E de sa simple contenance.
          (Roman de la Rose, 2695-96)[40]

Deus! tant vilain morsaus transglotent
Es povres maisons qu'il destruent
Quant il dou lor les despens fuent.
Il n'ont contenance mäure;
Il ne vivent selonc droiture.
(Guiot de Provins, La Bible, 836-40)[41]

Contenant also seems to mean in some cases "behaviour":

Mult parlèrent estreitement
E desputèrent clergeaument
Lesqualitez e les contenanz
E les mours de les enfanz,
Lur colurs e lur afferes.
(Continuation anonyme du Brut de Wace)[42]

Uns riches cuers en povres pances,
Qui font si orguilleusement
Des contenans lour jugement
Qui sunt touz temps enflammez d'ire,
Preis de tencer et de maldire,
Et Dieu meïsmes mal gracient.
(Conte from the Tombel de
Chartrose collection, XXII, 32-37)[43]

Although inconclusive, the evidence presented in the
foregoing pages is perhaps sufficient to question the rejection by Renson and others of the meaning "face, expression"
for contenance and contenant. When Roques states categorically that "la contenance est le 'maintien,' c'est-à-dire la
façon dont on se tient"[44] or when Spitzer tells us that "un
mot comme contenance ne sera jamais exclusivement ni 'maintien' ni 'figure,' 'mine,' ni 'effort de se contenir,'
maîtrise de soi' ni 'silence,' ni 'continence,' ni 'renoncement,' il sera toujours possible d'assumer tous ces sens
ensemble,"[45] we may be equally far from a full understanding
of a given Old French example. If a word attested, for
example, in the Chanson de Roland is found in later Old
French or in Modern French, it would be wise to assume that
its meaning and syntax should be the object of careful investigation and that it has undergone probably several shifts
in emphasis before its usage corresponds to Modern or later
Old French patterns. Such a shift might have taken place or
be beginning to take place by the second half of the twelfth

century. Considered in this light, a study of the first
examples in French of a word such as contenance can help us
to understand better the precise patterns of thought interpreted for us by an Old French writer.

No Old French dictionary covers adequately the range
of possible meanings for the terms contenance and contenant.
Only the dictionary of Tobler-Lommatzsch mentions for
contenant the meaning "contents, extent" ("Inhalt") of
which there are at least two possible examples:

> La cele est d'or et derriere et devant,
> Oevres i ot de molt divers semblant,
> Taillie a bestes de riches contenant.
> (Raoul de Cambrai, 500-502)[46]

> Or faites pais, segnor, por Diu le grant;
> S'oiiés cançon de moult fier contenant.
> (Huon de Bordeaux, 1087-88)[47]

The present study has concentrated on twelfth-century
examples, but it should be noted that new meanings for
contenance develop later. These are cited by Godefroy
("séjour, manchon, écran") and the FEW, but are not mentioned by Grandsaignes d'Hauterive or Greimas. The term
contenant, deriving from (sei) contenir, "to behave, to
display an attitude," seems to have disappeared by the end
of the fourteenth-century at the latest. The form contenant (contenir, "to contain") survives in Modern French.
Finally, if contenance in French could mean "face," as some
scholars think (and Cotgrave in the seventeenth-century
thought so too: "the countenance, looke, cheer, visage,
etc.") this would cast doubt on the opinion expresssed in
the Oxford English Dictionary that the development of this
meaning is peculiar to English.

Notes

1. Jean Renson, Les Dénominations du visage en français et dans les autres langues romanes: Etude sémantique
et onomasiologique. 2 vols. (Paris, 1962), II, 427-28.

2. Ibid., p. 427. Renson admits that in some cases
the meaning of the word contenance is "difficile à
expliquer" and quotes two examples, from the Facétieuses
Nuits and the Heptaméron of Marguerite de Navarre, which
offer in his view grounds for hesitation (p. 427).

3. Ibid., p. 427.

4. La Chanson de Roland, ed. J. Bédier: text and
translation (Paris, 1921; definitive edition, 1937). The
following discussion also cites the edition or translation
of L. Bacon (New Haven, 1914), G. Bertoni (Florence, 1935),
E. Boehmer (Halle, 1872), W. Calin (New York, 1968),
L. Clédat (Paris, 1886; traduction archaïque, Paris, 1887),
J. Crosland (London-Boston, 1907), L. Gautier (Tours, 1872,
etc.), J. Geddes, Jr. (New York, 1906), F. Génin (Paris,
1850), G. Gröber (Strasbourg, 1908), R. Hague (London,
1937), R. Harrison (New York-Toronto, 1970), A. Hilka
(Halle, 1926), T. A. Jenkins (Chicago, 1924; 2nd ed. 1929),
G. F. Jones and A. Demaître (Englewood Cliffs, 1971), W. S.
Merwin in Medieval Epics (New York, 1963), F. Michel (Paris,
1837; 2nd ed. 1869), G. Moignet (Paris, 1969), C. S.
Moncrieff (London, 1919), Th. Müller (Göttingen, 1851; 2nd
ed. 1863; 3rd ed. 1878), D. D. R. Owen (London, 1972),
A. Pauphilet in Poètes et romanciers du moyen âge (Paris,
1952), L. Petit de Julleville (Paris, 1878), H. S.
Robertson (London, 1972), D. L. Sayers (London, 1957),
C. Segre (Milan-Naples, 1971), E. Soufflet (Angers, 1943),
E. Stengel (Leipzig, 1900), A. S. Way (Cambridge, 1913),
F. Whitehead (Oxford, 1942; 2nd ed. 1946). For quotations
from other MSS of the Roland I have used R. Mortier, 10
vols. (Paris, 1940-44). The glossary of L. Foulet is found
in J. Bédier, La Chanson de Roland commentée (Paris, 1927).

5. Commentaires, p. 198. Bédier writes assonance
here by mistake. The emendation produces a metrically
acceptable line.

6. The first example of contenement in French seems
to occur in the Jonas fragment: "E si contenement fisïent,
si achederent veniam et resolutionem peccatorum suorum"
(ed. K. Bartsch and L. Wiese in Chrestomathie de l'ancien
français, 10th ed., Leipzig, 1910), p. 5, ll. 35-36.

7. G. S. Burgess, "Orgueil and fierté in Twelfth-
Century French," ZRP, 89 (1973), 103-122.

8. Edited by E. Langlois. 2nd ed., rev., CFMA (Paris:
Champion, 1925). See also ll. 354, 550, 1260, 1739, 2084.

9. Edited by D. McMillan (Paris, 1972). See also ll.
663, 676, 761, 798.

10. Edited by C. Régnier (Paris, 1967). See also
l. 875.

11. Edited by G. Favati (Bologna, 1965). I have also
used the editions of F. Michel (London-Paris, 1836), E.
Koschwitz, 7th ed. (Leipzig, 1923), A. S. Cooper (Paris,
1925), and P. Aebischer (Paris-Geneva, 1965).

12. In MS A^4 of the _Prise_, 1. 1480, the reading _cors_
fier is found (for _couchier_ A^{1}A^{2}A^{3}B).

13. G. F. Jones, _The Ethos of the Song of Roland_
(Baltimore, 1963), p. 66.

14. _Elie de saint Gille_, ed. G. Raynaud, SATF (Paris:
Picard, 1879), 11. 1304-1305: "Ne vous dementés si comme
veve caitive: / Faites bel contenant, franc chevalier nobile";
Floire et Blancheflor, ed. F. Krüger (Berlin, 1938), 11.
574-575: "L'uns jouste l'autre se seoit, / Gente contenance
fesoit" (MS B used by M. M. Pelan, Paris, 1956, has _riche_
contenance); _Ille et Galeron_, ed. F. A. G. Cowper, SATF
(Paris: Picard, 1956), 11. 1450-51: "Ylles fait gente
contenance, / Sasist l'escu et prent la lance" (_bele_
contenance P). Cowper glosses as "maintien, contenance,
mine" this last example and that in 1. 431: "Cascuns par
fiere contenance / Point le ceval, basse la lance" (_por_
faire contenance P). The phrase _par fiere contenance_ (W)
may mean "with fierce expression." The meaning of _pour_
faire contenance in P (1. 682, ed. E. Löseth, Paris, 1890)
is not clear from the context and the phrase is translated
unsatisfactorily by Tobler-Lommatzsch as "sich eine Haltung
geben."

15. Cooper translates the phrase as: "Elle avait vis-
à-vis de lui une attitude engageante et amicale." The
expression _far contenensa_ with the meaning "faire bon
accueil" is attested in the poetry of Marcabru, ed. J. M. L.
Dejeanne (Toulouse, 1909), IX, 29; XXVI, 44. See also
L. Spitzer, "Le Vers 830 du _Roland_," _Rom_, 68 (1944-45),
471-77, p. 477n.

16. Edited by H. Michelant and P. Meyer, SATF (Paris:
Picard, 1894).

17. Edited by D. McMillan. 2 vols., SATF (Paris:
Picard, 1949). For _contenant_, H. Suchier (Halle, 1911) has
semblant. We should note that the line in the McMillan
edition is metrically impossible.

18. It is true that in 1. 3117 Charles rides "mult
aficheement." Bédier translates the adverb here as "ferme
sur l'étrier" (followed by Moignet, Owen, etc.) whereas the
term may mean simply "resolutely" (Whitehead). See I.
Short in _RPh_, 25 (1971-72), 134.

19. The adjective _fier_ and _bel_ are almost interchange-
able. For _beles cuntenances_ in 1. 3086 _P_ has _lor fiere_
contenance and T _leur fier contenement_. The adjective _bon_
in 1. 3116 is replaced by _fer_ in V^4 and _bel_ in P.

20. Cf. the review of Clédat's edition by G. Paris in
Rom, 15 (1886), 141, and Bédier, _Commentaires_, p. 208. The
reading _enfuit_ is rightly considered as an incorrect form
and as too modern an idea by Foerster in his review of
Müller's 3rd edition, _ZRP_, 2 (1878), 173. Clédat's reading
en fuit is perhaps more plausible, but the verb _foïr_ does
not fit well with _contenance_. The syntax _foïr aucune rien_

has, however, been attested since the Eulalia: "Il i
enortet, dont lei nonque chielt, / qued elle fuiet lo nom
christiien" (13-14, ed. Bartsch-Wiese).

21. Rom, 54 (1928), 578-79, p. 579. The cause of
Charlemagne's attitude is, according to Roques, physical
or moral weariness or sickness: "'Rester sous son manteau,'
ne pas redresser son buste, ne pas dégager son cou, ses
mains, ses bras, ne pas donner de l'aisance à ses membres,
c'est ne pas avoir une 'fière contenance,' c'est le fait
d'un malade, d'un fatigué physiquement ou moralement"
(pp. 578-79).

22. G. Bertoni, "Nota sul verso 830 della Chanson de
Roland," Archivum Romanicum, 9 (1925), 216. On the verb
cuter see A. Thomas, Rom, 42 (1913), 387-90.

23. Note to his edition, 1. 830.

24. Op. cit., pp. 474-75.

25. Ibid., p. 475.

26. Rom, 66 (1940-41), 549. If Charles does conceal
his face beneath his cloak, it is unlikely that he would
do so in order to display "une attitude calme et digne."

27. In spite of Spitzer's approval of his interpretation, we should note that Bertoni translates cuntenance as
"face."

28. Roques, p. 578: "Attitude peu recommendable pour
guider sûrement son cheval à moins qu'il ne s'agisse d'un
manteau à capuchon" (cf. also Jenkins, p. 70, n.). The
scribe of MS T replaces suz sun mantel with desoubz son
elme.

29. Edited by W. Roach. 4 vols. to date (Philadelphia,
1949-1971), vol. II. Cf. also MS E 16485-86: "De son
mantel son chief covri, / Ainz mes hom ne fu si marri";
Galeran de Bretagne, ed. L. Foulet, CFMA (Paris, 1925),
7059-60: "S'a son mantel mis sur son chief; Veoir la joie
lui est grief." See also Tobler-Lommatzsch, art. mantel,
and Foulet's glossary to the First Continuation (vol. III,
pt. 2).

30. L. Foulet, glossary to the Roland, p. 378. Cf.
Jenkins, p. 317, Spitzer, op. cit., p. 472, 476, and Roques
in a supplementary remark to Spitzer's article, p. 472. I
am grateful for remarks on the question of the definite
article and the pronoun en to my colleague, Dr. J. Linskill,
and to Dr. R. Harris of the University of Oxford.

31. Edited by J. Gildea. 2 vols. (Villanova, 1967-68).

32. Edited by M. Roques, CFMA (Paris: Champion, 1960).
A similar example occurs in the Eneas: "Teus sont dolant
qui font samblant / Contenance de joie grant" (9823-24),
ed. J.-J. Salverda de Grave. 2 vols. CFMA (Paris: Champion,
1925-29). It may well be preferable to emend 1. 9824 to [E]
contenant de joie grant. Cf. also Chrétien de Troyes,

Philomena, ed. C. de Boer (Paris, 1909), 11. 904-906: "Li
fel tint la teste beissiee / Et fist sanblant et contenance
/ D'ome qui et duel et pesance."

33.   La _Vie de saint Alexis_, C. Storey (Geneva, 1968).
Ll. 3796-97 of the _Roland_ were the subject of a paper entitled "Remarques sur deux vers de la _Chanson de Roland_,"
which I presented to the 6th Congress of the _Société
Rencesvals_, held at Aix-en-Provence, 28 August-4 September,
1973, published in the _Actes_ (Aix-en-Provence, 1974),
pp. 65-78.

34.   Edited by M. Roques, CFMA (Paris: Champion, 1952)
and translated by W. W. Comfort (_Arthurian Romances_, London:
Everyman's Library 1914). The term _contenance_ in 1. 5489
("Seul de veoir sa contenance, / Sa grant biauté et sa
sanblance. . .," 5489-90) is rendered by Comfort as "countenance," by R. Louis (Paris, 1954) as "attitude."

35.   Edited by E. Walberg (Lund, 1900). Cf. also _Bueve
de Hantone_, ed. A. Stimming. 5 vols. (Dresden, 1911-20),
IIIa, 10444-45: "Li rois saut sus, qui moult ot hardement,
/ L'espee a traite par fier contenement," quoted by M.
Wandruszka, _Haltung und Gebärde der Romanen_ (Tübingen,
1954), p. 11.

36.   Edited by R. C. Johnston and D. D. R. Owen
(Edinburgh-London, 1972). The glossary gives "appearance,
visage."

37.   Edited by J. H. Fox (Paris, 1950), who in his
glossary offers "apparence."

38.   Edited by P. Champion. 2 vols., CFMA (Paris:
Champion, 1966), vol. I. D. Poirion in his _Lexique de
Charles d'Orléans dans les Ballades_ (Geneva, 1967) gives
for this example "expression du visage, manifestation
d'un sentiment par une attitude."

39.   Edited by F. Lecoy, CFMA (Paris: Champion, 1962).

40.   Edited by E. Langlois. 5 vols. SATF (Paris:
Picard, 1914-1924).

41.   Edited by J. Orr (Manchester, 1915).

42.   Edited by F. Michel in _Chroniques Anglo-Normandes_,
3 vols. (Paris, 1836), I, 81.

43.   _Contes pieux en vers du XIVe siècle tirés du
recueil intitulé le Tombel de Chartrose_, ed. E. Walberg
(Lund, 1946). The glossary definition of _contenant_ here is
"qui observe la continence," which I consider less likely
than the meaning "behaviour." There is however no doubt
that the form _contenance_ is found with the meaning "continence": e.g., Pierre d'Abernum of Fetchan, _Le Secré de
Secrez_, ed. O. A. Beckerlegge (Oxford, 1944), 1. 796:
"Descretiun e contenance aveir." Cf. also 1. 815: "E
cuntinance garder, sanz folur."

44.   Op. cit., p. 578.

45. Op. cit., pp. 476-77.

46. Edited by P. Meyer and A. Longnon, SATF (Paris: Picard, 1882). The editors suggest that 1. 502 is corrupt (glossary, art. contenant). However, if we give to the expression de riches contenant the meaning "rich in significance" or "on a liberal scale" (i.e., embracing a wide range of beasts), and emend riches to riche, the line is probably acceptable. Such a meaning would also render less surprising the presence in the same laisse of contenant in the sense of "expression" or "attitude": "R.i saut par si fier contenant, / Puis a saisi l'escu a or luisant' (506-507).

47. Edited by P. Ruelle (Bruxelles-Paris, 1960), who cites the suggestion of Tobler-Lommatzsch, but offers himself the unlikely meaning "apparence." Fier here probably means "remarkable, extraordinary" rather than "noble" (glossary).

QUELQUES ASPECTS DU "VERS ORPHELIN" DANS GARIN DE MONGLANE[1]

William L. Hendrickson

Dans son premier volume des Chansons de geste de Guillaume d'Orange Jean Frappier présente le "vers orphelin" de la manière suivante: "la facture de la laisse est caractérisée par la présence d'un vers final plus court que les précédents, un hexasyllabe après des décasyllabes; il est en outre de terminaison féminine indépendante de l'assonance ou de la rime de la laisse. . . . Ce 'petit vers,' dit aussi 'vers orphelin,' donne lieu à beaucoup de discussions."[2] Bien que "le vers orphelin" ait donné lieu à beaucoup de discussions, la plupart de ces dernières ont porté sur les poèmes épiques du "Cycle de Guillaume d'Orange" pour lesquels il y a souvent deux versions, une avec le petit vers et l'autre sans celui-ci.[3] La question principale est de savoir laquelle des deux versions est la plus ancienne. Pour une bonne mise au point concernant quelques manuscrits je renvoie le lecteur à l'étude de Mlle Madeleine Tyssens.[4] Néanmoins cette question est sans importance pour l'arrière-grand-père de la geste et pour sa propre chanson, Garin de Monglane, car il s'agit d'un poème assez tardif, probablement du milieu de XIIIe siècle, et d'autre part, tous les manuscrits et les fragments que nous connaissons contiennent ce "vers ophelin" à la fin de chaque laisse dodécasyllabique rimée.

Lors de la préparation d'une édition critique de Garin de Monglane, j'ai étudié le "vers orphelin" d'assez près. Une de mes conclusions est que le "vers orphelin" est une partie intégrante de chacune des laisses de Garin de Monglane. Comme démonstration, j'ai pris les 141 laisses publiées jusqu'ici.[5] Pour ces laisses, 48 des "vers orphelins" sont constitués par la fin des propos que tient un personnage de l'épopée. Afin de demontrer le lien

étroit entre la laisse et le "vers orphelin," j'ai inclus
dans mon étude le vers qui précède ce petit vers dans chaque
laisse et j'ai établi la relation entre eux. Les résultats
sont basés sur la ponctuation fournie par les éditeurs.
Selon moi, le choix de la ponctuation par les éditeurs
devait révéler leur impression concernant la présence ou
l'absence d'un lien entre le "vers ophelin" et l'avant-
dernier vers de la laisse.[6] La ponctuation qu'on y trouve
est la suivante:

absence de ponctuation	50 fois
virgule	48 fois
point-virgule	30 fois
deux points	1 fois
point	7 fois
point d'exclamation	5 fois

Ces résultats démontrent une conception de la laisse qui
place sa conclusion narrative dans le "vers orphelin." On
ne trouve que de rares exemples où le dernier vers dodécasyllabique de la laisse possède cet aspect de "vers de conclusion," comme l'appelle Jean Rychner.[7] Tout comme on peut
affirmer que le "vers orphelin" est inséparable du "Cycle
d'Aimeri," on peut dire que l'auteur de Garin de Monglane a
suivi la tradition en ajoutant d'autres aventures à la geste
dans une forme qui faisait partie de cette tradition.

Quoique le "vers orphelin" apparaisse comme un élément
structural pour les laisses de Garin de Monglane, il y a
néanmoins une certaine ressemblance entre les vers finals de
ces laisses. Ceci suscite une question sur plusieurs autres
aspects de ce petit vers. Abordant ce sujet, Jean Frappier
affirme: "L'hexasyllabe orphelin pourrait être, dans une
forme atténuée, une persistance du refrain qui semble avoir
existé à date ancienne à la fin des laisses épiques (on en
trouve notamment des traces dans Gormond et Isembart); s'il
s'agit d'une mode récente et passagère, elle serait
l'aboutissement d'une facture archaïque, ou un pastiche
discret de cette facture."[8] La répétition de certains "vers
orphelins" identiques aussi bien que la réapparition de

"vers orphelins" similaires ou semblables dans <u>Garin de Monglane</u> évoquent l'idée d'une espèce de refrain. Les exemples, tous fortement formulaires, démontrent ce phéno- mène. Pour les besoins de cet article, je me suis servi des 298 "vers orphelins" du manuscrit de la Bibliothèque Nationale (fonds français 24403, ancien La Vallière 78). Selon moi, ce manuscrit se rapproche le plus du poème original, surtout en ce qui concerne son dialecte. Mal- heureusement, il lui manque un demi-cahier. D'abord les vers identiques:

El roiaume de France	2 fois
Et molt ara pesance	2 fois
Si com porrés entendre	2 fois
Ainçois la nuit serie	2 fois
A nul jor de sa vie	2 fois
A nul jor de ma vie	2 fois
A ce ne faura mie	2 fois
N'en escaperai mie	2 fois
N'en puet estordre mie	2 fois
Qui molt fort le justissent	2 fois
Car ce sera droiture	3 fois

D'autres vers sont presque identiques, par exemple:

Car ce seroit damages
Car ce seroit outrages

Je te di sans soutance
Je vos di sans doutance

Dex de mort le deffende
Et de mort le deffende

Je li tolra la vie
Qui li tolra sa vie

Benoite soit ta vie
Maudite soit sa vie

Qu'ensi n'en irés mie
Ensi n'en iront mie

Savoir que volrai dire
Savoir qu'il valront dire

Et tornés a martire
Et torner a martire
Et traira a martire

Por mener a martire
Por morir a martire

Fille a roi ni a conte
Fille au roi ne a conte

```
Tuit i morront a honte
Tot i morront a honte
```

Il y a d'autres vers encore qui manifestent de fortes
ressemblances formulaires:

```
Ce samblë un diable
Ce est un vis diables

Molt lor fait grant damage
Dont ce fu grant damages
Dont ce sera damages

Mais ains en ara paine
Tant en ara grant paine

Li bers de bon afaire
Tant fu de bone afaire
Qui est de pute afaire

Por Garin a mort traire
Des franchois a mort traire

Por ce que il nel perde
Paor a ne le perde

Que il n'i fist demeure
N'i fist longe demeure

Qu'il ne m'espargnast mie
Ne l'espargnassent mie

Des caillex et des pieres
De la tere et des pierez

Au cuer en a grant ire
S'en ot au cuer grant ire

Espris de molt grant ire
Il fu plains de grant ire
Molt fu grains et plains d'ire

Ou je morrai a honte
Et morrai ci a honte

Il li fera grant honte
Et si li fera honte
```

Enfin, nous avons des "vers orphelins" pour lesquels
la ressemblance principale est dans le dernier mot. La
plupart de ces mots se trouvent dans les différents exemples
déjà cités, ce qui me dispense d'énumérer une longue liste
de "vers orphelins" supplémentaires. Ces mots finals, pourtant, ainsi que d'autres mots dont la dernière syllabe est

la même, prédominent et cela constitue une particularité
extrêmement intéressante.

Maintenant, nous donnons une liste de terminaisons des
"vers orphelins" et la fréquence de chaque terminaison dans
les 298 laisses du manuscrit de Paris:

-ie	48	fois	(16,1 pour cent)
-anc(h)e	17	fois	
-aire	16	fois	
-ire	14	fois	
-age	13	fois	
-oie(nt)	13	fois	
-onte	11	fois	
-aine(nt)	9	fois	
-ure	9	fois	
-ere	8	fois	
-ele(s)	6	fois	
-iere(nt)(s,z)	6	fois	
-endre	6	fois	
-orce	5	fois	
-aille(s)	4	fois	
-ee	4	fois	
-ende(nt)	4	fois	
-eure	4	fois	
-able(s)	3	fois	
-ece	3	fois	
-este	3	fois	
-ine(s)	3	fois	
-is(s)e(nt)	3	fois	
-oisse	3	fois	
-ome(z)	3	fois	
-orre	3	fois	
-oute(nt)	3	fois	

Signalons d'autre part que seize autres terminaisons se
répètent deux fois chacune. Si on examine la liste de près,
on note que les dix premières terminaisons comprennent 158,
ou 53 pour cent, des "vers orphelins." L'ensemble de la
liste contient 224 répétitions, ou presque 75 pour cent des
vers. Des 298 petits vers, 42 seulement ne se répètent pas
au moins deux fois.

Il est difficile de déterminer si cette répétition de
sons est due en partie aux exigences de la forme du "vers
ophelin." Il est certain que la terminaison féminine limite
le nombre de mots qu'on pouvait employer à la fin du vers.
Quelques-uns des "vers orphelins" se trouvent dans d'autres

chansons de geste, mais moins souvent qu'on ne pourrait le
penser. On remarque facilement que les "vers orphelins" qui
se terminent en "-ie" dominent. Treize de ces vers ont "mie"
comme mot final, formule sans doute très facile. Ce fait est
évident dans le manuscrit du British Museum (Royal 20 D XI).
Le texte y est en effet abrégé et les "vers orphelins" sont
souvent changés. Par exemple, dans les 127 premières laisses
du manuscrit de Londres on remarquera que six "vers orphelins"
de plus que dans le manuscrit de Paris se terminent en "mie."
"mie Bien qu'aucun des petits vers ne révèle une originalité
particulière (un vers seul se termine par "Monglane" et un
autre par le nom du géant "Robastre"), l'écho de plusieurs
vers et la répétition de certaines terminaisons semblent être
plus qu'une simple coïncidence. En dépit de la variété des
mots finals aussi bien que des terminaisons, certains d'entre
eux prédominent et créent une cadence lyrique et même musicale. Ce dernier trait rappelle les paroles de Jean de
Grouchy sur la musique de la chanson de geste: "Les vers,
dans la chanson de geste, qui se compose d'une suite de
laisses, se terminent par le même vocalisme et par des mots
qui présentent la même consonance. Cependant, dans certaines
chansons, on termine la laisse par un vers d'une consonance
différente de celle des autres vers, par exemple dans la
geste de Girart de Vienne."[9] Ne suffit-il pas de se souvenir que Girart de Vienne est le fils de Garin de Monglane--
le fils précède le père comme il arrive souvent dans les
lignages épiques--et que la forme des deux chansons est
presque identique?[10] La présence de terminaisons asso-
nantes ainsi que la possibilité d'une phrase musicale différente pour le "vers orphelin," comme dans Aucassin et
Nicolette par exemple, suggèrent l'une et l'autre l'aspect
d'un véritable refrain. Il se peut bien que l'auteur ait
tenté de raffiner le petit vers en lui donnant une qualité
plus lyrique par le moyen de la répétition et de l'assonance.
En tout cas, dans Garin de Monglane le "vers orphelin" semble
jouer un rôle musical aussi bien qu'un rôle narratif par sa
relation avec la laisse et avec la chanson dans son ensemble.

Notes

1. Le fond de cet article fut présenté en 1970 au Ve Congrès International de la Société Rencesvals à Oxford, dont les Actes n'ont jamais paru. Je tiens à remercier le National Endowment for the Humanities pour son aide.

2. Jean Frappier, Les Chansons de geste du cycle de Guillaume d'Orange (Paris: SEDES, 1955), I, 44-45.

3. Deux études intéressantes qui traitent du "vers orphelin" d'une autre manière sont celles d'Aurelio Roncaglia, "Petit vers et refrain dans les chansons de geste," dans La Technique littéraire des chansons de geste (Liège-Paris: Société des Belles Lettres, 1959) et de Peter F. Dembowski, "Le Vers orphelin dans les chansons de geste et son emploi dans la 'geste de Blaye'," une communication faite au Congrès du Kentucky au printemps 1970. Monsieur Dembowski a eu la bonté de m'envoyer un exemplaire de sa communication.

4. Madeleine Tyssens, La Geste de Guillaume d'Orange dans les manuscrits cycliques (Liège-Paris: Société des Belles Lettres, 1967), chapitres VI et XIII. Les grandes lignes de cette étude furent d'abord exposées dans La Technique littéraire des chansons de geste (Liège-Paris: Société des Belles Lettres, 1959), pp. 429-56.

5. On trouve les 127 premières laisses dans les thèses suivantes: Erich Schuppe, Die Chanson de Monglene nach den HSS. PRL--Teil I (Greifswald: Buchdruckerei Hans Adler, 1914); Max Müller, Die Chanson G. de Monglene nach den HSS. PLR--Teil II (Greifswald: Buchdruckerei Hans Adler, 1913); Hermann Menn, Die Chanson G. de Monglene nach den HSS. PLRT Teil III--(Die Monglene-Episode) (Greifswald: Buchdruckerei Hans Adler, 1913); et William L. Hendrickson, "A Critical Edition of the fragment of Garin de Monglane in the Garrett 125 manuscript," Dissertation Abstracts, 30 (1969), 2024-2025A (Princeton University). Le fragment de Princeton qui consiste en 1.032 vers apporte 317 vers de texte critique supplémentaire pour en donner 5.010 de suite, v. Rom, 96 (1975), 163-93. L'article de Mlle X. Pamfilova, "Fragments de chansons de geste," Rom, 57 (1931), 518-38, en ajoute 786 de plus.

6. Je me rends compte que la ponctuation varie selon l'éditeur, mais j'ai examiné tous les endroits mentionnés, et je considère leur ponctuation comme une indication de la continuation ou de la non-continuation de la narration.

7. Jean Rychner, La Chanson de Geste. Essai sur l'art épique des jongleurs (Genève-Lille; Droz-Minard, 1955), p. 72.

8. Jean Frappier, Les Chansons de geste du cycle de Guillaume d'Orange (Paris: SEDES, 1955), I, 57, n. 1. Monsieur Frappier, avec qui je me suis entretenu à ce sujet, insiste sur la différence entre le refrain et le petit vers, celui-ci étant peut-être la transformation et le souvenir de

celui-là. Selon Monsieur Frappier, il y a en tout cas un
changement de système.

9. Je cite la traduction française de René Louis qu'il
présente dans "Le Refrain dans les plus anciennes chansons
de geste et le sigle AOI dans le Roland d'Oxford," Mélanges
Istvan Frank, Annales Universitatis Saraviensis, VI (Sara-
ïevo, 1957), p. 345. A la page suivante Monsieur Louis
donne comme exemple un "vers orphelin" de Girart de Vienne
et il dit qu'il n'y a que cinq pieds!

10. Girart de Vienne est cependant décasyllabique.

Part II

Word/Geste

INTERPRETIVE STUDIES OF OLD FRENCH EPIC,

MORAL LITERATURE AND HAGIOGRAPHY

ROLAND VS. THE BARONS

William W. Kibler

In an article intended originally for the present
Festschrift, but which the editor consented to release for
earlier publication in Olifant,[1] I sought to establish a
relationship of analogy between the First Council Scene of
the Chanson de Roland and the culminating Judgement of
Ganelon scene.[2] In the council scene, the first major
episode of the epic (laisses VIII-XXVI), emissaries from
Marsilie propose a truce on what appears at first to be
favorable terms for Charlemagne's Christian army. Charles
calls together his advisers to consider the proposal.
Although the men acknowledge that "Il nus i cuvent guarde"
(v. 192),[3] Roland is the only individual to speak against
the majority decision, which is to accept Marsilie's proposal. In the Judgment Scene, the last major section of
the poem (laisses CCLXXVI-CCXCVI), Charles again is faced
with a difficult decision which he submits to his advisers:
what is to be done with Ganelon? Persuaded by Ganelon's
impassioned pleas, or unwilling to face the consequences
of adjudging him guilty, Charlemagne's men declare,

> . . . "Sire, nus vos prïum
> Que clamez quite le cunte Guenelun."
> (vv. 3808-3809)

Tierri alone opposes the majority decision.

The two episodes in question are closely related one
to the other, and not only by the overall similarity of
situation just sketched. Laisse XII, which names the
twelve peers who counsel Charlemagne and ends

    Guenes i vint ki la traïsun fist.
    Des ore cumencet le cunseill que mal prist.
                              (vv. 178-79)

is echoed by laisse CCLXXXII:

    Bavier e Saisnes sunt alét a conseill
    E Peitevin e Norman e Franceis;
    Asez i ad Alemans e Tiedeis,
    Icels d'Alverne(ne) i sunt li plus curteis;
                              (vv. 3793-96)

and by lines 3747-48:

    Des ore cumencet le plait e les noveles
    De Guenelun ki traïsun ad faite.

Laisse XIII, in which Charles addresses his barons, stating
the situation and requesting their advice, has its analogue
in laisse CCLXXVIII; Ganelon's proud speech in laisse XV is
balanced by laisse CCLXXIX. The first episode prepares the
treason which will culminate in the disaster at Roncevaux;
the second makes good the wrong which has been perpetrated.
It is the necessary counterpoise to the first.

    There is, to be sure, one principal and necessary
difference between the two scenes in question. In order
for the treason to take place, Charles must ignore Roland's
warning; in order to avenge Roland, he must accept Tierri's
offer of aid. This distinction, however, is on the level
of the plot, and does not affect the moral posture of the
two barons. While it would be excessive to pretend that
Tierri is a "second Roland,"[4] it does seem evident that the
poet intended us to recognize a close relationship between
the two: both stand alone against the majority opinion, and
both are ultimately proven right; both are eloquent speakers
in the defense of Justice; both are concerned with their
parenté. Roland bravely faces the overwhelming odds represented by Marsilie's troops, while Tierri, described as
"heingre, graisle e eschewid" (v. 3820), boldly challenges
the more powerful Pinabel.

It is my belief that the role of Tierri in the Judgment
Scene in a sense "glosses" that of Roland. The use of analogous scenes to enhance understanding and to deepen the significance of parallel episodes or repeated motifs has been
capably demonstrated by Professor Eugene Vinaver in his The
Rise of Romance,[5] although his characterization of the epic
as a form "which sought not to enlighten, but to move and to
impress" (p. 14), might make him hesitate to attempt to discover enlightening analogies in a poem such as the Roland.
Yet I believe that in a well-wrought epic like the Roland,
analogy and echoing possess elucidating roles similar to
those Vinaver has shown them to have in romance. But whereas
in a romance the poet seeks to motivate and explain the
actions of his characters, in the epic analogy is used to
heighten an effect, to prove by repetition that the particular action is a part of God's greater plan. It is the
scene with Tierri which, by analogy, enables us to appreciate the wisdom and insight of Roland. Like Roland, Tierri
defends an unpopular position and, like him, is proven to be
right. God's miracle on his behalf ("Deus i ad fait vertut"
v. 3931) is the unmistakable sign that He acknowledges the
truthfulness of Tierri's position (laisse CCLXXXIV) rather
than Ganelon's (laisses CCLXXVIII-CCLXXIX), and that He will
not permit Evil to prevail over Good ("E! Deus," dist Carles,
"le dreit en esclargiez!" v. 3891). In the same way, God's
miraculous interventions earlier in the epic--at Roland's
death (laisse CLXXVI) and to make possible Charlemagne's
triumph over the Saracens (laisse CLXXIX)--show His approval
of Roland's position, which is to assure the total victory
of Christianity at whatever cost. By establishing the
analogies which we have seen between Roland and Tierri, the
poet seems clearly to intend us to recognize God's approbation of both the victory and methods of Roland through his
approval and intervention in those of Tierri.

The strength of the analogy is in the opposition of
two situations, the former clouded and open to debate, the
latter clear, immediate and incontrovertible. If we accept

the Tierri-Roland analogy, we can find in the Judgment Scene
the vindication of Roland's earlier actions in the First
Council Scene and in his refusal to sound his horn. The
principal consequence of the analogy is, thus, to reaffirm
from a new angle the position held by many before me, viz.,
that Roland's actions are wholly blameless and that therefore he should not be accused of desmesure. Why, then,
does he initially refuse to sound his horn; and later, when
all is lost, reverse his position? Two explanations,
admirably summed up in a paper given by Professor Wolfgang
van Emden at the Sixth International Congress of the Société
Rencesvals,[6] have been defended: a) that Roland is a sort
of Christ-figure, an exemplary champion of Christianity;
and b) that the underlying esprit of the Roland is essentially feudal, so that Roland is motivated by feudal ties
to his country, his family and himself, and to speak of
pride or desmesure is to ignore the context.

In closing my article in Olifant I suggested, in accord
with the analogy proposed, that Roland must sacrifice himself and his men in order to force Charlemagne to a revenge
he would not otherwise have taken. Following others, I
depicted a war-weary Charlemagne, weakened in his authority
and eager to return to Aix.[7] In a reply to my article,
Professor van Emden objected most particularly to this
characterization of Charlemagne and presented a studied
portrait of a strong feudal king, wisely willing to listen
to consilium, and bound to the feudal forms in which he
must operate.[8]

I cannot but admit to being swayed by Professor van
Emden's careful and detailed argumentation, yet in a certain
respect it actually underscores the feudal character of the
poem as I see it. Roland's argument is not so much with
Charlemagne as it is with the barons, for Charles is only
following the majority counsel of his men. Therefore it is
they, rather than Charlemagne, whom Roland must convince.
In several important scenes in the Roland Charlemagne acts
on advice from his barons, chiefly Naimon. In the First

Council Scene Charlemagne follows the advice of Ganelon
(laisse XV), seconded by Naimon and the assembled baronage
(laisse XVI). In the Second Council Scene it is again
Ganelon's counsel (laisse LVIII), seconded by Naimon (laisse
LXII), which forces Charlemagne, apparently against his own
better judgment (see, for example, lines 745-47, 771-73,
823-25, 832-41), to name Roland to the rearguard. Laisses
CXXXIII-CXXXV, in which the sound of Roland's olifant
reaches Charles' ears, are three powerful laisses similaires,
studied by Rychner.[9] The core of the laisses, as his analysis
shows, are the verses beginning "Ço dist li reis":

>   Ço dit li reis: 'Bataille funt nostre hume.'
>   (v. 1758)
>   Ce dist li reis: 'Jo oi le corn Rollant!
>   Unc ne'l sunast, se ne fust cumbatant.'
>   (vv. 1768-69)
>   Ço dist li reis: 'Cel corn ad lunge aleine.'
>   (v. 1789)

These lines stress Charlemagne's passive hearing of the
olifant blast. Significantly, he does not himself propose
action, but once more follows the advice of Naimon, who
speaks here again for the Frankish barons:

>   'Bataille i ad par le men escïentre;
>   Cil l'at traït ki vos en roevet feindre.
>   Adubez vos, si criez vostre enseigne,
>   Si sucurez vostre maisnee gente!'
>   (vv. 1791-94)

Charles' hands are effectively tied by the consilium of
his men, particularly that of Naimon.

    Roland, thus, must act to sway the majority opinion,
represented always by Naimon. He has learned from the
First Council Scene that his words will have no effect, so
he turns now to the most desperate action he knows: the
sacrifice of himself and his men.

    When Charlemagne and the barons arrive on the field
of Roncevaux, Charles is yet again counseled to action by

Naimon, speaking for the others as well, in a pattern which
has by now become familiar:

> Naimes li dux d'iço ad fait que proz,
> Tuz premereins l'ad dit l'empereür:
> 'Veez avant, de dous liwes de nus
> Vedeir püez les granz chemins puldrus,
> Qu'asez i ad de la gent paienur.
> Car chevalchez, vengez ceste dulor!'
> (vv. 2423-28)

Roland's sacrifice has thus succeeded in instilling in
Charlemagne's barons the desire to fulfill their duty to
complete the conquest of Spain by pursuing Marsilie and
his men into Saragossa, the key to total Christian victory.

For the Chanson de Roland, as it is preserved in the
Digby 23 manuscript, is above all a poem of Christian
duty.[10] The Christians, personifications of the Good, must
utterly destroy the Infidel, the incarnation of Evil. From
the opening lines of the poem Saragossa symbolizes the
unfinished conquest:

> Carles li reis, nostre emperere magnes,
> Set anz tuz pleins ad estét en Espaigne,
> Tresqu'en la mer cunquist la tere altaigne.
> N'i ad castel ki devant lui remaigne,
> Mur ne citét n'i est remés a fraindre,
> Fors Sarraguce, ki est en une muntaigne.
> (vv. 1-6)

Although the number seven traditionally represents com-
pletion, perfection, fulfillment,[11] Charlemagne's campaign
is not yet over: Saragossa, Marsilie's city (v. 10), has
not fallen.

Roland's sacrifice culminates not in his death, but
in the final capture of Saragossa. He alone recognizes
that one cannot serve both God and mammon.[12] His sacrifice
ensures the total, rather than partial, victory of the
Christian forces and is thus, in the greater context of
the Oxford poem, both necessary and justified. The capture of Saragossa is indeed the final achievement of
Charles' Spanish campaign:

E Carles ad sa bataille vencue,
De Sarraguce ad la porte abatue. . . .

Li emperere ad Sarraguce prise.

                    (vv. 3649-50, 3660)

As I sought to show in the Roland-Tierri analogy, God's intervention on Tierri's behalf indicates divine approbation not only of Tierri's actions, but of Roland's. Whether these be to convince Charlemagne directly, or through his barons, what is ultimately essential is that they ensure the final and total triumph of the forces of Good over Evil.

Notes

1. "Roland and Tierri," Olifant: A Publication of the Société Rencesvals American-Canadian Branch, 2, 1 (1974), pp. 27-32.

2. Because of the limited circulation of Olifant I shall repeat in the following several paragraphs the principal points of my argument.

3. This and all subsequent quotations from the Chanson de Roland are taken from the edition by F. Whitehead, La Chanson de Roland (Blackwell's French Texts; Oxford: Basil Blackwell, 1968).

4. As we find for example in Marianne Cramer Vos, "Portraiture de la royauté de Charlemagne," in Société Rencesvals, VIe Congrès International, Actes (Aix-en-Provence: Imprimerie du Centre d'Aix, 1974), p. 96.

5. (New York: Oxford University Press, 1971.) See particularly chapter VI, "Analogy as the Dominant Form."

6. "'E cil de France le cleiment a guarant': Roland, Vivien et le thème du guarant," in Société Rencesvals, VIe Congrès International, Actes (Aix-en-Provence: Imprimerie du Centre d'Aix, 1974), pp. 31-61.

7. This position has for many years been in favor among Roland specialists. Pertinent references are furnished by van Emden in n. 6 of his response to my article, "Roland and Tierri," entitled "Pro Karolo Magno: In Response to William W. Kibler, 'Roland and Tierri'," Olifant, 2, 3 (1975), pp. 175-82.

8. See preceding note. A very different and much less persuasive defense of Charles' greatness is to be found in Marianne Cramer Vos, art. cit., pp. 83-107.

9. Jean Rychner, La Chanson de Geste. Essai sur l'art épique des jongleurs (Geneva: Droz, 1955), pp. 94-100.

10. This point is argued well by Emanuel J. Mickel,
Jr., "Christian Duty and the Structure of the Roland,"
RomN, 9, 1 (1967), pp. 126-33. The following quotation
makes clear his position, and mine: "It is Charlemagne's
duty to persevere until the conquest has been completed
and the evil pagans are either converted or destroyed. In
his decision to bargain with the forces of evil, Charlemagne
is shirking his duty as emperor of Christendom and God's
temporal representative. Only the heroic sacrifice of
Roland and his example of unswerving duty prevent the
Saracens from succeeding in their ruse. For it is Roland's
death at Roncevaux which forces Charlemagne to return to
his duty and complete the conquest of Marsilius and ultimately of all Saracens under their supreme commander,
Baligant" (p. 130). Other scholars who take a similar
stand are mentioned by van Emden, "Le thème du guarant,"
pp. 34-35 and nn. 8-18.

11. One need scarcely document the prevalent Christian-
Crusade attitude toward the Saracens, curtly expressed in
Roland, v. 1015, "Paien unt tort e chrestïens unt dreit."
In the words of the great apologist for the Crusades,
Humbert of Romans, Saracens were the summa culpabilis, and
opposition to them was the just and holy war par excellence,
the bellum justissimum. To the unlettered, and indeed to
most learned Christians in the period, there was no common
ground: one was either Christian (= just, right, Good) or
pagan (= heretic, Muslim, Evil). See esp. chapter IV, "The
Place of Violence and Power in the Attack on Islam," in
Norman Daniel, Islam and the West, The Making of an Image
(Edinburgh: The University Press, 1960). For the attitude
toward Islam expressed in the Old French epic, see also C.
Meredith Jones, "The Conventional Saracen of the Songs of
Geste," Spec, 17, 2 (1942), pp. 201-225, and Barbara P.
Edmonds, "Le Portrait des Sarrasins dans 'La Chanson de
Roland'," FR, 44 (1971), pp. 870-80.

LES RAPPORTS ENTRE LA STRUCTURE, LES PERSONNAGES ET LA MATIERE D'ALISCANS

Friederike Wiesmann-Wiedemann

Toute oeuvre d'art vaut par l'effet qu'elle produit et non par ses origines. Le critique doit s'y attacher avant toute autre chose. Et puisque une chanson de geste s'adresse à un auditoire dont le jongleur veut retenir l'attention, ne serait-ce que pour des raisons pécuniaires, il faut que chaque partie soit asservie à ce dessein. Il en est résulté un art littéraire qui n'a pas besoin de s'intéresser autant à l'unité de l'ensemble qu'à l'effet immédiat de chaque scène. Les chansons de geste peuvent présenter des incongruités qui choquent le goût classique et qui contredisent notre sens de la logique en ce qui concerne la suite des événements aussi bien que la psychologie des personnages. Par contre, les chansons de geste sont pleines d'actions (gesta!) qui nous impressionnent et nous émeuvent. Rappelons les vers initiaux d'Aliscans:

> A icel jor ke la dolor fu grans
> Et la bataille orible en Alicans
> Li quens Guillaumes i soufri grans ahans.[1]

C'est un début dramatique qui nous introduit in medias res présentant l'action en train de se dérouler. C'est aussi un début pathétique, provoquant pitié (dolor, orible, ahans), curiosité et anticipation (bataille). L'auditeur embrasse tout de suite la cause de Guillaume et espère une fin heureuse pour la guerre. Il n'en est pourtant rien. L'épopée dépeint la prouesse des chrétiens en face de la défaite due au nombre écrasant des païens. Le vrai héros de la bataille est Vivien qui, restant fidèle à son serment de ne jamais fuir, meurt en martyr. Toutes les sympathies de l'auditeur vont vers ce personnage jeune et brave, vraie

incarnation de la chevalerie chrétienne. La mort de ce
héros appelle la vengeance. Ainsi la tension ne s'affaiblit
point avec le désastre de la bataille--seul d'entre tous les
combattants chrétiens Guillaume y échappe--mais elle monte:
où Guillaume va-t-il trouver des troupes pour s'engager
dans un nouveau combat qui délivrera les prisonniers, vengera
Vivien et chassera les païens? L'attente anxieuse de
l'auditeur accompagne Guillaume à Orange, ville assiégée où
il revoit sa femme, de de là à Laon où Guillaume va demander
de l'aide à son père, à ses frères et au roi. La scène de
Laon s'avère ainsi comme le point culminant. L'auditeur est
impatient de savoir ce que deviendra Guillaume que le roi et
la reine traitent d'une manière ignoble. Il semble vraiment
possible que Guillaume ne soit pas secouru. Une fois les
obstacles éliminés, l'action se déroule comme il faut. Les
armées se rassemblent à Orange, la bataille s'engage sur
l'Archamp, les prisonniers sont délivrés, Vivien vengé et
les païens chassés. Nul intérêt particulier donc dans cette
deuxième partie. La tension se relâche pour disparaître
complètement.

Ainsi, il y a un mouvement qui monte jusqu'au milieu
de l'action pour descendre jusqu'au moment où il s'arrête.
Ce mouvement est une fonction de l'action; il coïncide avec
le développement de celle-ci. Les relations personnelles
capables de créer des tensions psychologiques n'y jouent
aucun rôle.

Si l'épopée ne veut pas devenir franchement ennuyeuse
pendant la deuxième partie où la tension décroît, elle doit
captiver l'intérêt de l'auditeur par un autre moyen. Notre
chanson se sert du divertissement, et c'est à ce titre
qu'elle présente le personnage de Rainouart. Par sa descen-
dance il est prédestiné à la grandeur sociale et à l'héroïsme
sur le champ de bataille. Ayant pourtant vécu sept ans dans
la cuisine de Louis, il est asoté par le milieu où il a
grandi. Ce décalage qui pourrait se trouver à la base d'un
caractère pathétique, tragique même, produit dans notre
chanson un être admirable et grotesque à la fois. C'est à

Rainouart qu'est due la victoire finale des chrétiens et
l'auditeur est stupéfait par la prouesse de ce héros qui
confond des adversaires monstrueux aux armes inouïes. Mais
en même temps la sottise de ce géant, son manque de mémoire,
son arme peu conventionnelle, sa force et sa rage exterminatrices, son énorme capacité de dévorer des nourritures
solides et liquides font de lui un vrai personnage de farce
qui provoque à coup sûr le gros rire.

Rainouart domine la deuxième partie d'un bout à l'autre
et même au delà, puisque après la victoire nous assistons à
son baptême et à son mariage. En effet, la fin de la
chanson représente le début d'une nouvelle action, d'une
nouvelle bataille où figureront Rainouart et un géant païen
terrifiant. En outre, on nous annonce la naissance future
du fils de Rainouart et des batailles où figurera ce fils.
La fin de la chanson n'est donc aucunement une conclusion
puisque la deuxième bataille sera suivie d'une troisième et
ainsi de suite, tout comme le début n'était aucunement un
commencement. La première bataille avait commencé avant le
premier vers de notre chanson (cf. 235s, 1591ss) et il est
évident qu'il y en a eu d'autres.

La chanson n'est donc pas une oeuvre autonome, centrée
sur un événement privilégié, ce n'est qu'une tranche d'un
récit bien plus long dont elle ne raconte ni le début ni la
fin. Sa forme est "ouverte." Et voilà la raison pour
laquelle l'auditeur n'est nullement choqué de voir Guillaume
supplanté par Vivien pendant la première bataille et par
Rainouart pendant la deuxième. Il ne l'est pas davantage
par le changement du ton de la chanson qui est sérieux dans
la première partie et comique dans la deuxième--et s'il lui
arrive d'en être surpris, c'est qu'il applique à la chanson
des critères esthétiques qui sont à lui au lieu de permettre
à la chanson de faire son effet ou plutôt ses effets sur lui
selon ses propres lois.[2]

Le ton sérieux de la première partie est dû d'abord à
la situation, c'est-à-dire à la défaite des chrétiens et
ensuite aux personnages de Vivien et de Guillaume. Vivien
est le chevalier de Dieu par excellence. Deux qualités le

distinguent: son amour pour Dieu et sa famille et sa haine
pour les païens.   Arrivé à la place idyllique où il mourra,
il prie:

> 'Diex, dist il, Sire, vrais peres omnipotent,
> Par qui est toute créature vivant,
> La toie force ne va mie faillant;
> Secor mon oncle, se toi vient à commant.'
>   (402-405)

Au moment donc de sa mort, il loue la magnificence de son
Seigneur et l'implore, non pour lui-même, mais pour son
oncle.   Ses dernières pensées vont vers Guibourg.   Après
la communion,

> Puis bat sa coupe, si laissa le parler,
> Mais ke Guiborc li [à Guillaume] rova saluer.
>   (860-61)

Sa mort est due avant tout à son serment téméraire de
ne jamais fuir "le long d'une lance" devant les païens.
Jean Frappier voit dans ce serment "une faute de démesure."[3]
Mais comment peut-on être démesuré quand on lutte pour Dieu?
Vivien se met entièrement au service du summum bonum.
"[L]a vraie trouvaille de l'auteur d'Aliscans," dit Frappier
(p. 248), "est d'avoir consenti à laisser reculer Vivien,
sans qu'il sache . . . s'il a rompu ou non son voeu."   Le
jongleur permet pourtant à Vivien de rester fidèle à son
serment; il rassure l'auditoire: (85) N'ot pas fuï une
lance tenant.   Frappier pense (p. 248) que "ce doute affreux
le poursuit dans son agonie."   Mais ce doute est-il vraiment
aussi affreux?   D'abord ce n'est qu'un doute et pas une
certitude, ensuite Vivien est sûr d'avoir la grâce divine.
Quand Guillaume lui demande s'il a communié,

> Dist Viviens: 'Je n'en ai pas gosté;
> Or sai jou bien que Diex m'a visité
>   Quant vos à moi venistes.'
>   (819-21)

Vivien meurt donc en héros et en saint:

En paradis le fist Diex hosteler,
Aveuc ses angles entrer et abiter.
                                    (866-67)

Son destin ne comporte ni démesure ni dénouement tragique
comme le croit Jean Frappier;[4] ce destin est fait d'héroïsme
et de gloire. En effet, comment une oeuvre littéraire qui
chante le christianisme pourrait-elle montrer un chrétien
dans une situation tragique?

Il va de même que le caractère de Vivien fait son
effet sur les émotions de l'auditoire. Sa prouesse provoque
l'admiration, sa jeunesse la pitié.

Guillaume participe à son tour au caractère pathétique
de la scène, lui qui souffre de voir mourir son neveu, qui
remplit une fonction religieuse, liturgique même lors de la
confession et de la communion de Vivien:

    Or dist Guillaumes: 'Or te fai bien certain
    De tes pecchiés vrai confès aparmain.
    Je suis tes oncles,[b]n'as ore plus prochain,
    Fors Damedieu, le [verai soverain];
    En lieu de Dieu serai ton capelain,
    A cest bautesme vuel estre ton parin,
    Plus vos serai ke oncles ne germain.'
                                    (825-31)

Il a le même sentiment profond pour sa femme. Ses pensées
sont toujours près d'elle (cf. 503, 554), il jure en son
nom (595), il pense à la souffrance qu'elle ressentira en
apprenant l'issue de la bataille (cf. 755ss, 773s, 1563ss),
il la regrette quand il est loin d'elle (cf. 2069s, 2463),
il l'admire (1919ss, 8414s), il lui demande de l'aider
(4434s, 7735s), il cherche son approbation (1878), il la
protège jusqu'à être prêt de rester à Orange et de s'exposer
à la mort certaine plutôt que de l'y laisser seule et d'aller
chercher du secours (1941ss). Il se prête sans hésiter à ce
qu'elle lui demande: devant la porte d'Orange, elle ne le
reconnaît pas et dit que s'il était vraiment Guillaume il
délivrerait les chrétiens enchaînés qu'elle voit passer.

'Je ne leroie por la teste à coper,[5]
S'en me devoit trestoz vis desmembrer,
Que devant lui ne voise ore joster.
Por soe amor me doi je bien grever. . . . .'
(1683-86)

Le serment qu'il prête avant de quitter Orange (1987ss) et
qu'il tient si scrupuleusement est la meilleure preuve de
son amour.

Mais cet homme qui peut être le meilleur et le plus
tendre des amis (cf. aussi son attitude envers son cheval,
504ss, 657ss, 990ss, 1094ss, 1370ss, 1498, 1512ss) est
aussi le pire et le plus acharné des ennemis.

Ainc n'ot .i. jor vers paiens de losier.
Quant les tenoit, nes faisoit pas langir,
Nes faisoit mie en sa prison jesir,
Ainc n'en fist un à raechon venir,
Mais à droiture l'ame dou cors issir.
(633-37)

A la cour de Laon il n'hésite pas à calomnier sa soeur
qu'il menace de tuer (2772ss).

Guillaume est néanmoins le vrai successeur de Charlemagne. C'est lui qui se bat contre les païens, tandis que
le roi reste dans la sécurité de son palais. C'est par son
intervention que Louis porte la couronne, alors qu'il porte,
lui, l'épée Joyeuse. "C'est à mon sens," dit Joseph Bédier,[6]
"l'un des symboles les plus significatifs du cycle: Charlemagne, vieux, a pressenti l'avenir; il a deviné l'indignité
de son fils Louis et la loyauté de Guillaume: il laisse donc
sa couronne à son fils, mais son épée à Guillaume. Avec
cette épée, c'est la force de la France qui, de la famille
royale, passe à la famille des Narbonnais; mais les Narbonnais la mettront toujours au service du roi couronné."

Guillaume est ainsi un homme qui se laisse guider par
ses émotions. Ses actions sont toujours extrêmes. Aussi
n'est-il pas surprenant de le voir comme héros d'une scène
de farce, celle notamment qui a lieu lors de la libération
des chrétiens sous les murs d'Orange. Une fois les prison-

niers délivrés, Guillaume poursuit les païens qui le
prennent pour Aerofle dont il porte l'armure. Voilà le sol
juché de païens morts. Guillaume commande aux vivants, en
leur langue bien sûr, de descendre de leurs chevaux. Ses
pauvres victimes se hâtent d'obéir:

> Paien s'escrient: 'Si com vos commandez;
> Fetes, biau sire, totes vos volentez.'
> (1732-33)

Guillaume ne se le laisse pas dire deux fois. Il les lie et
les massacre sans délai, menant leurs bêtes avec les sommes
de ravitaillement dans la ville: à trompeur, trompeur et
demi!

Frappier appelle Guillaume (p. 88) un héros "populaire"
et il a certainement raison. Guillaume n'a rien de la
réserve, de l'attitude distante, de la dignité même d'un
Charlemagne, ni de la prouesse en dehors de toute mesure d'un
Roland, ni même de la froide raison d'un Olivier. Il n'est
pas visité par les anges, mais Dieu lui donne le cheval qu'il
lui demande (1176ss). Il préfère la fuite à la mort certaine
(620) et il ne raisonne pas avec ceux qui ont tort: il leur
fait sentir la pesanteur de son bras. C'est un homme de
chair et de sang. Guessard dit de la peinture de ce
caractère, en parlant de la scène de Laon (préface à son
édition, p. lix): "telle qu'elle est, elle nous frappe,
nous émeut, nous prend par les entrailles, comme dit
Molière." C'est dire qu'elle s'adresse à notre sentiment
plutôt qu'à notre raisonnement, que nous y répondons par des
émotions plutôt que par des réflexions.

Quant à la "prise par les entrailles," c'est encore
plus vrai pour Rainouart. Il s'agit pourtant d'entrailles
moins raffinées, si j'ose dire. Ce personnage produit à coup
sûr ce qu'en anglais on appelle belly laugh, le gros rire.

Il est vrai, bien sûr, que Rainouart est un excellent
guerrier. C'est lui qui fait revenir les couards (4810ss),
c'est lui qui délivre les Aymerides prisonniers (5347ss).
Il sauve même Guillaume de la mort certaine (5746ss).

C'est en effet grâce à lui que les chrétiens remportent la victoire (5688ss).

Mais dans l'ensemble ses actions et son enthousiasme sont si exagérés que Rainouart devient un héros nettement comique:

'Se jo n'oci ces paiens .x. et .x.,
Bien doit mes fus et jo estre honis.
Monjoie! escrie, or me suis trop tapis;
Se je ne venge Guillame le marcis,
Si m'aït Diex, jo esragerai vis.'
(5258-62)

Rainouart est l'incarnation de la force brute. Son arme est le tinel qu'il aime tendrement (cf. 3456s, 3848, 4407s etc.), il en fait son coussin (cf. 4366s, 4444 etc). Une fois il le blâme:

'Or ai ocis les miens amis charnez
Et à mon pere ai brisié les costez!
Icist pechié ne m'iert ja pardonnez.
Et qu'ai je dit? Ce a fait mon tinez;
Mal soit de l'eure que il fut charpentez.'
(6658-62)

Il y a dans cette riposte quelque chose qui relève d'une psychologie enfantine.[7] D'ailleurs, Rainouart se corrige bien vite quand il voit arriver Haucebier avec ses hommes:

'Amis, dist il, nous somes acordez. . . .'
(6681)

Le tinel est d'habitude son meilleur argument dans les discussions (cf. 3810ss, 4312ss, 4841ss, etc.), mais il se sert aussi de ses poings. Au fait, ses activités exterminatrices sont illimitées. Le roi dit de lui:

'Molt par est fel et plains de cruauté. . . .'
(3279)

Mais ce n'est pas le seul défaut. En le décrivant, le jongleur dit:

'. . . une tece l'a forment enpiré:
Ja tant n'auroit une cose amenbré,
Ains, c'on éust une traitie alé,
Ke maintenant n'éust tout oublié. . . .
                              (3222-35)

Comme la cruauté, ainsi le manque de mémoire sert à la
présentation de scènes bouffonnes. Trois fois Rainouart
oublie son tinel, ce qui produit le gros rire. Mais
l'auteur en tire le prétexte de quelques autres scènes
grotesques.[8] Un autre événement bouffon dû au manque de
mémoire de Rainouart suit la scène de la libération des
prisonniers. Les neveux ont besoin de bêtes, mais Rainouart
tue toujours homme et cheval, oubliant le conseil de Bertran
de bouter les chevaliers de leurs montures (5476ss).

   Un troisième trait ternit le caractère de notre ami:
la gloutonnerie. Louis explique à Guillaume:

     'En ma quisine là est tous asotés.
     Autant mangüe com .x. vilain barbé. . . .'
                              (3275-76)

et, bien sûr, il s'ensuit des aventures bouffonnes.[9] Même
quand Rainouart est finalement accueilli à la table de
Guillaume, honneur qu'il avait tant réclamé, il se dit
qu'après tout:

     Il amast miex le deduit de l'estable
     U la quisine ki samble foisounable.
     Ne serra mais des mois, s'il puet, à table,
        Car forment li anoie.
                              (7870-873)

Rainouart est ainsi le sujet de beaucoup de scènes de farce.
Il faut mentionner encore sa première apparition où il porte
les vestiges de la moquerie du maître queux qui l'a tonsuré
et lui a noirci le visage (3158ss). Il faut parler de son
essai d'équitation où il monte le cheval de rebours (6146ss),
de son baptême où il tombe dans la cuve (7908ss) et de sa
malheureuse tentative de navigation (7738ss).[10]

Plusieurs critiques ont voulu voir un trait "démo-
cratique" dans le caractère de Rainouart quand il donne à
manger aux pauvres devant la porte du monastère de sorte
qu'ils s'écrient:

> 'Ciex Damediex, ki maint en Bailliant,
> Cest aumosnier garisse longuement!
> Ainc ne vi si preudoume.'
> (3720-722)

et lorsqu'il aide le fermier aux fèves (7375ss).[11] Ces
scènes se trouvent pourtant dans un contexte de farce. Il
y a une exagération nette et comique dans les événements.
Les épisodes suivent le modèle du trompeur trompé. Ils
produisent le rire plutôt que la pitié. Je ne pense ainsi
pas qu'ils s'inspirent d'un sentiment social. Il est vrai
qu'on est content du secours que Rainouart offre aux pauvres,
mais ce plaisir ne fait qu'ajouter à l'amusement que nous
procurent ces bouffonneries.

Il faut pourtant insister sur le fait que Rainouart
n'est pas tout comique. L'auteur lui a donné une âme très
sensible. C'est pourquoi Rainouart se rend toujours compte
du décalage entre la situation qu'on lui a faite et celle
qui lui est due. Il dit à Guillaume:

> 'Sire Guillames, je me vuel esprover;
> Trop longement m'ai laissié asoter,
> Si m'aït Diex, nel puis mais endurer.
> Ja en quisine ne quir mais converser;
> Se Diex voloit, je vaudroie amender:
> Mal soit dou fruit ki ne veut méurer.'
> (3356-61)

Ce motif revient bien des fois (cf. 4384ss, 4832ss, 4878ss
etc.). Mais avant de réclamer le respect qu'il mérite,
Rainouart veut s'en rendre digne. Il cache ainsi à sa
soeur sa vraie identité (4494ss, cf. aussi laisses
CLXXXIV[b]ss, pp. 494ss de l'édition de Halle).

Son bon caractère se montre aussi dans sa résistance
à la tentation (par les couards 4830ss et par plusieurs de

ses adversaires, surtout par Baudus, 6911ss) et dans son
comportement envers les femmes. Lorsque Aelis lui demande
de lui pardonner tous les torts qu'elle a pu lui faire, il
y consent sans hésiter (3920, cf. aussi 7571s), et il
n'oublie jamais la bonté de Guibourg (cf. 4871ss, 7575 etc.).
Rainouart fait son effet sur l'émotion de l'auditeur
qui l'admire, se moque de lui et le plaint tout ensemble.
Nous trouvons ainsi dans ce caractère une curieuse contradiction. D'un côté, il a des traits héroï-comiques, de
l'autre, il est sensible et sérieux. De la tâche que
l'auteur s'était donnée Guessard remarque (p. 1xv de la
préface à son édition): "Il s'agissait, d'une part, de
montrer que bon sang ne peut mentir, et, de l'autre, qu'on
ne tombe point dans la boue sans en garder des souillures."
C'est pourquoi le caractère semble impossible à un homme de
notre temps qui cherche l'unité.[12] Mais, l'unité de caractère n'intéressait pas le jongleur. Ce qui comptait pour
lui, c'était le récit. Comme Rainouart allait être le héros
de la bataille, il fallait lui donner un bon caractère qui
provoquât l'admiration et le respect. Mais, comme il
fallait aussi s'assurer l'intérêt de l'auditoire dans la
partie de la chanson qui allait suivre le point culminant du
récit, il fallait faire de Rainouart un héros comique dont
on pouvait rire. L'aspect touchant de ce personnage résulte
de ces deux données. La multitude des variantes dans les
différents manuscrits au sujet de Rainouart prouve que les
auditeurs ont demandé et redemandé du Rainouart.

La vie de ces trois hommes est étroitement liée à celle
de Guibourg. Elle a élevé Vivien dont la dernière pensée
va vers elle. Elle se réjouit et souffre avec Guillaume.
Elle se sait unie à lui par la foi et le mariage (1804ss).
Elle lui rend le courage. Quand elle apprend la défaite
à l'issue de la première bataille, elle pleure avec
Guillaume, mais

            Puis a parlé à loi d'enperéis.
            'Sire Guillames, dist Guibors la gentis,
            Or ne soiés ne fous ni esbahis. . . ,'
                          (1901-1903)

et elle lui conseille d'aller chercher du secours. Après
la deuxième bataille elle console Guillaume, triste d'être
tout seul après le départ de sa famille, et lui suggère de
rebâtir Orange (8402ss). Pendant l'absence de Guillaume,
elle défend la ville. L'auteur lui garde pourtant sa
fémininité. Ainsi, lors du départ de Guillaume qui veut
aller chercher du secours, elle a peur que son mari ne lui
devienne infidèle (1969ss) et lorsqu'il revient avec
l'armée du roi et qu'elle croit que ce sont les ennemis,
elle s'évanouit de peur (4038).

Les scènes les plus touchantes où elle figure sont
celles qui la mettent en présence de Rainouart. Elle
l'emmène dans sa chambre, lui demande s'il a frères et
soeurs, ce qu'il affirme en parlant d'elle-même sans
pourtant s'en rendre compte:

> Adont se taist et tient la chiere encline.
> Et Guibors ouevre son mantel de porprine,
> Se l'afubla, car ses cuers li destine,
> Car chou estoit ses freres.
>   (4473-76)

Elle n'insiste pas quand Rainouart refuse de dire qui il
est, respectant la réserve de son frère, mais elle lui
prouve son amour en l'armant. (La scène de leur reconnaissance dans les mss. bBTLVCdeM [laisses CLXXXIV[b]s,
pp. 494ss de l'édition de Halle] reprend tous ces motifs
d'une façon très heureuse.)

Il y a un passage qui jure avec cette peinture du
caractère de Guibourg, c'est celui où la comtesse et
l'écuyer essaient de lever le tinel, évidemment sans y
réussir (4725ss). Autre preuve qu'une esthétique du moyen
âge ne prenait pas à tâche de présenter ce que nous
appelons "un caractère uni."

Guibourg est pour ainsi dire l'âme de la chanson.
Elle est forte quand il faut être fort et faible quand le
récit l'exige. Elle comprend toujours, aime toujours et
pardonne toujours. Comme les autres personnages, elle
nous touche plutôt qu'elle ne nous fait réfléchir.

Ermengart et Aelis représentent la même attitude. Ce
sont des femmes actives et raisonnables. C'est Ermengart
qui rappelle à sa famille qu'il ne faut pas pleurer mais
agir (2707ss), c'est elle aussi qui se jette entre Guillaume
et Blancheflor, sauvant la vie de sa fille (2805s). Le
respect qu'on lui offre à cause de sa position de mère et à
cause de son âge (cf. 2721), Aelis le doit à sa seule beauté
(cf. 2880ss). Elle explique à sa mère le tort que celle-ci
a fait à Guillaume (2831ss), elle est prête à faire tout ce
que Guillaume pourrait lui demander à condition qu'il
pardonne à Blancheflor (2914ss). Elle approuve hautement
Aimeri qui demande qu'on aide Guillaume, passage où elle
s'oppose à son père (3080ss). Quand elle tombe amoureuse
de Rainouart sans même y réfléchir en admirant son torse nu
(3861s), elle fait encore un choix raisonnable, puisque
Rainouart va prouver qu'il est digne d'une fille de roi.

Ermengart impressionne l'auditeur par sa réaction immédiate et émotive au récit de Guillaume. Elle règne sur sa
famille et la sert en même temps. Son seul mobile est
l'amour du lignage. D'où son ardent désir de vengeance, qui
émeut l'auditeur dont elle suscite immédiatement l'admiration
et la bienveillance. Quant à Aelis, il va sans dire qu'elle
intéresse les sentiments de l'auditeur. Quoi de plus con-
vaincant en effet que la jeunesse, la beauté et l'amour?

Comme les autres femmes de la chanson, la reine est
une femme forte et active, mais à la différence des autres,
elle est vaine et égoïste. Elle ne salue pas son frère
parce qu'il est pauvrement habillé. Elle s'oppose au roi
qui veut aider le comte:

'Voire, dist ele, [^b s'iere] desiretée!
'Or ont déable faite ceste accordée. . .';
                        (2768-69)

lorsqu'elle change son attitude, ce n'est pas par charité
ni par amour fraternel, mais parce qu'Aelis lui rappelle
son devoir de reconnaissance:

'Par lui sui jou essauchie et montée,
'Roïne et dame par la terre clamée.'
(2842-43)

Comme les autres personnages de la chanson, Blancheflor est
guidée par ses émotions. A la différence des autres pourtant, elle agit pour des motifs qui sont condamnables.
Elle crée ainsi dès sa première apparition une forte anti-
pathie chez l'auditeur. Ce jugement est maintenu même
quand la reine consent à aider son frère, secours qu'elle
lui offre par devoir seulement.

Le roi joue un rôle encore plus repréhensible et plus
lâche. Quand il apprend l'arrivée de Guillaume: (2393)
. . . vers terre est clinés; ce qui d'ailleurs semble être
son action favorite. Il maudit son beau-frère vilainement
(2396ss), se moque de lui en lui parlant d'une fenêtre
(2473ss), mais perd le courage quand il se trouve devant
le comte. Il lui promet son secours pour les mêmes raisons
que la reine: il se rend compte de son devoir de reconnaissance lorsque Guillaume lui rappelle ses services (2765s).
Il ne fait rien pour son épouse quand Guillaume l'attaque,
craignant, semble-t-il, pour sa propre vie, et répète sa
promesse sur l'insistance d'Aelis et d'Ermengart (2948).
Mais lorsque tout semble arrangé, il hésite tout à coup:

'Et le matin savoir le vos lairon,
Ma volenté se jo irai ou non.'
(3048-49)

Et cela après que Guillaume l'a appelé li fiex au roi
Charlon (3044)! La formule se jo irai ou non explique
l'hésitation: Louis a peur de la guerre. C'est finalement
par crainte ou par appréhension qu'il promet une armée parce
qu'il se voit implorer de toute sa famille (3096ss). Il
s'excuse pourtant, il ne pourra pas accompagner l'armée, ce
qui pèse d'autant plus lourd qu'Ermengart était prête à
mettre l'armure elle-même (2717ss) et qu'Aimeri avait juré
de considérer comme traîtres ceux qui refuseraient de se
battre (3072ss). Louis n'est courageux que lorsqu'il n'y

a pas de danger; la plus petite difficulté prouve sa
pusillanimité. Son action la plus lâche, c'est bien sûr de prédestiner
Rainouart, qui dépend entièrement de lui, à la damnation
certaine. Il s'y prête tout en connaissant la haute extrac-
tion du jeune homme qui lui a souvent demandé le baptême
(cf. 3261ss). L'opposition entre Guillaume et Louis est évidente.
Ainsi, plus l'auditeur soutient la cause de Guillaume, plus
il méprise le roi. Ces jugements se forment automatique-
ment, autre preuve que la peinture des caractères vise
l'émotion de l'auditeur. La chanson est une oeuvre passionnée et passionnante.
Ce sont les émotions qui motivent le comportement des personnages, émotions qui n'existent qu'en fonction du récit.
Il est clair que je ne parle pas ici de la genèse de la
chanson, mais de l'art du jongleur qui l'a composée.
Lorsqu'il lui a fallu un général brave, intelligent, lié
étroitement à la maison royale, il a créé le Guillaume de la
chanson. Pour donner de l'agrément au récit, il a donné au
comte une femme tendre, intelligente et active. Afin de
relever l'intérêt du récit et créant en même temps un
développement à retardement, il a présenté un roi lâche et
une reine égoïste. Voulant chanter le lignage, il a doté
le héros d'une famille noble. Finalement, il a suscité
l'intérêt de l'auditoire quand la matière racontée ne s'y
prêtait pas en inventant un héros comique. Les personnages
de la chanson agissent à l'avenant du récit, ils ne l'inflé-
chissent pas. C'est pourquoi leur psychologie et leur
raison jouent un rôle minime. C'est pourquoi un caractère
peut être contradictoire. Chaque scène du poème se soutient
elle-même, fait son effet individuel, sans entrer en relation avec d'autres scènes avec lesquelles elle peut ainsi
jurer. Le conte existe avant les personnages. Ils en
remplissent le moule.[13]
En parlant entre autres des sculptures aux portes
occidentales de la cathédrale de Chartres, datant d'à peu

près 1145-1150, Henri Focillon dit que c'est "un art qui,
prenant l'image de l'homme et celle de la femme, les con-
figure selon le gabarit et les proportions des colonnes
contre lesquelles elles sont adossées. . . . Il semble que
nous ayons là le dernier mot de ce conformisme architectural
qui, dans l'art roman, impose à l'être vivant, non seulement
l'attitude, mais le canon exigé par la fonction."[14] Ne se
trouve-t-on pas comme forcé de comparer ces statues aux
personnages et l'architecture à la chanson, les personnages
assumant la forme et servant les exigences du poème?

Notes

1. Aliscans: Chanson de geste publiée d'après le
manuscrit de la Bibliothèque de l'Arsenal et à l'aide de
cinq autres manuscrits, éd. F. Guessard et A. de Montaiglon,
Les Anciens Poëtes de la France, 10 (1870; réimprimé Nendeln,
Liechtenstein: Kraus, 1966). Toutes les citations sont
empruntées à cette édition. J'ai consulté aussi Aliscans:
kritischer Text (Halle: Niemeyer, 1903), éd. Erich Wienbeck,
Wilhelm Hartnacke, Paul Rasch.

2. Philipp August Becker ("Der Liederkreis um Vivien,"
Akademie der Wissenschaften in Wien, philosophisch-
historische Klasse, Band 223 [1944]) croyait à deux auteurs
(cf. pp. 11ss). Voir aussi Friedrich-Whilhelm Fischer,
"Der Stil des Aliscans-Epos," diss. Rostock (1930), p. 83.

3. Jean Frappier, Les Chansons de geste du cycle de
Guillaume, I. La Chanson de Guillaume, Aliscans, Chevalerie
Vivien (Paris: SEDES, 1955), p. 248.

4. Ouvr. cité, p. 248 "[U]ne faute de démesure entache
la beauté de son sacrifice et sa tragédie se situe à un
autre plan que dans la Chanson de Guillaume."

5. Guessard souligne le texte quand il emprunte de
longs passages au ms. b.

6. Joseph Bédier, Les Légendes epiques: Recherches
sur la formation des chansons de geste, I. Le Cycle de
Guillaume d'Orange, 3e éd. (Paris: Champion, 1926), p. 69.

7. Un passage analogue se trouve dans les mss. deCm
après que Rainouart a triomphé de son frère Walegrape
(laisse CIL^a, pp. 390s de l'éd. de Halle). Pour le même
détour psychologique, cf. 4702ss où Rainouart accuse
Guillaume d'avoir oublié son tinel.

8. A Laon: Rainouart au monastère, le tinel caché
dans du fumier, Rainouart et le maître queux qui veut le
retenir; à Orange: Rainouart qui blâme Guillaume de ne pas
lui avoir rappelé le tinel, Guion et Guibourg essayant en

vain de lever le tinel, Rainouart renversant charrette et
cheval dans sa joie de revoir son arme; finalement entre
Orange et l'Archamp: Rainouart rencontrant les couards.

9. Rainouart s'enivrant la nuit avant le départ de
l'armée et ne se réveillant qu'au bon milieu d'une rivière
à l'eau froide, l'aventure au monastère, les heures
passées auprès du feu et les expériences qu'il y rencontre:
le maître queux d'Orange lui brûle la barbe et Rainouart le
jette au feu; entre Orange et l'Archamp, Rainouart se
réveille au milieu d'un incendie, l'armée étant partie
depuis quelque temps.

10. Le ms. C. présente même une scène où Rainouart se
refuse au mariage pour des raisons nettement misogynes
auxquelles Guillaume se hâte de convenior (laisse CLXXXIX[b]
vv. 9ss, pp. 519s de l'éd. de Halle).

11. Cf. Guessard, préface à son éd., pp. lxxjs;
Fischer, diss. citée, p. 16 et Frappier, ouvr. cité, p. 276.

12. Il m'est incompréhensible comment Werner Schröder
("Das epische Alterwerk Wolframs von Eschenbach," dans
Wolfram-Studien, éd. Werner Schröder [Berlin: Schmidt,
1970], pp. 199-218) peut affirmer "der kraftstrotzende
Naturbursche Rainoart ist durchaus eine lebensvolle Gestalt
aus einem Guss." (p. 204) Voir aussi Alfred Adler ("Rückzug
in epischer Parade: Studien zu Les Quatre Fils Aymon, La
Chevalerie Ogier, Garin Le Lorrain, Raoul de Cambrai,
Aliscans, Huon de Bordeaux," Analectica Romanica, Heft 11
[1963]; l'épopée d'Aliscans est traitée aux pp. 225-56),
qui essaie à son tour de voir dans Rainouart un caractère
unifié qui unifie la chanson. Ce critique s'approche de la
chanson à l'aide d'une esthétique qui n'a rien à voir avec
celle de l'épopée.

13. Jean Rychner (La Chanson de Geste. Essai sur
l'art épique des jongleurs [Genève: Droz; Lille: Giard,
1955]) explique la composition lâche de nos chansons par
leur présentation orale en plusieurs séances: "Les
jongleurs ne se souciaient pas plus que leurs auditeurs
de l'unité de couleur, de style, de la cohérence narrative
d'une oeuvre insaisissable en son entier; ils étaient au
contraire très fiers de rajouter à l'ancienne tradition des
morceaux tout neufs" (p. 47). Pour la genèse d'Aliscans,
voir Philipp August Becker, "Das Werden der Wilhelm- und
Aimerigeste," Abhandlungen der Sächsischen Akademie der
Wissenschaften, philosophisch-historische Klasse, Band 44,
no. 1 (1939), l'art. cité du même auteur et Jean Frappier,
ouvr. cité. On y trouvera d'autres notices bibliographiques.

14. Henri Focillon, Art d'occident: Le Moyen Age
roman et gothique (Paris: Colin, 1947), p. 165.

THE HUNTING SCENES IN L'ESTOIRE DE GRISELDIS

Donald Maddox

Although overshadowed by a thriving tradition of medieval
mystery and miracle plays, the late fourteenth-century
Estoire de Griseldis (1395) is nevertheless an important
milestone in the history of medieval French drama. Called
by Grace Frank "the first example of a French play that is
serious yet non-religious,"[1] Griseldis is unique not only
because of its lack of a prominent biblical or hagiographic
context, but also because it probes the moral and dramatic
value of serious secular narrative, thereby broadening the
spectrum of the dramatist's potential sources. Griseldis
reflects a narrative prose tradition originating in the last
novella of Boccaccio's Decameron (1353), whence Petrarch
adapted the story into Latin prose twenty years later.
Petrarch's Latin version served as the basis for two French
prose translations, one of which has been plausibly attributed to Philippe de Mézières.[2] From this version the
dramatist, perhaps Philippe himself,[3] derived over two-
thirds of the play, often with close adherence to the
phrasing and vocabulary of his prose model.[4]

Despite such extreme fidelity to source, the dramatist
frequently displays a keen awareness of dramatic potential
latent in the prose tradition. Hunting scenes, pastoral
interludes and two depictions of childbirth, all of which
are either unstressed or totally absent in previous versions,
betray a serious attempt to enhance the story's impact by
dramatic development of secondary elements. The two richly
detailed hunting scenes near the beginning of the play are
particularly effective as major enlargements of a constant
yet minor feature of the prose tradition, and they afford
valuable insight into the playwright's conceptualization

of the human depth and esthetic value of the popular story
of Griselda.

In the first known literary version of the story,[5]
Boccaccio introduced the seemingly insensitive and often
enigmatic Marquis as an avid hunter:

> Giá è gran tempo, fu tra' marchesi di Saluzzo il
> maggior della casa un giovane chiamato Gualtieri,
> il quale, essendo senza moglie e senza figliuoli,
> in niuna altra cosa il suo tempo spendeva che in
> uccellare e in cacciare, né di prender moglie né
> d'aver figliuoli alcun pensiero avea. . . .[6]

Subsequent authors retain the concept of a Marquis for
whom hunting precludes thoughts of matrimony, though they
emphasize this major flaw by contrasting it with the positive qualities of the Marquis. Petrarch's Valterius is both
handsome and noble in manner, though "incuriosissimus
futurorum erat. Itaque venatui aucupioque deditus, sic
illis incubuerat ut alia pene cuncta negligeret. . . ."[7]
Chaucer's Walter, brought to life in the Clerk's Tale some-
time after 1380, is drawn from Petrarch and the anonymous
French prose translation.[8] He is "the gentilleste yborn of
Lumbardye, / A fair persone, and strong, and yong of age, /
And ful of honour and of curteisye. . . ." The Clerk nevertheless blames him for his indifference to "tyme comynge"
and his "lust present . . . / . . . for to hauke and hunte
on every syde." His neglect of administrative duties is
overshadowed by the fact that he "Wedde no wyf" which was,
according to the Clerk, "worst of alle."[9]

Both French prose translations of Petrarch's Latin
version offer few significant departures from this tradition, though Philippe de Mézières describes the Marquis'
qualities in greater detail:

> Le dit Gautier, marquis de Saluce, estoit biau de
> corps, fort et legier, noble de sang, riche d'avoir
> et de grant seignourie, plains de toutes bonnes
> meurs et parfaictement garnis de dons de nature,
> de fortune et de grace.[10]

This cumulatively superlative and idealized portrait of
Gautier is immediately undercut by the same singular passion
that mars all previous portrayals of the Marquis:

> Une chose avoit en lui, car il amoit fort solitude
> et n'acontoit riens au tamps à venir et quant on
> lui parloit de mariage, il n'en voloit ouir parole.
> Toute sa vie estoit dediée en bois et en rivieres,
> en chiens et en oisyaux, et du gouvernement de sa
> seignourie paou se melloit, pour quoy ses barons et
> son peuple estoient en grant tristesce, et par
> especial de ce qu'il ne voloit entendre à mariage.[11]

In addition to the double emphasis placed on Gautier's
adamant refusal to marry,[12] this passage introduces original
topographical elements of woods and rivers to accompany the
Marquis' indulgence in hunting and hawking.

These new environmental details, which are absent from
corresponding passages in the anonymous French version[13] and
from the versions by Boccaccio, Petrarch and Chaucer, reinforce Grace Frank's belief that _Griseldis_ "was written or
directly inspired by Philippe de Mézières himself."[14] The
playwright's indebtedness to Philippe's prose is already
apparent in the 100-line prologue, which includes a portrait
of the marquis that frequently echoes the primary source:

> Si estoit cil marquis Gautier
> Beau de corps, fort, preu et legier,
> Noble de sanc et de lignie,
> D'avoir riche et de seignourie,
> De bonnes meurs parfaictement,
> Enrichi naturellement
> Des biens de nature et de grace.
>   . . .
> Mais il avoit son deduit mis
> Seul en chacier et en voler,
> Seulement se voult deporter
> En oyseaux et en chiens chassans.
> La riviere li fu plaisans
> Et le bois au deduit des chiens.
> Mais point ne lui plot li liens
> Ne li estas de mariaige.
> Souffrir n'en vouloit le servaige
> Ne n'en vouloit oÿr parler.
> Et pou le veïst on meller
> De gouverner sa seignourie,

Qu'en deduit demenoit sa vie
Par champs, par boiz et par rivierez
A son gré en maintes manieres.[15]

The dramatist has twice repeated Philippe's allusions in
prose to environmental details as if he were consciously
attempting to prescribe the decor of the play's opening
scenes. In the play itself, the two hunting scenes are
introduced by verbal reference to their topographical location. Gautier opens the first hunting scene with the suggestion that it is time "D'aler voler sur la riviere"
(v. 103), while the second begins with the huntsman's
report of having seen a large stag "es bois" (v. 644).

It is conceivable that as Philippe introduced environmental details into his prose version he was already mindful
of a possible future adaptation of the story into dramatic
form. While these details function as mere incidental
description in both the prose version and the prologue to
the play, in the play itself they provide a means of linking
the dramatization of hawking and hunting with a plausible
scenic background.

To anyone already familiar with the story of Griselda
by Boccaccio, Petrarch, or even Philippe de Mézières, the
hawking and hunting scenes in the play appear at first
glance to be nothing more than a disproportionately larger,
though engaging and picturesque, dramatization that adds
little to previous versions of the story. Yet a closer
examination of these scenes reveals that they serve to
enhance the esthetic appeal of the play while elucidating
certain traits in the character of the Marquis so that, on
balance, they constitute a definite improvement upon ante-
cedent tradition.

Immediately following the 100-line prologue, Gautier,
accompanied by his falconer and two barons, proceeds to the
river in hopes of taking a heron with one of the trained
falcons. After some good-natured boasting about the
superior training of his falcon, the falconer leads his

impatient companions to a likely vantage point, whereupon
the second baron announces a suitable prey:

> J'ay veu maintenant devaler
> Trop beau hairon sur la riviere.
> (vv. 130-31)

Although confident that his own bird would easily capture
the heron, the second baron urges Gautier to release his
falcon ". . . aprez celle proye/ En tel maniere qu'il la
voye" (vv. 139-40). The marquis eagerly complies, and the
falconer declares that

> Vostre faulcon a ja saisi
> Le hairon et mis dessoubz lui.
> Si fault aler querre la proye.
> (vv. 145-47)

The scene concludes with the falconer's boast of superior
wisdom in falconry and his anticipation that the heron will
provide a hearty repast. The entire scene occupies only 54
lines of vivid dialogue.

Equally entertaining is the second hunting scene
(vv. 638-717), in which the Marquis and two huntsmen,
probably among a large group of barons, engage in the chase
of a stag. Following a detailed report by the huntsmen on
the condition of the stag and a lengthy identification by
name of thirty hounds, the hunters set out in pursuit of the
pack, uttering cries of encouragement and gentle reproach
to various dogs along the way. When the stag is finally at
bay, the Marquis advances for the kill:

> Descochier feray ja si fort
> Ma saiette au large barbel
> Que je croy puis le temps Abel
> Ne vistes plus beau cop ferir.
> (vv. 704-7)

He then issues an order to sound the _prise_, while the second
huntsman looks forward with relish to feasting and drinking

upon returning from the forest. Like the first hunting
scene, this episode is detailed yet brisk and animated.
Even the enumeration of hounds by name is colorful by virtue
of the names involved, which include Gauvain, Tristran,
Yseut, Genievre, Lancelot, Fernagus, etc.

Barbara Craig's observation that the two scenes are
"fast-moving and fairly realistic, obviously the creation of
someone who has actually witnessed or participated in such
sport"[16] is supported by late medieval treatises on hunting.
One of the most comprehensive handbooks of hunting, and one
which is nearly contemporaneous with the play, is the Livres
du roy Modus et de la royne Ratio, written between 1354 and
1377.[17] The allegorical King Modus instructs his apprentice
on every conceivable aspect of hunting, both with birds as
well as with dogs and horses, while Queen Ratio occasionally
pronounces moral allegories derived from matters relating
to the hunt.

A brief chapter of Modus et Ratio (I, ch. 95) is devoted entirely to the method of training falcons to pursue
and seize herons. Certain details in this chapter shed
light on the dialogue between Gautier, his barons, and his
falconer in the first hunting scene. King Modus tells his
apprentice that the falcon must be trained to chase the
heron by being allowed to feed on certain portions of the
bird's carcass. It is therefore necessary to deprive the
falcon of food prior to this type of hunting. "Et retieng
que tout faucon qui volle pour heron doit avoir greigneur
fain et plus aspre . . ." (I, 196), so that it is best to
seek the heron "Au matin, quant il sera heure de pestre ton
faucon . . ." (I, 194). These details serve to explain why
the Marquis specifies that a propitious moment to seek the
heron is at hand: "Je croy qu'il feust heure et saisons
. . . / D'aler voler sur la riviere, / Savoir s'en aucune
maniere/ Prendre y peüssons le haron" (vv. 101-105).

In this first hunting scene at least three falcons are
mentioned, one each for Gautier, the second baron, and the
falconer. Each bird has apparently been trained, or "duit,"

by its owner, who is understandably willing to vouch for
the superior performance of his own falcon. The falconer
is particularly pleased with his bird:

>   Je vueil qu'on me pende au plus hault
>   Du beau gibet de Monfaucon
>   Se voler ne faiz mon faulcon
>   Encore mut mieux qu'onques maiz!
>   (vv. 118-21)

The second baron is not to be outdone, however:

>   Je vueil que je soye batu,
>   Se bien tost ne l'a abbatu,
>   Car assez est duit du voler.
>   (vv. 135-37)

According to Modus, the quest for the heron normally involved several falcons in a "debatois." The well-trained
falcon "devroit bien debatre le heron au debatois ovec un
autre faucon," though in the play, the "debatois" is fore-
stalled by the second baron in order to allow Gautier's
falcon first chance at the heron:

>   Sire, pour Dieu, laissiez aler
>   Vostre oyseau aprez celle proye
>   En tele maniere qu'il la voye.
>   (vv. 138-40)

The second baron's description of the heron, which he has
seen "devaler sur la riviere" (v. 131), probably in pursuit
of food, and his admonition to Gautier to release his falcon
"en tele maniere qu'il la voye" (v. 140), are reminiscent of
Modus' instructions for engaging one's falcon in the pursuit:
"Mes se le heron se desconfist et que il funde a l'iaue . . .
oste donques le chaperon a ton faucon, et se il le veut et
s'embat, si le lesse aler au debatois" (I, 195). The second
baron's invitation to the Marquis might therefore have been
accompanied by Gautier's removal of the hood covering the
head of his falcon.

Many traditional elements in the chase of the stag with
hounds are included in the second hunting scene (cf. Modus
et Ratio, I, chs. 3-31). Immediately prior to this scene,
the Marquis' letter to the Count and Countess of Panice is
dated "Le quatorziesme jour de may" (v. 633), well within
the limits of the hunting season, which extended from
Holyrood Day, May 3, to Holyrood Day, September 14.[18] The
stag hunt was usually preceded by the report of the harborer, whose duty it was to seek and identify worthwhile
game, after which he would submit an oral account of his
findings to the assembly of hunters. The harborer might
examine the stag's lair and its traces, or hoofprints, in
order to determine its size, while its fewmets, or droppings, revealed its age and health. It was also important
to render detailed account of the antlers, including the
number of tines, to determine the animals' age and maturity
(pp. 266-67). In the play, the harborer's report is given
by the first huntsman, who describes the "erres," or traces
of the stag, its "fumees," or droppings (v. 650), and who
indicates that it is "sommé de quinze cors" (v. 660).

A successful chase depended heavily on the quality of
the hounds, and they sometimes received as much attention
and consideration as would a fellow hunter.

> A great point was made of caressing one's hounds
> and speaking to them affectionately at all times.
> . . . It was very important to cheer the dogs on,
> to be well acquainted with the name, the voice,
> and the character of each one, and to call them
> continually by name (Thiébaux, p. 268).

It is not uncommon to find catalogues of names for dogs in
treatises on hunting, though our playwright has chosen many
of the names for Gautier's pack from medieval epic and
romance. Thiébaux cites "par ci," "voylela" and "haro" as
some of the typical cries to the pack, while the dramatist
has the second huntsman typify the chase in full swing with
similar directives (cf. Thiébaux, pp. 271, 274):

> Harou, Clabaut! Voyci la beste!
> Va la, Tirati, et l'arreste!
> Haire, Lancelot! Haire! Haire!
>   (vv. 685-87)

Once the dogs had surrounded the stag, a huntsman would
kill it with a knife or sword (cf. Ratio, I, ch. 25), though
it was sometimes already wounded by bowmen (cf. Thiébaux,
p. 271). As in the first scene, it is Gautier himself who
finishes the stag with a single arrow, after which he issues
orders to "Cornez Prise tost . . ." (v. 712). The blowing
of the Death signaled the end of the chase.

> Se tu veulz corner de prise . . . l'en doit corner
> un bien lonc mot et puis corner jusques a dis mos,
> les plus cours que l'en puet corner et assés a lesir,
> puis deux bien lons mos au derrain . . . et tous
> ceulz qui ont cors doivent corner tous ensemble,
> si est belle melodie; et ainsi corne l'en de fois
> a autres en s'en alant a l'oster.
>   (Modus, I, ch. 26).

This description of the blowing of the Death enables one
to imagine how the chase in Griseldis might have sounded
if hunting horns were used. The use of live hounds and
imaginative actors familiar with the chase would also have
provided a very animated and realistic scene.

The dramatist has clearly made the two hunting scenes
authentic and detailed without reduplicating every aspect
of the hunt as set forth in hunting handbooks. His primary
objective has been to delight the eyes and ears of a public
undoubtedly well acquainted with the finer points of hawking
and hunting and thus capable of mentally supplementing the
necessarily more and rudimentary effects of staging.

Along with the esthetic benefits derived from the
hunting scenes, the playwright is able to use them as a
means of graphically portraying the Marquis' single-minded
pursuit of pleasure. Enlarging upon previous depictions of
the Marquis, the playwright's portrait of Gautier in the
prologue repeatedly emphasizes his delight in hunting (see
vv. 70-84, cited above) and opposes the deduit of hunting

and hawking to the idea of marriage, described as a <u>servaige</u>
and as <u>li liens</u> which "point ne li plot." In the play,
Gautier's opening speech resembles that of a king summoning
his jester:

> Y a il nul en ceste place
> Qui beau gibier trouver nous face
> Ou avoir puissons beau deduit?
> (vv. 107-109)

Indeed, like the royal fool, Gautier's subordinates are
eager to please, witness the reply of his falconer: "vous
aurez plus beaulz deduis / Que vous n'eüstus mais pieça"
(vv. 112-13). Later, the second baron assures him "tantost
bel deduit" if he releases his falcon (v. 141), while the
same promise is made by the first huntsman prior to the
chase.

It would be wrong, however, to assume that Gautier's
passion for hunting is meant to depict him in an unfavorable light. King Modus speaks for medieval courtly society
in general when he ranks the chase among "les plus biaus
deduis" (I, ch. 3). Far from showing the Marquis' hedo-
nistic pursuit of a deleterious pastime, his activities
would have appeared to a contemporary audience as ennobling
enterprises that foster physical fitness, preclude the vice
of idleness, and liberate the hunter from the sin of sensuality. In every respect, as Thiébaux suggests, the
"passion for hunting is linked to excellence" (pp. 260-261).
The opposition between hunting and marriage is therefore a
conflict between two fundamentally <u>positive</u> ideals which
the Marquis cannot reconcile in his own mind.

As in previous versions, a spokesman for the subjects
of the Marquis brings the issue of marriage to his attention,
though the playwright has invented the elderly and venerable
Quint Chevalier to assume this function (vv. 276-549). In
response to Gautier's fear that

> . . . puis que je seray liez,
> Petit auray de bon plaisir.

. . .

> Et mon deduit en perderoy,
> Et me fauldra mes jeux abatre,
> Auzquelz je me souloie esbatre.
> Müer me faulra mon coraige
> Par la vertu du mariaige,
> Et mon cuer faire feminin,
> Se je veuil tenir le chemin
> D'avoir en mariage paix.
>   (vv. 356-57, 364-71)

the Quint Chevalier promises him "Bonne amour, lyece et plaisance" (v. 409), as well as the power to choose a pleasant and good mate "Selon vostre noble personne" (vv. 410-11). To the objection that marriage would render him effeminate, the Quint Chevalier assures him that precisely the opposite would occur:

> Car bien scez que pas ne domine
> La femme, maiz ce fait li homs;
> Si changent les complections
> Du subget par le dominant.
>   (vv. 420-423)

Out of love for his subjects, who fervently desire that the Marquis produce an heir, Gautier submits to this appeal, though it is apparent that he remains doubtful that marriage will not permanently deprive him of his independent and carefree existence (cf. vv. 436-48).

In a markedly significant departure from tradition, the playwright has framed Gautier's conversation with the Quint Chevalier between the two hunting scenes. This alternating sequence renders the conflict between hunting and marriage more acute and emphatic than in previous versions. The opening scene at the river firmly establishes Gautier as the Hunter, while the second, which follows immediately upon the heels of Gautier's declaration that he will marry "D'uy en quinze jours" (v. 516), reveals how little the Quint Chevalier's discourse on the virtues of marriage has influenced him. Having dictated a letter announcing his marital plans, Gautier abruptly addresses his huntsmen:

> Chiens et oyseaux nous fault avoir
> Et aler prendre aucun deduit,
> Que bonne piece y a, ce cuit,
> Que n'eümes deduit de chace.
>   (vv. 638-41)

This sudden transition brilliantly captures Gautier's urgent desire to obliterate from his thoughts the perilous new direction his life has just taken.

As in all previous versions of the story of Griselda, the matter of hawking and hunting occurs only at the outset and is then displaced by the traditional account of Griselda's steadfast love for her spouse as he repeatedly tests her obedient devotion and constance. Yet the hunting scenes and the discourse of the Quint Chevalier occupy nearly one-fourth of the entire play, which is proportionately a far greater place than is accorded to analogous elements in previous versions. Their prominence at the beginning of the play leaves an indelible, highly original mark on the play as a whole. Aside from their graphic realism and their incisive reflection of the Marquis' character, they embody a strikingly poetic kind of beauty replete with emblematic overtones that surpass the literal dimension of the play.

The earliest inkling that they are meant to serve as a commentary on later events in the play occurs in an original scene that takes place on the morning of Gautier's wedding, yet prior to his having chosen a bride. Gautier, perhaps on his way to the forest, asks his huntsman if he knows anything about the identity of the young peasant woman nearby. The 26-line reply of the huntsman (vv. 752-77), in which he recounts Griseldis' poverty as a young shepherdess and narrates her activities from dawn to dusk, acquires deeper significance precisely because these lines are spoken by the huntsman. Just as he has faithfully reported to his master the condition of the stag on the morning of the hunt, he now reports the condition of unsuspecting Griseldis on the morning of her wedding to Gautier.

This metaphorical equation between Griseldis and the game in Gautier's preserve invites us to consider the preceding hunting scenes in a new light. The haunting description of the heron soaring above the river as it falls prey to Gautier's falcon now seems to foreshadow the fate that awaits Griseldis after she becomes the Hunter's wife and, in a sense, his prey. By way of contrast, Gautier's frenetic pursuit of the stag recalls the legend of Saint Eustace, whose chase of the white stag with the cruciform projection between its antlers culminates in his miraculous conversion by the admonition of this marvelous beast:

> 'Voiz, por l'amor de toi sui je venuz en
> en ceste beste, que tu voies et que tu me conoisses. . . .
> Or me sui venuz a toi mostrer par cest cerf.
> Tu bees a la prise del cerf e je bé a fere de
> toi ma proie: tu ne lieras ne ne prendras
> cerf, mes je t'en menrai pris et lié. . . .'[19]

Like Placidas-Eustace, Gautier is a hunter who is ultimately "converted" by the love bestowed upon him by his prey.

After his marriage, Gautier no longer appears in his role as the Hunter, yet his hunting instincts are no less apparent as he stalks his wife at a distance, looking for evidence of less than absolute devotion to him. His repeated testing of her constancy as he deprives her of their two children, then secures the annulment of their marriage, and finally confronts her with his plans to remarry, constitutes an attempt to exercise the same control over his mate as he had previously exercised over the game in his preserve. To justify his dismissal of Griseldis from the household, he alludes to the instability of Fortune, declaring that "nul sort n'est perpetuel / A homme n'a feme" (vv. 2091-92). In effect, he is attempting to place himself above Fortune and mutability by instituting the ill fortune of his former wife.

Yet it is precisely her indifference to the whims of Fortune, both in the palace of the Marquis and in the humble cottage of her father, and her faith in "l'amour de Dieu" (cf. vv. 2265-71), that enable her to maintain her cheerful

obedience to Gautier. Like the heron in the bestiaries that
"is wise above all other birds and does not seek numerous
resting places, but where it dwells it feeds,"[20] Griseldis
is quite content to relinquish the splendid garments and
elegant residence of nobility and return to her father's
humble dwelling clad only in her tattered chemise.

Ironically, it is Gautier who, after having striven
so desperately, as he says, not to "müer mon coraige"
(v. 367), must abandon his inflexible control and acknowledge the triumph of his prey:

> O Griseldis! asses! souffist!
>
> . . .
>
> Et croy que soubz le ciel n'ait homme
> Qui par tant d'experimens comme
> Je t'ay ferme et constant trouvee
> Ait en autre femme esprouvee
> La bonne amour de mariage.
>   (vv. 2452, 2459-63)

Having passed all of Gautier's tests, Griseldis now finally
becomes the new mediatrix of poverty and wealth, forest and
hearth, prowess and love.

As Gautier's devotion to hunting is brought into re-
lief in the play, it becomes apparent that the playwright
is attempting to improve upon previous versions of the story
of Griselda by furnishing an explanation of why the Marquis
deems it necessary to test his wife. The dramatist is
reviving the question frequently entertained in courtly
romance concerning the relationship of prowess and conjugal
love. As long as prowess is exercised apart from marriage,
it is non-problematic. Yet as Chrétien de Troyes had shown
in Erec et Enide and Yvain over two centuries earlier, the
married Warrior or Hunter must strive to maintain his prowess
in order to avoid the pitfall of recréantise, or cowardice.
Gautier's pre-marital fear of becoming effeminate in marriage
("mon cuer faire feminin," v. 369) causes him to test
Griseldis in order to reassure himself of his own masculi-
nity, for as long as Griseldis impassively obeys even the

most outrageous of his whims, he is able to preserve a
positive masculine self-concept. As the unmarried Hunter,
Gautier could easily obtain such reinforcement with each new
victory over beast and fowl. In marriage, however, one does
not dominate and control one's mate with falcons and hounds.
Some other means must be found to measure one's supremacy.
Thus, for Gautier, testing becomes a kind of surrogate for
hawking and hunting inasmuch as it allows the married Hunter
to acquire positive reinforcement at regular intervals without forsaking the hearth. By magnifying Gautier's zest for
hunting, the playwright has brought us closer to piercing
the mystery that shrouds the Marquis' strange marital behavior in all versions of the story. It becomes clear that
during the first twelve years of his marriage, he manages
his domestic life in much the same manner and for the same
reasons that motivated his youthful pursuits through field
and stream. Yet the contrast between the early, robust
pleasures of the chase and Gautier's later, almost voyeur-
istic manipulation of his human "prey" enables the dramatist
to disclose the moral boundaries of ego-fulfillment. Ultimately, the play, far more than its prose sources, implies
that the experience of Gautier is not unlike that of a
Placidas, for example, inasmuch as each, in his vigorous
quest of the Self through the prey he pursues, is quite
unexpectedly brought to an irresistible, irreversible transformation in his recognition of the Other.[21]

Notes

1. The Medieval French Drama (Oxford, 1954), p. 156.

2. See Elie Golenistcheff-Koutouzoff, Histoire de
Griseldis en France (Paris, 1933), pp. 42-53.

3. See Grace Frank, "The Authorship of Le Mystère de
Griseldis," MLN, 51 (1936), 217-22. "The question has
occurred to me: could Philippe himself have written the
play? No categorical answer can be given. . . . Yet it
seems highly probable to me that Philippe, if not the actual
writer of the play, was its instigator and intimately concerned in its performance" (p. 219).

4. For rapprochements of the prose translation with passages from the play, see Golenistcheff-Koutouzoff, p. 120, and Frank, "Authorship," pp. 218-19.

5. For theories of possible antecedents to Boccaccio's novella in folklore, see L'Estoire de Griseldis, ed. Barbara M. Craig, Univ. of Kansas Humanistic Stud., no. 31 (Lawrence, 1954), 1-3.

6. Giovanni Boccaccio, Il Decameron, ed. Charles S. Singleton (Bari, 1955), II, p. 308.

7. Cit. from J. Burke Severs, The Literary Relationships of Chaucer's Clerkes Tale, Yale Univ. Stud. in Engl., 96 (New Haven, 1942), 256.

8. Cf. Severs, pp. 33-37.

9. The Works of Geoffrey Chaucer, ed. F. N. Robinson. 2nd ed. (Boston, 1957), p. 101, vv. 71-84.

10. Golenistcheff-Koutouzoff, pp. 157-58.

11. Ibid., p. 158.

12. Cf. Petrarch, who mentions it only once in the corresponding Latin passage: "quodque in primis egre populi ferebant, ab ipsis quoque coniugij conscilijs abhorreret" (Severs, p. 256).

13. See Golenistcheff-Koutouzoff, pp. 195-213.

14. Frank, "Authorship," p. 222.

15. Craig ed., vv. 61-67, 70-84. Subsequent citations of passages in the play are from this edition.

16. Craig, L'Estoire, p. 9.

17. Les Livres du roy Modus et de la royne Ratio, ed. Gunner Tilander, SATF (Paris, 1932), I, 196.

18. Cf. Marcelle Thiébaux, "The Mediaeval Chase," Spec, XLII (1967), pp. 260-74. Esp. pp. 265-66: "This was their 'grease-time,' the period during which they were fattest, and they were said to be at their best around the Feast of the Magdalen, which was the 22nd of July."

19. La Vie de Saint Eustace, ed. Jessie Murray, CFMA, (Paris, 1929), pp. 5-6.

20. See Florence McCulloch, Mediaeval Latin and French Bestiaries, UNCSRLL, 33 (Chapel Hill, 1960), pp. 125-26.

21. The dramatist may have been prompted to expand the hunting theme in Griseldis partly as a result of his acquaintance with a familiar variety of altercatio in which falconers and huntsmen debate the question of whether hawking affords more pleasure than hunting. One such dispute appears in Modus et Ratio, I, chs. 117 and 118, in which a heated argument between hunters and falconers at an inn culminates in the reading of a long versified debate entitled "le jugement de chiens et d'oiseaus, lequel est plus biau deduit." In this debate, two noblewomen argue the pleasures

of hunting, one upholding the chase of the stag as superior,
the other championing the "deduit d'espreveterie." Their
arguments are recorded by a scribe and read to the Count of
Tancarville, who rules in favor of the pleasures of the chase
which are greater because they appeal to both eye and ear,
whereas hunting with birds is pleasing only to the eye.

The same esthetic doctrine, according to which the
involvement of two higher senses--hearing and seeing--is
superior to the involvement of only one, underlies the
playwrights' rationale for casting the story of Griselda
into dramatic form. After having declared in the prologue
that the story he is about to relate is of exemplary instructive value to "Celles a qui vient pestillence" (v. 14),
the author broaches the question of sensory experience:

> Si fait bon oÿr exemplaire
> Et bonnes vertus raconter,
> Dont on puet par raison monter
> En l'estat de perfection.
>   . . .
> Et pour ce que plus est meü
> Le cuer de l'omme par vĕoir
> Que par lire, sanz plus savoir,
> Et mieux s'i mettent les coraiges,
> Sera ci fait par personnages,
> Se Dieux nous en donne puissance,
> D'icelle hystoire la semblance.
>   (vv. 18-21, 26-32)

Dramatic representation of an exemplum involves both visual
and auditory faculties and is therefore more moving to the
spectator than is either reading or listening. In Modus the
principle is primarily esthetic, while in the prologue both
esthetic and instructive goals are involved.

Whether the prologue's reminiscence of the debate on
hawking and hunting and the expanded hunting theme in the
play constitute evidence of the direct influence of a hunting handbook such as Modus et Ratio remains an open question.
Yet there can be no doubt that the original hunting scenes
in L'Estoire de Griseldis enhance the esthetic and pro-
foundly human features latent in the story of Griselda and,
because of their dramatic effectiveness, provide the spectator plus biau deduit.

A SAINT NEGLECTED

Harry F. Williams

From the beginnings of French literature to the flowering
of the Renaissance, it is well known, writers produced an
enormous corpus of saints' lives, in both Latin and French,
verse or prose, either dramatic or narrative in form. Many
hagiographicae are still ignored, others have been only
partially edited and studied. The legendary life of Saint
Barbara falls into the latter category.

Patroness of armorers, artillerymen, carpenters, gun-
smiths, masons, miners, she was invoked against storms,
thunderbolts, sudden death and final impenitence.[1] Her
cult was popular early in the East, whence it passed, by the
seventh century, to the West; her feast day, December 16,[2]
was especially observed in Belgium and northern France;[3]
her name was adopted as a toponym in such scattered areas
of the New World as Venezuela, Mexico, Honduras, California.[4]
Told first in Greek, apparently, her story passed notably
into Syriac, Latin, Germanic and Romanic versions.[5]

The only daughter of a rich pagan named Dioscorus,
Barbara lived apart from the world in a tower built to protect her beauty from the eyes of men and to preserve her
from evil. Many suitors sought unsuccessfully her hand in
marriage. Before beginning a journey, Dioscorus ordered
for her the construction of a magnificent bath-house; on
his return, he learned that she had destroyed his cherished
idols and changed the plans from two windows to three in
order to symbolize the Holy Trinity.

He sought to kill her, but the floor broke away beneath
her and carried her miraculously to a mountain peak where
two shepherds guarded their flocks. The pursuing father
learned of her hiding place from the second shepherd, who

95

was promptly punished for his treachery by being turned to stone while his sheep became locusts. The cruel parent seized Barbara and dragged her back to the city. Handed over to the prefect Martianus, she was tortured to make her recant. At night, the Lord appeared, comforted her and healed her wounds; the next day she endured more suffering. Finally, her father decapitates her and, as punishment, fire from heaven consumes him utterly. A certain Valentinus buried the martyr, at whose tomb many miracles promptly occurred.

Her life was retold or recalled in epigrams, hymns, odes, prayers, songs, stories; in pictorial form; in dramas produced frequently in Belgium and France, above all.[6]

French non-dramatic literature about Saint Barbara is known in modern printed form only by A. Denomy's[7] edition[8] of an octosyllabic rhymed-couplet _Vie_, 512 verses, from the fifteenth-century manuscript Brussels 10295-304,[9] plus three minor French poems[10] of the same century.

Yet unpublished[11] are a verse[12] and a prose life of Saint Barbara.[13] The former, in MS Musée Calvet (Avignon 615), was donated by the Celestins of Avignon in 1793. It consists of 112 dodecasyllabic monorhymed quatrains, in handwriting which strongly suggests the sixteenth century. The prose version in question is in MS BN 975, which once belonged to Jeanne de France (1464-1504). It was committed to paper in the late fifteenth or early sixteenth century, judging from the script and the language.

It is not without interest to compare salient features of these works, B[russels], A[vignon], P[aris], illustrations of different treatments of essentially the same story, which provide further insights into medieval literary composition.

The B story alone is introduced by a claim to novelty, a story different from accounts of Ogier, Roland, Oliver; A begins with the prayer that Saint Barbara's devotees be favored; P first etymologizes her name, an effort buttressed by Biblical references.

After her entombment, B adds first the account of a
miracle: the beheaded knight whose head is rejoined to his
body before he expires, following confession and extreme
unction, and next a prayer to the saint. A terminates
abruptly (in mid verse) after the burial. P adds, at that
point, crusaders' translation of her bones from Nicodemia
to Rome; their further removal, minus the head, by Charlemagne (in 895!) to Piacenza; and then thirteen miracles
involving Saint Barbara.

B does not localize the action in time or space; A
situates it in Nicodemia; P sets it in the time of Emperor
Maximian, son of Diocletian, and in the Egyptian city of
Solis now named Nicodemia.

Barbara's mother is absent from B; in A she tries to
change (Quatrains 21-29) her daughter's new religious inclinations; in P the mother, linked to the line of Jesse,
from which sprang also the Virgin Mary, is no longer living.

Dioscorus, prior to a trip, in B, tells masons to
consult his daughter concerning the bath-house (lavatoire)
construction; in A, before leaving to unearth Christians in
his lands, he grants her the boon of an additional window to
the building (tour); he leaves, in P, on the emperor's service, after ordering a tower addition (une cisterne bagnore).
As she enters the completed bath-house, the water gushes in,
according to B; it was already there in abundance, for which
she thanks God, says the author of A; the water is lacking
until she prays to God, when it comes rushing in four streams,
recalling the four rivers of the terrestrial Paradise,
according to version P. In B she traces with her finger a
cross in the bath's marble and Saint John the Baptist comes
to baptize her; in A she is visited by the voice of God,
which baptizes her; in P an angel visits her, also Christ in
a child's form, and Saint John confers baptism, after she
has imprinted in the stone a cross with her finger and
another with her foot.

Her travail recalls to the author of B not only Saints
Agatha, Agnes, Catherine, Juliana (who shares Barbara's

fate), Margaret, but also the forsaken gods Apolin, Jupin,
Mahom. These references are reduced in both A and P to
Saint Agnes only. When the father first tries to kill her,
the stone beneath Barbara's feet transports her suddenly to
a mountain top, where the false shepherd's flock were later
turned into locusts, according to B; in A she flees to the
mountain and a stone there splits to hide her; in P the
divided stone bears her to the mountain where the sheep in
question became locusts and their perfidious master was
turned into a marble statue.

The magistrate Martianus is unnamed in A alone; Origen
appears only in P; Valentin appears in all three versions.
Only in P are Latin quotations and attempts to elevate
Barbara's lineage; only P gives her age (15) and the date of
her martyrdom (December 4, 267). In A alone is there confusion between the tower and the bath-house. In A her
nakedness is covered by her hair; in the other two versions
by a white stole sent from Heaven. The episode of the
suitors is displaced sufficiently in A to cause some inco-
herence. In B the decollation takes place, as in the other
versions, on the mountain but without express mention of the
second trip there.

The verse B and A are of the same approximate length,
prose P is more than twice as long. These three versions
follow somewhat different traditions whose sources can
hardly be identified, with the exception of P's. This
account has close affinities with the Latin story added to
later editions of Jacobus de Voragine's <u>Legenda</u> <u>aurea</u>
(L).[14] P is a typical medieval translation[15] of L, with
significant additions.

Comparison of P and L shows that the order of events is
exactly alike, except for the former's displacing the
episode of the suitors rejected. In other respects, there
are changes, subtractions, additions and minor divergences.

P changes from parents to philosophers Barbara's
philosophical dialog; from Valentin to Saint John her baptism; a cross placed in the new East window to one imprinted,

with thumb and then foot, in a pillar and the bath-house
floor; two miracles to thirteen others.

Among P's subtractions are such details as her early
life in a tower; her messenger to Origen finding him preach-
ing the doctrine of Christ in the palace of the emperor's
mother; the name of Origen's messenger to Barbara; her
cursing the treacherous shepherd; designation as apocryphal
the metamorphoses of the shepherd and his sheep; the pro-
vost's initial reaction to her great beauty and his subsequent desire to behead her himself.

Additions to P are mainly: the etymologizing first two
chapters; identification of Nicomedia with Solis; ancestry
and death of Barbara's mother; the ruse employed to introduce Origen's messenger into Barbara's apartment; the bath-
house visitation by angelic beings; comparison of the four
rivers of Paradise and the bath water, its curative powers;
recollection of Saint Agatha's fate; breaking of the idols
and distribution of their gold and silver components to the
poor; salt poured into flagellated Barbara's wounds and
rough clothing put on her body; her presence in the street
and square named Dilasion; angels bearing her soul to Heaven;
her age, the date of her martyrdom, her burial by the priest
Valentin; the erection of a temple (habitacle) where miracles
took place for the blind, the halt, the deaf, the possessed,
and the ill; the forging by the bourgeois of Nicomedia of a
suspended and illuminated shrine (fierte [< *firmitata] =
"virole de fer"); restoration to life of dead crusaders
brought to her tomb; removal of her bones to the cemetery of
St. Sixtus in Rome, later translation by Charlemagne to the
Benedictine monastery of St. Sixtus in Piacenza; and the
claim that God granted her prayer to permit her devotees to
leave this world only after confession, repentance and last
rites.   None of these addenda are in B except Agatha (plus
Agnes, Catherine, Juliana and Margaret),[16] burial by
Valentin, another miracle.   In A: angels bear her soul to
Heaven, Valentin buries her.

Hence, one sees that changes are minor except for
additional data which occur throughout but which are most

striking at P's beginning and end. The initial additions
could have been drawn from the author's evident learning.
He could hardly have followed L so closely, however, without
that text or its source before him, a supposition bolstered
by his Latin words left untranslated. The end (after her
martyrdom) must derive from another source which must surely
have been Latin, in view of the frequent quotations.[17]

Miracles recounted in the L text are: I. A count of
Saxony imprisoned in a tower his enemy who, in a few days,
begged vainly for food and drink, for the love of Saint
Barbara. When he was thought dead, the count ordered his
body removed. By a cord it was dragged to a cliff and
thrown over, but when it reached the ground he arose and
walked, saying that he could not die until he confessed
and had communion. Receiving these sacraments, he expired.
II. In the time of Roman kings, when Count Adolphe was
governor of an eastern province, a soldier was accused of
rape. A prison confessor, thinking him innocent, advised
him to become a devotee of Saint Barbara. A woman pressed
for conviction, which did ensue; however, an unknown
appeared, proved the soldier's innocence and then disappeared. The prisoner, freed, passed the remainder of
his days in Barbara's service.

The P text presents thirteen other miracles involving
Saint Barbara's devotees. I. A knight's severed head is
rejoined to his body so that he can confess and receive
communion before death is possible. II. Although broken
on the wheel, a criminal in Cologne could not die before
receiving final rites. III. Saved from drowning by Saint
Barbara, a monk of Brabant becoming abbot near Louvain
incited his brethren to serve her also. IV. Forty years
after the event, a severed giant's head revealed to a bishop
that it could not expire before enjoying the Church's sacraments. V. Contrary to the third commandment, merchants
sailed from the English port of St. Bechut on Christmas eve
and so perished in a storm, except two Louvanistes who
existed three days on planks and then told fishermen they

would die only after having last rites, and so it came to
pass. VI. At a customary feast for Saint Barbara, an
unbeliever in Cologne (where her head rests) blasphemes her
miracles, whereupon he ends his own life with a knife, thus
showing that God approved the miracles attributed to her.
VII. A bourgeois subject of Duke Guerles in the town of
Nouveau Manoir, bereft of his senses, transpierced himself
with a knife, for which the duke pardoned him and then the
priest administered the last rites so that he could die, and
so he converted to Saint Barbara's service several notable
people. VIII. Three Cistercian abbots, including Jehan of
Arbrede near Grounghe (= Groningen?), were traveling in a
Frisian forest when a merchant's head, severed three days
before by robbers, asked to be rejoined to its body, whereupon the man arose, walked to a nearby town, confessed his
sins, had communion and then died. IX. In the valley of
Malines (Brabant), where rests the body of Saint Moluc, inn
guests, reciting the virtues of Saint Barbara, debated
whether to fast or merely to abstain from meat, and so incited their host to mock their beliefs by eating a capon,
which action caused his death that night in bed. X. Wrongly
accused of a tavern theft, a man was hanged but did not die
and so he was freed; later the real thief confessed the
crime. XI. A Norman invader, defeated by the Flemish at
Tabbaye near Balgant, lay wounded fifteen days before a
priest, brought by fishermen, gave him the last rites so
that he could die. XII. A locust mysteriously appeared
just long enough to inspire a painter who had forgotten the
forms of such insects which accompany portraits of Saint
Barbara. XIII. Accused of rape and condemned to transfixion
by a stake, a German from the Asian city of Vualphangon told
passers-by on the third day why he was not dead and so a
priest gave him last rites to end his suffering.

   Differences among these three lives of Saint Barbara
(B, A, P) are not untypical of saints' lives generally, nor
of other medieval genres. Variant versions of epics and
romances, for example, suggest also that medieval authors

freely reshuffled old materials to create new works. Such
methods of composition must be taken into account by editors
who seek to recover our medieval heritage. They must respect
the integrity of each version, debate not only the Scylla
and Charybdis choice between a composite version and a "best"
manuscript, but at times edit multiple texts. That was done
in Ham's Five Versions of the Venjance Alixandre, Roach's
Continuations of the Old French Perceval of Chrétien de
Troyes, and, more recently, by various editors of Saint
Alexis: C. Storey (Geneva, 1968, on MS L), C. E. Stebbins
(Iowa dissertation, 1970, on P), D. Gatto-Pyko (Florida State
University dissertation, 1973, on M). Justice to the story
of Saint Barbara dictates a critical edition of each version.

Notes

1. See Agnes B. C. Dunbar, A Dictionary of Saintly
Women (London, 1905), I, 99-100, Le Comte de Lapparent,
Sainte Barbe (Paris, 1926), and A. Butler, Lives of the
Saints (N. Y., 1938), XII, 56.

2. Or December 4 in some martyrologies. See Denomy,
MS, 1 (1939), 148.

3. The New Catholic Encyclopedia, II, 86.

4. Cf. Phebe E. Spaulding, Patron Saints of California
(Claremont, Calif., 1934).

5. Fed. Morellus, Graecos trimentros è Bibl. regia
(Paris, 1614); W. Weyh, Die syrische Barbara-Legende
(Schweinfurt, 1912).

6. See Petit de Julleville, Mystères (Paris, 1880),
II, 478, 486; E. Ernault, Archives de Bretagne, 3 (1885);
P. Seefeldt, Studien über die verschiedenen mittelalterlichen
dramatischen Fassungen der Barbaralegende (diss. Greifswald,
1908); Grace Frank, The Medieval French Drama (Oxford,
1954), pp. 200-201. Cf. J. P. W. Crawford, Spanish Drama
Before Lope de Vega (Philadelphia, 1937), p. 146.

7. MS, 1 (1939), 148-78.

8. Comparison with the MS reveals only these textual
errors: v. 72 for tous read tout, 461 E r. Ez, 470 Qui pas.
Nowhere does he use the customary acute accent. The emend-
ment proposed for v. 68 is unnecessary since peres a may
elide, 80 read esparnïes, 139 malades i elides, 321 il =
elle, 18 is still hypermetric (r. dire ?). Some vv. termed
assonated may be considered as permissible free rhymes (as
was v. 180): 130, 284, 388, 398.

9. Analyzed by P. Meyer, _Rom_, 30 (1901), 295-316, who, followed by Denomy, dated the original as latter 13th century, date properly challenged as too early by de Gaiffier (p. 38, n. 3); cf. infra, n. 14.

10. From BN n.a. lat. 615, BN f. fr. 24865, BN lat. 1321. All are prayers and only the first and longest (126 + 26 verses) out lines her story.

11. See now the present writer's critical edition of Avignon 615 and BN 975, "Old French Lives of Saint Barbara," _PAPS_, 119:2 (1975), 156-85.

12. Noted by Meyer, _Rom_, 30:295; G. Paris, _HLF_, 33 (1906), 340; and Langfors, _Les Incipit des poèmes français antérieurs au 16e siècle_ (Paris, 1917), p. 184.

13. In the Burgundian library at Bruges in 1467 was inventoried a _Vie Sainte Barbe_, of which two Gothic editions were known. Cf. J. Barrois, _Bibliothèque protypographique_ . . . (Paris, 1830), no. 825.

14. See B. de Gaiffier, _Analecta Bollandiana_, 77 (1959), 5-41. He believed that the latter 15th-century Augustinian, Jean de Wackerzeele or de Louvain, circulated a life and passion of Barbara which contained new legendary traits (as her ancestry, her translation to Piacenza).

15. Cf. Paul Chavy, "Les Premiers translateurs français," _FR_, 47 (1974), 557-65.

16. See Denomy, nn. 71, 80, 81, 82, 87.

17. See the 23 miracles listed in _Bibliotheca hagiographica latina_, 932-55 and the larger number outlined by W. B. Lockwood, "A Manuscript in the John Rylands Library," _BJRL_, 36 (1953), 23-37.

Part III

Motif/Image

STUDIES ON THE VARIETIES OF MEDIEVAL POETRY AND ROMANCE

LE REVE D'AMOUR DANS LE ROMAN COURTOIS

Herman Braet

Les longs discours que Jean de Meun met dans la bouche de ses personnages contiennent, on le sait, quantité d'indications précieuses: non seulement sur l'auteur lui-même, sur ses idées et connaissances, mais encore sur celles de son temps. C'est ainsi que Nature aborde à un moment donné la question des phénomènes oniriques. Les dormeurs, explique ce personnage, reçoivent les impressions les plus variées; certains par exemple,

> Quant d'amors ardanmant s'antraiment,
> Don mout ont travauz et enuiz,
> Quant se sunt endormi de nuiz
> En leur liz ou mout ont pansé
> (Car les proprietez an sé),
> Si songent les choses amees
> Que tant ont par jour reclamees. . . ."
>
> Le Roman de la Rose, éd. F. Lecoy,
> CFMA [Paris, 1970], Tome III, 18366-72)

Ce genre d'images, précise-t-on, peuplent les nuits de "cil qui fins amanz se claiment." Jean de Meun se souvient ici de ses lectures: l'expérience qu'il vient d'évoquer se trouve en effet souvent décrite dans la littérature courtoise--tant chez les poètes que chez les romanciers.

Avant de passer à ces derniers, rappelons la valeur et l'importance du rêve d'amour dans la poésie lyrique. Les Provençaux, nous l'avons montré ailleurs, l'intègrent à leur poétique de l'inaccessibilité et de la distance: à la faveur du songe, l'amant voit s'abolir les obstacles qui le séparent de sa dame.[1] De plus, on tend à faire coïncider le monde du sommeil et celui de la poésie (ou fiction): le rêve devient un véritable ravissement de l'esprit, permettant au poète de sublimer son désir dans l'univers engendré par

sa parole. Son importance est peut-être la même chez les
lyriques d'oïl, encore que le nombre de textes soit trop
réduit pour pouvoir conclure. On peut citer cet anonyme
qui exprime l'exaltation que lui procure son expérience;
à la seule vue de l'être aimé il se sent transporté de joie:
"Qu'en mon dormant la regart et remir, Et m'est a vis que
soie en paradis Quant je la voi, si me fet resjoïr. . . ."[2]
Comme les troubadours, les trouvères font ressortir
le prix de ce moment d'extase en l'opposant à ce qui suit.
L'image tant désirée disparaît à l'instant même où le dormeur atteint au bonheur suprême--"quant je cuit estre en ma
tres plus grant joie. . . ."[3] Le lendemain apporte, avec le
réveil, une amère déception: ". . . cruelment le m'estuet
comparer Au resvoillier, quant je ne puis trover Ce qu'en
dormant m'estuet avisoner," nous confie Gace Brulé.[4]
Rares sont ceux qui osent suggérer que leur vision
puisse un jour se transformer en réalité; dans la poésie
d'oïl, cette invitation à la dame ne se rencontre qu'une
seule fois.[5] L'amant demandera plutôt qu'on le laisse
dormir.[6] "Bien met pitié en oubli Qui tel dormir remue,"
écrit Gace Brulé;[7] sans doute sait-il que le bonheur réel
lui fera toujours défaut. Gontier de Soignies, lui, est
convaincu qu'il devra se contenter de ce que lui offre la
nuit: "D'amors n'ai, lais, autre desduit Fors penseir et
songier la nuit."[8]

* * *

Rappelons encore que l'exploitation littéraire du
rêve d'amour remonte fort haut.[9] Les héroïnes des épîtres
d'Ovide recherchent les délices nocturnes, dont elles
regrettent au réveil le caractère fugitif. Les auteurs
latins du moyen âge chantent la brève vision d'un bonheur
insaisissable; ils exaltent la nuit et le sommeil, qui
accordent à l'amant ce qu'on lui refuse de jour.
Poète lui aussi, à ses heures, l'historien Giraud de
Barri assigne à ce genre de rêve une fonction bien précise.
Dans la pièce De subito amore, il décrit ce que l'on pourrait appeler les symptômes du mal d'amour. La tête tantôt

s'échauffe, tantôt se refroidit, le teint vire de la pâleur
à la rougeur, des soupirs s'échappent de la poitrine de
l'amoureux. De plus, son esprit, quand il n'est pas tra-
vaillé par l'insomnie, est égaré par des songes.[10] Cette
peinture très ovidienne se trouve ainsi complétée, puisque
le rêve y est appelé à figurer parmi les signes obligés de
la passion. D'autre part, André le Chapelain en souligne la
valeur dans son traité: ". . . si coamantem somnium re-
praesentet amanti, oritur inde amor et ortus sumit augmenta."
(Un trouvère lui fera écho: "S'en nest l'amor et croist,
qui ja n'iert mendre.")[11]

C'est au titre de signe conventionnel que nous allons
le retrouver dans le roman.[12] Le parfait amant, prescrit
Aimon de Varennes, est censé rêver de l'objet de sa flamme:

> En dormant en ait grant desduit,
> Que voit de jor, songet la nuit.
> (2825-26)

L'auteur applique ce précepte dans son roman de
Florimont. Romanadaple est fort éprise: la passion
l'empêche de dormir et, quand enfin elle s'assoupit, l'image
de Florimont hante son sommeil:[13] "De dormir n'avoit gaires
cure, Et quant se dort per aventure, En dormant mout se
delitoit; Qu'avis li ert qu'ele baissoit Son amin, le Povre
Perdu, Si estrangnoit per grant vertu Contre son cuer
ansdous les bras."[14] Pour Renaut de Beaujeu, le rêve est
également révélateur de la passion et de son intensité. Le
héros du roman se croit visité par sa belle:

> Amors le destraint et travaille,
> Mais lasés ert, si s'endormi.
> En dormant a veü celi
> Por cui ses cuers muert et cancele;
> Entre ses bras tenoit la biele.
> Tote nuit songe qu'il le voit
> Et qu'entre ses bras le tenoit,
> Tros qu'al main que l'aube creva.[15]
> (2464-71)

On trouve des descriptions semblables un peu partout:
Jean Renart, l'auteur de Blancandin et l'Orgueilleuse
d'amour et celui de Durmart le Gallois, Robert de Blois et
même Adam de la Hale, montrent qu'ils sont au courant de
la dernière mode littéraire.[16]

*
* *

Quelquefois, le dormeur voit apparaître une belle et
lointaine inconnue, qui lui inspire une passion soudaine;
sitôt réveillé, il n'aura de cesse de la rejoindre. Il
s'agit d'un thème ancien, qui se rencontre dans le domaine
gréco-latin comme dans les lettres arabes, persanes et
celtiques.[17] Au moyen âge, c'est tout d'abord Vénance
Fourtunat qui l'utilise: le roi Sigebert se serait épris
en rêve de celle qui allait devenir par la suite son
épouse.[18] Au XIIIe siècle, un romancier français contera
les aventures de Cristal: elles ont pour origine une
merveilleuse beauté aperçue en songe, que le jeune homme
cherche partout à retrouver.[19] Dans le Roman des Sept
Sages, il s'agit des rêves complémentaires d'un chevalier
et d'une belle dame qui, eux non plus, ne se sont jamais vus
auparavant.[20]

Il arrive donc que les images oniriques correspondent
à la réalité: elles révèlent au dormeur l'existence d'une
personne inconnue et le poussent à partir à sa recherche.
Mais le plus souvent, l'expérience nocturne se termine tout
autrement. Déjà chez les auteurs latins et médiolatins, le
bonheur qu'elle laisse entrevoir s'avère insaisissable;[21]
au dire des poètes de langue vulgaire, le rêve d'amour ne
laisse subsister qu'un profond désenchantement.[22] Ecoutons
le troubadour Folquet de Romans peindre son désarroi, au
moment où il explore vainement sa couche: ". . . Per pauc
no.m volh los olhz crebar . . . E vauc vos per lo leich
cerchan, E quan no.us trob, reman ploran. . . ."[23]

Il est curieux de voir combien de fois revient dans le
roman courtois ce trait du rêveur qui se retrouve les mains
vides. A partir de quelques vers de l'Enéide,[24] l'auteur du
Roman d'Eneas a imaginé toute une scène, où il nous montre

Didon tourmentée par un songe. "Anpor l'amor au chevalier,
Cuide que cil qui ert absenz Anz an son lit li fust presenz"
(vv. 1244ss). Elle croit même l'étreindre, illusion qui est
ramenée à une cause matérielle: en réalité, "elle acole son
covertor" et couvre de baisers . . . son oreiller! Le
lecteur assiste enfin à ce que l'on peut appeler, dans toute
l'acception du terme, la déception de la reine abandonnée:

> An son lit le taste et quiert;
> Quant nel troveq des poinz se fiert;
> Ele plore et fait grand duel.[25]
> (1249-51)

Plus loin dans le roman, il en ira de même de Lavine
que l'on voit, elle aussi, se persuader de la présence
d'Enée: "Si acolot son covertor; Et quant ele se
reporpansoit (var. s'apercevoit) Qu'il n'i ert pas, si se
pasmot. . . ." (vv. 8416ss)

Sans la traiter pour autant en termes plaisants,[26]
l'adaptateur de Piramus et Tisbé évoque une expérience
analogue; la jeune fille, en voyant se dérober l'image tant
désirée, doit constater à son grand dépit l'inconsistance
des songes. "Dont m'est a vis que je vois voi, Et que poez
touchier a moi," raconte-t-elle. Mais lorsqu'elle croit
pouvoir la saisir, la vision est déjà évanescente: "Dont
tent les mains que je vos bail, Et quant vos doi prendre
si fail."[27]

Pour l'auteur d'Athis et Prophilias, les songes
n'apportent aux amants que des joies éphémères et trom-
peuses. Chaque fois, l'apparition s'évanouit dans les
airs: "Prandre la cuit, si n'en truis mie," se lamente
Prophilias.[28] Athis a beau tendre les bras à sa belle,
"il ne la trueve ne ne sant." Sa déception est profonde,
explique l'auteur: "Sa fause joie torne en plor, Car qui
faut la ou mout espoire, De fause joie a dolor voire."[29]
Gaïte, enfin, connaît la même mésaventure: "Prendre le
voil, n'i tieng noient." A ses yeux, c'est cependant la
réalité qui déçoit, non le songe; comme les poètes, elle

conclut: "Quant je recort ma volenté, Que en veillant
m'estuet faillir, Si vodroie tous tans dormir."[30]

*
* *

Cette insistance sur le réveil solitaire se retrouve
dans beaucoup d'oeuvres plus récentes.[31] Le <u>Roman</u> <u>d'Eneas</u>
aurait-il exercé, une fois de plus, son influence?[32] Un
rapprochement direct ne semble pas indiqué, car ces textes,
comme ceux que l'on vient de lire, ne traitent pas le motif
dans le même esprit.[33] Si l'on y marque si fortement le
contraste entre la joie et le désenchantement de l'amoureux,
ce n'est pas pour en faire rire, mais pour mieux souligner
l'irréalité et, surtout, le caractère subjectif de l'événement.

Il convient de rappeler sous ce rapport les théories
oniriques de Macrobe, que le Moyen Age connaissait bien.[34]
Dans son Commentaire sur le <u>Songe</u> <u>de</u> <u>Scipion</u>, cet auteur
décrit de façon détaillée le phénomène appelé <u>insomnium</u>,
dont il souligne le caractère éphémère et trompeur: c'est
une chimère, qui disparaît au réveil. L'<u>insomnium</u> n'est
autre, ainsi Macrobe, qu'une réminiscence de la conscience
vigile ou encore, un simple produit du coeur. Et de citer,
à titre d'exemple, les songes dont se leurrent les
amoureux.[35] C'est d'ailleurs à ce passage que renvoie
visiblement le discours de Nature, chez Jean de Meun: les
visions attribuées aux "fins amanz" possèdent les mêmes
traits. Engendrées par la vie intérieure, elles traduisent
les sentiments profonds du dormeur: "Si songent. . . .
Que tant ont par jour reclamees." Mais elles n'ont pas
plus de consistance que l'air: "Ainsinc con de l'ome qui
songe, Qui voit, ce cuide. . . .   Et sent antre ses braz
s'amie, Toutevois n'i est ele mie" (vv. 18334-58).

A la différence des chansons de geste et des vies de
saints, le songe, dans la littérature courtoise, n'apparaît
plus comme une révélation d'origine surnaturelle. L'optique
a d'ailleurs changé: on n'admet plus l'immixtion du divin
dans l'histoire humaine. La littérature subit l'influence
de l'esprit profane et mondain, qui tend à réintégrer

l'individuel: dès lors, on considère que le rêve a son
origine dans l'homme même, qu'il exprime ses besoins ou
ses désirs.

*
* *

A l'époque du Roman de la Rose, le rêve inspiré par
l'amour représente, on l'a vu, un thème parfaitement con-
stitué. Comme l'indiquent sa fréquence et le caractère
conventionnel de la description, il tend à devenir un
topos figurant parmi les autres "accidenz d'amor": on
peut dire que dès Aimon de Varennes, le songe fait partie
intégrante de l'arsenal érotique.

A côté de l'exploitation lyrique,[36] on perçoit, dans
le roman, une certaine objectivation de l'événement, qui ne
traduit plus l'état d'âme de celui qui écrit: le romancier
s'interpose entre le rêveur et nous. Comme l'expérience
survient à un tiers, elle est considérée avec un certain
détachement. Dès lors, nos auteurs insistent davantage
sur la déception que sur l'exaltation, ou encore se plaisent
à évoquer celle-ci pour mieux l'opposer à celle-là. (Tout
se passe comme s'ils voulaient illustrer encore une fois les
théories anciennes sur l'insomnium). Si le songe apparaît
en tant que révélation du désir, on nous montre surtout
qu'il ne l'assouvit que dans l'imaginaire.

Notes

1. Pour les origines gréco-latines du thème et sa
fortune chez les troubadours, v. notre étude "Visio Amoris:
Genèse et signification d'un thème de la poésie provençale,"
Mélanges . . . Ch. Rostaing (Liège: Assoc. des romanistes
de l'U. de Liège, 1974), pp. 89-99. Aj. ce que l'on dit
dans le roman de Flamenca: Le héros voit exaucer en songe
son voeu le plus cher: "E vi si dons a son talen, Que nulla
res non la.il defen"--éd. R. Nelli et R. Lavaud, Les Troubadours, I (Paris, 1960): vv. 3447ss.

2. R. 959, IV, 21-23; éd. A. Jeanroy et A. Langfors,
Rom, 45 (1918-19), 359.

3. R. 1648, IV, 25. J. Beck, Les Chansonniers des
Troubadours et des Trouvères (Paris-Philadelphie, 1927),
II, 158.

4. R. 1572, V, 33-35. H. Petersen Dyggve, Gace
Brulé, Trouvère Champenois (Helsingfors, 1951), p. 327.
De même l'anonyme déjà cité (R. 959, 24-25): "Au resveillier me truiz si esbahi Qu'en veillant n'ai ce qu'en
dormant choisi."

5. R. 2036, VI, 32-34: "Quar fust or mes guerredons
Teus que vous fust la visons Quen songant vous ai baisie
. . .". [Trébutien], Les Chansons de Messire Raoul de
Ferrières (Caen, 1847); G. Huet, Chansons et descorts de
Gautier de Dargies (Paris, 1912), p. 42.

6. Tel l'auteur anon. de R. 1648 (IV, 27-28). Plutôt
que de veiller, dit-il, je préfère dormir, "car en dormant
me plait a li parler, Puis qu'en voillant ne os vers li
aler."

7. R. 772, IV, 67-68. Petersen Dyggve, éd. cit.,
p. 200.

8. R. 2115, Inc. "Quant li tens torne a verdure"
(Gontier de Soignies), refrain (ms.C). H. Spanke, Eine
altfr. Liedersammlung. Der anon. Teil der Liederhs. KNPX
(Halle, 1925), pp. 181-82. Note: ces vers sont repris
littéralement dans le roman de Durmart le Gallois, I, éd.
J. Gildea (Villanova, Pa., 1965), vv. 9035ss.

9. Voir les textes cités dans notre étude "Visio
amoris."

10. ". . . Surripit si quando sopor, sopor omnis in
illa est, Quae mihi non soli sola placere potest. . . ."
Opera, I, éd. J. S. Brewer (Londres, 1861), p. 353
(vv. 57ss).

11. De Amore, lib. II, 2, éd. E. Trojel (Copenhague,
1892), p. 242. R. 1754, IV, 27. A. Lerond, Chansons
attrib. au Chastelain de Couci (Paris, 1964), p. 21;
Petersen Dyggve, éd. cit. (LVI).

12. La littérature occitane connaît peu d'exemples où
le rêve s'insère dans un cadre narratif. Hormis Flamenca,
nous ne pouvons citer que cette cobla anonyme (P.-C. 461,
245): "Un cavaler conosc que l'altrer vi Una donna bel' e
precios' a fi . . . . E songet la la noit, can el dormi."
A. Kolsen, "25 unedierte provenzalische Anonyma," ZRP, 39
(1917), 296 (no. 23).

13. A. Hilka, éd., Goettingue, 1933, vv. 7791ss.

14. Le héros lui-même fait un rêve semblable dans
lequel il croit étreindre la fée de l'Ile Celée (vv.
3988ss). Dans son introduction, le savant éditeur rassemble
des exemples tirés de plusieurs autres romans.

15. Le Bel Inconnu, éd. G. Perrie Williams, CFMA
(Paris, 1929).

16. Pour Le Lai de l'Ombre, v. infra, n. 31.
Blancandin, éd. F. P. Sweetser (Genève, 1964), vv. 3930ss.
Il y a plusieurs passages dans Durmart, notamment: "Le jor

le voit en sa pensee Et maintes fois songoit la nuit Qu'il
ert o li en grant desduit. . . . ." A quoi l'auteur ajoute:
"Cant il songoit qu'il ert o li, Todis vossist dormir ensi,
Et quant le jor a li pensoit, Sa pensee tant li plaisoit
Qu'il ne vossist jamais dormir" (éd. cit., vv. 9066ss).
(Voir également vv. 9032ss et l'extrait cité plus loin).
Beaudous rêve de Beauté: "Tot en pensant c'est endormis.
. . . Li oil dorment et li cuers veille," explique le
poète, en se rappelant sans doute le fameux verset du Cant.
Cant. (Voir également, sur le rôle du coeur, la note 40 de
notre étude "Visio amoris"). Robert von Blois: Sämmt-
liche Werke, I, éd. J. Ulrich (Berlin, 1899), vv. 2516ss.
Dans le Jeu de la Feuillée, le thème de la vision amoureuse
est caricaturé: "Adont me vint en avisions De cheli ke j'ai
a feme ore, Ki or me sanle pale et sore; Adont estoit blanke
et vermeille, Rians, amoureuse et deugie, Or sanle crasse et
mautaillie, Triste et tenchans." Ed. E. Langlois, CFMA
(Paris, 1923[2]), vv. 68ss.

     17. Lucien et Hygin rapportent que Médée devint
amoureuse de Jason en le voyant en songe. Hermotime 73 –
Luc. Opera, éd. C. Iacobitz (Leipzig, 1852), p. 382.
Hyginus, Fabulae, éd. H. I. Rose (Leyde, 1934), fable XXI:
"Quae[sc. Medea] cum eum[Iasonem] uidisset, agnouit eum quem
in somniis adamauerat." D'après Athénée, Deipnosophistarum
XIII 35, éd. G. Kaibel (Leipzig, 1887-90), Charès de Mytilène
observait déjà que beaucoup de gens s'éprenaient d'une
inconnue vue en rêve. Qu'on se reporte à Erwin Rohde, Der
griechische Roman, pp. 49ss; F. Liebrecht, trad. John
Dunlop's Gesch. der Prosadichtungen . . . (Berlin, 1851),
p. 107; Wikenhauser, "Doppelträume," Biblica, 29 (1948),
101. Voir d'autre part J. Pizzi, Storia della poesia
persana, II (Milan, 1887), 412ss, et R. R. Bezzola,
Origines et formation de la littérature courtoise, (Paris,
1960), II, 1, 186, n. 6. Pour la littérature irlandaise,
M. Dillon et N. Chadwick, The Celtic Realms (Londres, 1967),
pp. 145, 252 et 255; en gallois, le Songe de Maxen, trad.
J. Loth, Les Mabinogion (Paris, 1913[2]), I, 213-22. Peut-
être est-ce simplement une variante du thème de l'amour
conçu pour une personne qu'on a entendu louer (cf. T.11.1
et T.11.3 du Motif-Index de S. Thompson). G. Paris notait
déjà: "S'éprendre d'amour pour une princesse lointaine sur
le seul bruit de sa beauté est un trait qui se retrouve dans
les fictions romanesques de tous les peuples" (d'après O. M.
Moore, "Jaufré Rudel and the Lady of Dreams," PMLA, 29
(1914), 527.

     18. Voir notre étude "Visio amoris," n. 13.

     19. Cristal et Clarie, éd. H. Breuer (Dresde, 1915),
vv. 421ss. Après avoir rencontré Clarie, le jeune homme
manifeste les "symptômes" que l'on connaît; il sera de
nouveau visité par des rêves (vv. 7167ss et 7831ss).

     20. Ed. H. A. Keller (Tübingue, 1836), vv. 4222ss;
éd. H. A. Smith, RR, 3 (1912), vv. 1447ss; éd. J. Misrahi
(Paris, 1933), 4225ss. Aj. l'histoire du Chevalier de la
Trappe, chez P. J. B. Legrand d'Aussy, Fabliaux ou

Contes . . ., III (Paris, 1829[3]), p. 156. Wikenhauser, op.
cit. (supra, n. 17), montre l'origine ancienne de ces rêves
parallèles.

21. A peine le rêveur croit-il l'enlacer, que déjà
l'image lui échappe. Voir, dans notre première étude, les
exemples tirés de Virgile et d'Ovide, ainsi que les poèmes
de Ratisbonne et de l'Anònim enamorat de Ripoll.

22. Voir notre étude "Visio amoris."

23. Comjat, vv. 25ss. Gedichte, éd. R. Zenker (Halle,
1896). On lit chez Arnaut de Mareuil: ". . . Hobra mos
huelhs soptozamen, Cerc say e lay tot belamen, Trobar vos
cug, Dona, latz mey, Mas jes no.us truep ni no vos vey
. . . ." Salut I, vv. 163ss. (Les Saluts d'amour du troubadour A. de M., éd. P. Bec (Toulouse, 1961) (au v. 164,
nous adoptons la leçon de G). Pierre de la Vigne fera comme
Folquet: ". . . an hoc verum fuerit saepius per lectum
quaeritur, et dum non invenit manus quam tenuerat, genas
confestim laniat et deturpat." Vie et correspondance, éd.
A. Huillard-Bréholles (Paris, 1864), p. 420 (CIV).

24. "Anna soror, quae me suspensam insomnia terrent"
(IV, 9), "Illum absens absentem audit uiditque" (IV, 83);
voilà les seules indications que l'on trouve chez Virgile.
Pour l'Eneas, v. 1'éd. J.-J. Salverda de Grave. CFMA
(Paris, 1925-29).

25. E. Faral, Recherches sur les sources latines des
contes et romans courtois (Paris, 1913), p. 137, croit que
ce rêve fait écho à celui de Sappho (Hér. XV, 123-32). A
noter toutefois que le trait de rêveur qui explore sa couche
ne se retrouve pas, chez Ovide, dans les songes érotiques,
mais dans Hér. X, 9-14 (où Ariane est victime d'une autre
illusion) et dans Métam. XI, 674-82 (Alcyone visitée par
l'ombre de Céyx). Voir encore la Consolatio ad Liviam,
jadis attr. à Ovide: "Et modo per somnos agitaris imagine
falsa Teque tuo Drusum credis habere sinu, Et subito temp-
tasque manu sperasque recentum, Quaeris et in uacui parte
priore tori"--vv. 325ss, éd. J. H. Mozley, The Art of Love
and Other Poems (Londres, 1929).

26. On se rappellera également la mésaventure d'Alis,
dans Cligés (éd. A. Micha, CFMA [Paris, 1957]): sous l'effet
du philtre, l'empereur croit être avec Fénice, alors qu'il
n'enlace qu'un fantôme (vv. 3309ss). Selon Ph. Ménard, dans
la thèse citée infra, n. 33 (pp. 270ss: "Nuits de noces
comiques"), on cherche surtout à nous faire rire aux dépens
du mari trompé, impuissant à consommer le mariage. Mais
d'autre part, la description de ces ébats imaginaires
rejoint le topos du songe érotique, dont Chrétien ne retient
que l'aspect illusoire, comme pour mieux le tourner en
dérision. (Outre les reprises du verbe "cuidier" et de
"neant," cf. les vv. 3165ss où sont rapprochés "songe:
mançonge").

27. C. de Boer, éd. (Paris, 1921), vv. 552ss. Cf. la
"chanson d'histoire" d'Oriolanz (R. 1312, IV, 24-25):
". . . Et qant g'i fail au resveillier, Nule riens ne m'i
puet aidier." G. Saba, Le 'Chansons de toile' o 'Chansons
d'histoire' (Modène, 1955), p. 64 ou K. Bartsch, Altfr.
Romanzen u. Pastourellen (Leipzig, 1870), p. 14.

28. A. Hilka, éd. (Halle, 1912), vv. 751ss. Ce passage, ainsi que le suivant, a été repris littéralement dans
Cristal et Clarie (vv. 7831ss et 7169ss).

29. Vv. 3337ss. De même, le second rêve d'Athis,
vv. 3531ss: "Ses braz estant, n'en trueve mie; Sa joie
est a duel revertie."

30. Vv. 3320ss (D); cf. ms. C, vv. 3393ss.

31. "Li esveilliers me desembrace, En ce qui plus me
delitast; Lors quier par mon lit et atast Son biau cors qui
m'art et m'esprent; Mes, las! qui ne trueve ne prent; C'est
avenu moi et maint autre Mainte foiz" (Le Lai de l'Ombre,
éd. J. Bédier, SATF [Paris, 1913], vv. 180ss); Durmart vv.
4094ss: ". . . trueve son lit tot vuit . . . Deus! fait
il, com sui engigniés Quant je si tost sui esveilliés! A
tos jors mais dormir vodroie. . . ." Guillaume de Lorris,
dans une description des "symptômes": ". . . Lors feras
chastiaus en Espaigne Et avras joie de noiant. . . . Mes
poi i poras demorer; Lors comenceras a plorer," etc. (2430ss);
désillusions analogues dans Floriant et Florete, éd. H. F.
Williams (Ann Arbor-Londres, 1947), vv. 3498ss, le Roman de
Cassidorus, I, éd. J. Palermo (Paris, 1963), ch. VII, 81ss.
et le Méliador de Froissart, III, éd. A. Longnon (Paris,
1899), vv. 28605ss.

32. Elle est indéniable chez l'auteur de Guillaume de
Palerne. Son héros, lui aussi, "souvent embrace l'orillier."
La passion l'emporte tant et si bien qu'il finit par se
réveiller; mais même alors, l'illusion persiste: "Grant
pièce après li est avis De l'oreillier qu'ensi demaine, Que
ce soit la bele demaine. Soventes fois l'a embracié,
Estraint, acolé et baisié, Quarante fois, je cuit, et plus,
Ains qu'il se soit aperceus. . . ." Enfin, il constate
"qu'en vain travaille Et que ce est songes et faille,
Fantosmes, niens et vanités" (éd. H. Michelant [Paris,
1876], vv. 1118ss).

33. Contrairement à ce que semble suggérer Ménard, Le
Rire et le sourire dans le roman courtois . . . (1150-1250),
PRF (Genève, 1969), pp. 196-97. Nous faisons exception, bien
entendu, pour Guillaume de Palerne. On ajoutera le fabliau
de Guillaume au faucon: ". . . Estent ses brax, n'en trueve
mie; . . . Par tot son lit la dame quiert; Quant ne la
trueve, si se fiert Sor la poitrine et en la face. . . ."
A. de Montaiglon et G. Raynaud, Rec. gén. des fabl., II
(Paris, 1877), vv. 356ss. Rappelons à ce propos la déception
d'une jeune "mal-mariée," racontée dans une complainte
gasconne; ayant rêvé de son amant, elle entend, au réveil,
ronfler son vieux mari: Chansons du XVe siècle, éd. G. Paris,
SATF (Paris, 1935), p. 119.

34. Ainsi nous le rappelle Guillaume de Lorris qui, lui, est persuadé que certains rêves ne sont "fables" ni mensonges; afin d'étayer ce jugement, il invoque dans son prologue l'autorité de "Macrobes, qui ne tint pas songes a lobes." (Précisons que Macrobe distingue différentes sortes de songes, dont les révélations surnaturelles, véridiques, et les phénomènes subjectifs et trompeurs).

35. In Somnium Scipionis, lib. I, 3,4, éd. J. Willis (Leipzig, 1963).

36. Le thème reste vivant jusqu'à la fin du moyen âge. Il se retrouve, par exemple, chez un Charles d'Orléans, Ball. XII, II, 9-16 et Ch. XXVII; Poésies, I, éd. P. Champion, CFMA (Paris, 1923), pp. 29 et 220.

THE THEME OF CONCEALED LOVE IN TWO FRENCH POETS OF THE TWELFTH CENTURY

A. R. Press

The theme of concealed love figures both in French courtly romance of the twelfth century and in troubadour lyric poetry of the same period. Although it is in both genres a relatively minor and infrequent theme, a comparative study of the way in which it is handled will, it is hoped, contribute positively to the elucidation of a more general and, to some extent, still problematical topic, namely the relationship between the love-concepts of the northern French romance-writers and those of the southern French troubadours.

For practical reasons, the present article is limited to examining how the theme is treated in the works of two writers only, Guillaume IX, Duke of Aquitaine, and Chrétien de Troyes, but the limitation might well be considered as compensated for by the very special and closely comparable status of them both. For in the poetry of Guillaume IX, our earliest known troubadour (1071-1127), we find en germe, as Friedrich Diez[1] and many scholars after him have recognized, all the principal characteristics of later courtly lyric poetry, while the romances written by Chrétien in the last quarter of the twelfth century represent for us the earliest, most consistent, and most coherent attempt to infuse legendary narrative material with a new, courtly significance, born of the cultural milieu in which their author worked and destined to influence all subsequent literary manifestations of that milieu.

Before examining the relevant texts, one further preliminary remark is, I feel, necessary. That is that the theme of concealed love is in its essence a narrative theme; in the works of both writers to be examined, as

119

elsewhere, it forms part of an objectively described or
recounted situation or episode. In this fundamental respect
it is to be, from the outset, clearly distinguished from
the lyric motif of secrecy-in-love, li celers of the courtly
poets. To formulate this distinction in a different way:
the term "concealed love" characterizes a situation of
close privacy, seclusion, even of sequestration entered
into by the lovers willingly; secrecy-in-love, on the other
hand, denotes an attitude of discretion and reserve maintained, even in the public milieu of the court, by the
lovers as they react to external circumstances. (Chief
among the latter figures the malicious gossip of the
jealous, envious, losengiers.) This precision being made,
let us now consult the relevant texts.

Concealed love figures clearly in two of Guillaume IX's
eleven lyric poems, those numbered 2 and 5 in A. Jeanroy's
edition. In the first of these, the poet warns those who
would keep a noble lady in closely guarded confinement, out
of contact with all that pertains to prowess, that the outcome can only be for her to consort with malvestatz, with
baseness. If good company (or "fine goods," the exact
sense turns on the double meaning of conrei l. 16), is
priced too high, then she will accommodate herself with
what she finds to hand; if she cannot have a horse she'll
buy a hack and that, concludes the poet, as surely as one
who, because of sickness, is forbidden strong wine will
drink water rather than die of thirst. The general point
which the poet is making then, from what he claims to be a
specific case, is this: if noblewomen are kept in seclusion, not allowed to mingle freely with men of their own
social status, then they will seek satisfaction in furtive
liaisons with their social inferiors, the malvestatz, the
inferior company or goods, the hack rather than the fine
horse. [2] Clearly the poet takes the lady's part: he
expresses dismay at the complaint she makes against her
keepers (st. 1), portrays the latter as grossly inconsider-
ate and boorish individuals (st. 3), and warns them directly

against the outcome of the lady's seclusion (st. 4), which is thus presented to Guillaume's public as something to be deplored and avoided. Consequently, this poem can well be considered to be a lively, spirited, but nonetheless genuine plea for a more open form of court life, wherein noblemen and noblewomen may freely indulge in social and emotional relationships with one another, in strong contrast to the furtive, secretive, and concealed affairs which, the poet alleges, are the inevitable outcome of a socially primitive, sexually segregated form of life in the feudal castle.[3] In other words, we see already sketched out in Guillaume IX's poem no. 2 the notion that concealed love is the very opposite of that ideal form of love which should be experienced in noble society.

A similar notion emerges from a careful reading of poem no. 5, most of which is devoted to the telling of a rather scabrous tale: the poet tells how, when travelling in Auvergne one day, alone and somewhat furtively, he was met by two married noblewomen. Misled by his appearance, they greet him, in the name of a local saint, as <u>don pelerin</u>; further deceived by his feigned inability to speak, they find him eminently fitting for their secret purposes and take him home. There, having tested his apparent muteness to their entire satisfaction, they retain him for a week or more as their secret lover. Clearly a tale of concealed love, recounted seemingly in a spirit of coarse jest. However, two important structural features of the poem, the introduction and the conclusion, combine in their effect to indicate that once again our earliest known troubadour has a serious point to make. Firstly, he concludes the tale by simply, but twice, stating that he cannot express the sickness which befell him as a result of his encounter: <u>Ges no.us sai dir lo malaveg</u>, / <u>Tan gran m'en pres</u>. Neither here nor elsewhere in the poem is there a word of erotic pleasure, satisfaction, pride, or self-congratulation. This, coupled with the curiously passive rôle played by the poet-narrator, in the end a victim of

his own deceptions, leads one to ask what, precisely, is
the point of the tale. Short of dismissing it as a gross
and gratuitous jest, a possible answer can only lie in the
two introductory stanzas. Here, after a brief declaration
of intent to compose a vers, the poet launches into an
attack on those ladies who, rejecting the love of a loyal
knight, prefer that of a monk or a cleric; such ladies, he
affirms, should be burned. There then follows, beginning
with the first line of stanza 3, and without any explicit
link between introduction and main topic, the tale of concealed love. But link there must surely be; for one cannot
but associate, if only by virtue of their structural juxtaposition, the ladies condemned so strongly in the introduction with those two ladies of the central stanzas who,
thinking the poet to be a solitary pilgrim, choose him as
the one with whom to indulge in their concealed love. In
other words, as in poem no. 2, a particular case is narrated
in order to illustrate a general point; the two noblewomen
are examples of those who reject a loyal knight's love--in
this case their respective husbands'--in preference for
that of a man of religion, figured in the story by the bogus
pilgrim. Indeed many structural features of the poem seem
to indicate a conscious imitation of the medieval Latin
exemplum while, thematically, the poem is no doubt also
related to that other medieval tradition of poetic debates
on the respective merits, as lovers, of cleric and knight.[4]
In such debates, a frequently cited advantage of the cleric
is precisely his secretiveness. Unlike the clerical authors
of most of them, however, Guillaume IX not unsurprisingly
takes the knight's part and, perhaps less obviously though
in full accordance with the notion sketched out in poem no.
2, he opposes desirable, free, and open relationships
between noblemen and noblewomen to the joyless, deplorable,
secretive, and furtive liaisons between the latter and men
of another social status.

Concealed love is thus again presented as the negation
of the poet's own aspirations to that ideal form of love

which, as is made clear both in the poems considered and in
his more obviously courtly poems, should be exclusive to men
and women of the nobility. That ideal form of love does not
exclude secrecy--the _celers_ of poem no. 9, for example--but,
cultivated freely in the open context of civilized, polite,
and considerate court society, such as is evoked in poem no.
7, it can alone lead to all the joy of the world, _Totz lo_
joys del mon.

After Guillaume IX, the vast majority of troubadour
love-songs are devoted to the lyric formulation of that joy
or of aspiration to it; purely narrative elements are rare,
and the theme of concealed love perforce isolated and
sporadic. Further exploration would doubtless produce
further material to discuss,[5] but without more ado let us
now turn to the works of our second writer, Chrétien de
Troyes, in the first two of whose romances the theme of
concealed love is again clearly identifiable.

Towards the end of the "Joie de la Cour" episode of
Erec et Enide,[6] two conversations take place between,
firstly, Erec and Maboagrain whom the former has just
defeated and, secondly, Enide and Maboagrain's mistress.
From these conversations we learn that Maboagrain and his
mistress had been in love since a very tender age; that
love had been kept secret, and, once Maboagrain had attained
knighthood, his mistress had exacted from him a pledge which
he had previously granted her, without knowing its exact
terms (the rash-boon motif of Celtic legend). By these
terms Maboagrain is now obliged to retire with his mistress,
secretly, into the grove where he has just been dubbed; he
must forbid its access to any knight who dare challenge him,
and stay with his mistress there until he is defeated by any
such challenger. Thus, adds Maboagrain, his mistress
thought to retain him with her for a long time (_a lonc_
sejor), at her free and exclusive disposition (_a delivre_),
and _an prison_ (11. 6041-6047). So much for the factual,
narrative circumstances of what clearly constitutes a realisation of the theme of concealed love. But what would

Chrétien have us conclude as to the social, psychological,
and moral implications of this concealed love?

In the first place, it is clear that Maboagrain himself
has not been entirely at ease in the secret grove. It is he
who uses the term prison to characterise his situation vis-
à-vis his mistress, and who envisages issue therefrom as a
delivrance (1. 6052); he who recognises that his defeat at
Erec's hands will restore joy to his uncle's court and to
his friends, and who urges Erec on to perform the last
symbolic act (the blowing of the horn) by which that long-
awaited joy will be renewed. And, finally, it is Maboagrain
who, when referring to the knights he has slain, seeks
explicitly to disculpate himself, pleading that he could do
nothing else without breaking his pledge (11. 6234-37).

In the second place, the stress which Maboagrain's
mistress, for her part, places on the secrecy of their love-
life is immediately contrasted, in Enide's reply, with the
openness and publicity of her courtship and marriage, an
openness and publicity which, adds Enide, filled all who
knew of it with joy and happiness (11. 6242-47). It is not,
moreover, without significance that the only other piece
of information which Maboagrain's mistress has to impart,
after stressing the secrecy of her love-life, is that at
the time of her withdrawal into the grove she was "jeune
et petite" (1. 6237).

In the third place, although the grove has all the
appearance of an earthly paradise, and possibly did have
when the young lovers first withdrew into it, by the time
of Erec's arrival it has become a source of terror and
dread among the local populace. Its abundant fruits cannot
be shared with the outside world, and it is surrounded by
the most gruesome symbols of death--the spiked heads of
Maboagrain's victims.

Fourthly and finally, in the same way that Enide had
pointedly opposed the joy-inspiring openness of her courtship and marriage to the concealed love of her interlocutor,
so I would suggest, has Chrétien de Troyes himself exploited

here the theme of concealed love in order to illuminate
further the experience of his two main characters. For
surely one of the many and complex functions of the
Maboagrain story, as narrated by Chrétien, is to remind us
of the joy-destroying risks which Erec and Enide themselves
ran when, after their wedding, they too retreated into a
self-absorbed and introspective life of passionate love; a
life in which Erec neglected his knightly duties, and Enide
those of the lady; a life from which only the most heroic
efforts and the most loving trust and confidence were,
ultimately, to deliver them both.[7] The conclusion   then
seems clear and unavoidable: concealed love, as presented
in the romance of _Erec_ _et_ _Enide_, is a menace. It deprives
court society of that joy which it is entitled to feel at
the fulfilment of love between two of its members, and even
such knightly acts as it does inspire contribute in no way
to the well-being of that society. What is more, it deprives
the lovers, too, of any permanent, lasting satisfaction and,
inspired by a desire for total and exclusive possession of
the loved one, it strongly suggests a lack of trust, of
confidence, and of personal and emotional maturity. Though
its setting may appear to be one of earthly paradise, the
rest of society, far from sharing its fruits, sees in it
only a spectacle of death and horror. The joy of love, as
that of society as a whole, can only be achieved if that
love is lived openly in its proper, noble, social context,
in the fullest mutual trust and confidence, and with both
partners, inspired by their love, fulfilling their proper
functions in that social context. Concealed love is the
opposite of all this; as in Guillaume IX, it is to be
deplored.

Turning lastly to the romance of _Cligés_,[8] we find that
the theme of concealed love occupies a rather more important
place in the narrative. Fénice, the heroine, is married
against her will to the uncle of the man she loves. She has
already, with the aid of a potion, avoided giving her body
to one who has not her heart, but a new situation arises

when she subsequently learns that Cligés, the man she loves,
loves her in return. It is then that she resolves to feign
death and to have Cligés spirit her away to a secret place
where they can live their love in concealment, away from the
rest of the world. All this is done and, notes the author,
such is the lovers' joy that it _seems_ to them that the whole
world is thereby set to rights (1. 6254). However, immediately following this indication of the lovers' seemingly
total contentment, Chrétien introduces a note of dissatis-
faction. Fénice, after something more than fifteen months
of secret bliss lived in the marvellous tower which Cligés
has had built for her, now--for the first time--feels a
desire to walk and take her pleasure in a garden. It is
Spring, and, what is highly significant, a Spring described
in exactly the same general and conventional terms as those
used by the troubadours to introduce their songs of
fin'amors. More remarkable is the fact that scarcely is
Fénice's desire expressed when the faithful Jean, constructor
of the tower, reveals--for the first time--the presence of a
secret door leading into a secret garden. But most remarkable of all, however, is this: having taken four lines to
assure us that the garden is surrounded by a wall so high
that no one could penetrate into it (11. 6360-363), Chrétien
at a point no more than twenty-four lines further in the
narrative, recounts how a young Thracian knight scales this
same wall, discovers the sleeping lovers, and thus precipi-
tates the final dénouement. The lovers flee to Arthur's
court, seek armed assistance in order, at last, to wrest
from his uncle Cligés' rightful inheritance, but are saved
the prospect of battle by news of the uncle's death. The
marriage and coronation of Cligès and Fénice are briefly
reported, and they live happily ever after. Their love
increased day by day and, concludes Chrétien in a curiously
insistent return to the theme of concealed love, Cligés
never lost confidence in his wife and never secluded her--
as all later Emperors were to do.

Let us consider for a moment those remarkable events
which, shattering the apparent bliss of concealed love,
finally bring the lovers to the lasting and satisfactory
solution of their problems. I believe that we have long
passed the stage of dismissing all Chrétien's narrative inconsistencies as due to nothing more than clumsy and naive
ineptitude. There is, on the contrary, a growing awareness
that, all other things being equal, such inconsistencies
might well be ranged among those "artifices très conscients"
which the late Professor Frappier rightly attributed to
Chrétien and which he noted to be particularly frequent in
the romance of Cligés.[9] Artifices très conscients, that
is, skillful devices by which, without direct intervention,
the author arouses our curiosity and directs our attention,
through the narrative material itself, to a point which he
is seeking to make. This being so, then even as no more
than a reasonable working hypothesis, one is led to ask
what, precisely, is the point, if any, of the apparent
inconsistencies with which we are here concerned. To my
mind it is this: by forcing the lovers first out of the
secret tower and next out of the secret garden, by the
simple structural fact of deciding not to end his romance in
either of these two places (which, after all, was well
within his rights as a free creative writer),[10] Chrétien
makes clear that, as far as he is concerned, concealed love
was not the right solution to the problem which faced his
two lovers. That solution, characterized, as Gaston Paris
pointed out long ago, by a desire for "la pleine et exclusive possession des deux amants l'un par l'autre,"[11] deprived
the lovers of their rightful place in court society. To
this extent, it put them in a position no better than that
of Tristan and Iseut in the forest, a position which appalled
Fénice no less than it obsessed her creator. The only
satisfying, fitting, and lasting form of love, says Chrétien
once more through his story, is that lived in the open
context of court society. Concealed love is at best a
mistake, at worst an impossible and unworthy illusion.

On the basis of the foregoing analysis, a number of
general observations can now, by way of conclusion, be made.
Firstly, it is remarkable that the treatment of the theme
of concealed love in both our authors attributes no special
function or significance to the civil status of the lovers.
In the first of Guillaume IX's poems, we are not informed
whether the ladies kept in seclusion are married or not,[12]
while in the second, although the two women of the narrative
are married, there is no indication of whether the general
run of domnas blamed for preferring the love of clerics to
that of loyal knights are married or not. In Erec et Enide,
the lovers in the secret grove are clearly not married,
although we are led to understand that Erec and Enide themselves risked, even in marriage, the same joy-destroying
effects of seclusion as those incurred by the unwed lovers.
In Cligés, finally, while the situation of hero and heroine
is technically adulterous, the ideological (though not thematic or narrative) insignificance of this fact has long been
established by Gaston Paris for whom "l'idéal qu'incarne le
roman [de Cligés] est celui de l'amour tout court . . .
pour lequel mariage et adultère sont des considérations tout
à fait accessoires et même négligeables."[13] This first
observation might well, on further examination, cast light
on the whole problem of the place of adultery in the love-
concepts of troubadours and trouvères.

Secondly, in both our authors, concealed love is
portrayed as undesirable and unsatisfactory. It is so
portrayed by virtue of a strong contrast established
between it and another form of love, the latter being
presented as corresponding either to the poet's own
explicit aspirations or to the idealised and exemplary
conduct and destiny of his main characters.

Thirdly, the common root of this opposition lies in
the fact that concealed love denies the possibility of an
open, joyful, court life, of a life where men and women of
the nobility may mingle freely, and cultivate social, sentimental, and emotional relationships with one another. A

court life, moreover, where the rest of society derives joy
from such relationships, and itself benefits from the conduct which they inspire in those who maintain them. In
other words, the same theme is used by both authors to the
same effect: namely, to point up what they conceive to be
the highest form, the most satisfactory realisation, and
the most fitting circumstances of love.

Finally we can now see that such an ideal concept of
love is, in both Guillaume IX and Chrétien de Troyes, broadly
identical, in so far as it is illumined by their respective
treatment of the theme of concealed love. But, having made
this last qualification, one is led to ask how restrictive
it is. Not, in my view, to any considerable extent. For,
if the foregoing analysis is correct, then the question of
concealment, that is, of living a love away from the social
context of the noble court, touches on one of the most
distinctive features of the concept of ideal love as formu-
lated by our two authors. According to that concept, love
can only be fully realised in an open court society; for
this reason if for no other, it merits the term courtly
love, a term which in itself, as in the examples of it
proposed by troubadour and trouvère alike, indissolubly
associates the quality and value of a universal emotion
with a highly specific, narrowly circumscribed set of social
circumstances. Here then is a basic conceptual link between
our two, most influential, twelfth-century writers; here is
the conceptual resemblance which our study of one particular
theme has enabled us to identify, and which, I would suggest,
places in the same cultural, ethic, and aesthetic perspectives Guillaume IX's joy del mon and Chrétien de Troyes's
Joie de la Cour.

Notes

1. F. Diez, Leben und Werke der Troubadours. 2nd ed.
(Leipzig: Barth, 1882), p. 6; see also Les Chansons de
Guillaume IX, ed. A. Jeanroy. 2nd ed., CFMA (Paris:
Champion, 1927), p. xvii.

2. In his poem no. 1 also, Guillaume IX uses the horse to figure the object of sexual desire.

3. For a full account of such socio-cultural intentions, see R. R. Bezzola, "Guillaume IX et les origines de l'amour courtois," Rom, 66 (1940), 145-237.

4. The structural and typological resemblances between this poem and the medieval Latin exemplum are studied in the author's "Quelques observations sur la chanson V de Guillaume IX: Farai un vers pos mi sonelh," Mélanges Labande (Poitiers: Université de Poitiers, 1974), pp. 603-609; a full account of the knight-cleric debate is given in C. Oulmont, Les Débats du clerc et du chevalier dans la littérature poétique du moyen âge (Paris: Champion, 1911).

5. See, for example, Jaufre Rudel, Les Chansons, ed. A. Jeanroy. 2nd ed., CFMA (Paris: Champion, 1924), no. 4, and Raimbaut d'Orange, The Life and Works, ed. W. T. Pattison (Minneapolis: University of Minnesota Press, 1952), no. 30.

6. Text edited by M. Roques, CFMA (Paris: Champion, 1955).

7. This special function of the "Joie de la Cour" episode has been analysed by the author, "Le Comportement d'Erec envers Enide dans le roman de Chrétien de Troyes," Rom, 90 (1969), 529-38 and, more recently, by Professor Barbara N. Sargent, "Petite histoire de Maboagrain (à propos d'un article récent)," Rom, 93 (1972), 87-96.

8. Text edited by A. Micha, CFMA (Paris: Champion, 1957).

9. J. Frappier, Chrétien de Troyes, 2nd ed., Connaissance des Lettres (Paris: Hatier, 1957), p. 106.

10. One may recall, for example, Marie de France's Lanval, where the hero does in fact flee, finally, to the introspective fairy-land of his secret love.

11. G. Paris, Mélanges de littérature française du moyen âge (Paris: Champion, 1910-1912), p. 292.

12. Despite A. Jeanroy's unwarranted reference to the gardador of Guillaume IX's poem as 'mari' and 'jaloux' (in La Poésie lyrique des troubadours, 2 vols. [Paris: Didier, 1934], I, 95).

13. G. Paris, loc. cit.

"SENPRES EST CI ET SENPRES LA":
MOTIF REPETITION AND NARRATIVE BIFURCATION
IN BEROUL'S TRISTAN

Douglas Kelly

Beroul has Tristan and Governal club Ivain and the other
lepers to the ground rather than kill them. This, he
admits, is contrary to the commonly received version of
the incident.

> Li contor dïent que Yvain
> Firent nïer, qui sont vilain;
> N'en sevent mie bien l'estoire,
> Berox l'a mex en sen memoire:
> Trop ert Tristran preuz et cortois
> A ocirre gent de tes lois.
> (vv. 1265-70)[1]

Tristan's conduct contrasts with Marc's in handing Yseut over
to the lepers. Tristan treats the lepers in a manner befit-
ting their class and his rank, whereas Marc more willingly
listens to their advice than that of his own seneschal, and
in so doing deals with Iseut in a manner unbecoming to her
position. Similarly, descriptions of clothing in Beroul's
Tristan serve as amplified epithets of obvious class significance. They express the wearer's position in the social
hierarchy. François Rigolot has discussed the function of
vestmental description in the romance. But he concludes:
"Aucune signification particulière n'est attachée a priori
à la chose; on ne peut pas dire que tel vêtement 'signifie'
telle attitude."[2] The contrary is however true. Iseut is
queen of Cornwall, and she is attired accordingly, but the
treatment given her is undignified; or, Iseut is queen, but
not living as she should, a fact obvious from the way she is
dressed. The disparities are so obvious, or would have been
to Beroul's audience prepared to fix its attention on the
obvious, that they required no authorial elucidation.

The tension derives from incongruent configuration.
When Iseut is brought out to be burned without benefit of
escondit, as a result of her apprehension in the "flour on
the floor" episode,[3] Beroul places the queen before the
fire and, at this dramatic moment, inserts into the narrative a brief description of her attire.

> Iseut fu au feu amenee;
> De gent fu tote avironee,
> Qui trestuit braient et tuit crïent,
> Les traïtors le roi maudïent.
> L'eve li file aval le vis;
> En un bliaut de paile bis
> Estoit la dame estroit vestue
> Et d'un fil d'or menu cosue;
> Si chevel hurtent a ses piez,
> D'un filet d'or les ot trechiez.
> Qui voit son cors et sa fachon,
> Trop par avroit le cuer felon
> Qui n'en avroit de lïé pitié;
> Molt sont li braz estroit lïé.
>   (vv. 1141-54)

The description of Iseut's dress and hair style underscores
visually ("Qui voit . . .") her nobility. Yet she stands
before the fire because of Marc's condemnation without allowing her the escondit she requested, and because of the felony
of the "traïtor le roi" who encourage and approve the action.
Iseut's nobility, indeed her royalty, and its concomitant
vestmental accoutrements clash with the ignoble, felonious
treatment she receives. Dinas exclaimed earlier (and then
left Marc's service because his counsel was not heeded):

> Sire, merci de la roïne!
> Vos la volez sanz jugement
> Ardoir en feu; ce n'est pas gent,
> Qar cest mesfait ne connoist pas;
> Duel ert, se tu le suen cors ars.
>   (vv. 1096-1100)

Even Ganelon was permitted a trial by Charlemagne!
The denial of escondit to Iseut, the refusal to grant
her what is just as much her due as the royal clothing she
wears, climax when Marc condemns her to living death in

ignominy among the lepers. The new version of punishment,
still without escondit, will be long-lasting and even more
ignoble. As Ivain argues:

> Et que voudroit mex mort avoir,
> Qu'ele vivroit, et sanz valoir,
> Et que nus n'en orroit parler
> Qui plus ne t'en tenist por ber.
>   (vv. 1175-78)

The irony of Marc listening to his felons and to outcasts
about what is ber, rather than attending to his seneschal
Dinas, is patent. Ivain's description of Iseut's lot with
him and the other lepers stresses dress and thus underscores
the contrast between her life as queen and her fate with
them.

> Li drap nos sont au cors aers.
> O toi soloit estre a honor,
> O vair, o gris et o baudor.
>   (vv. 1198-1200)

The accumulation of discrete instances of this motif in so
few lines shows Beroul's terse but effective description of
Iseut before the fire to be no idle digression. Her dress
is essential to our sense of pity.

Appearance and its obvious signification are used as
motif in constantly varying configurations. In the forest
of Morois, the lovers bear the weight of their harsh life
in the woods, so different from what they knew at court:
constant movement; animal-like fear, even panic; hunting and
cooking without wine, bread, spices; living in a loge made
of sticks and leaves on the side of a mountain. But the
strength of the potion, still operating during the first
three years, sustains them, as Eugène Vinaver has demonstrated:[4] "Tant s'entraiment de bone amor, L'un por
l'autre ne sent dolor" (vv. 1365-66). They are as dead to
pain and want as to a sense of guilt for their love. This
fact is specifically linked to their dress and food.

> Molt sont el bois del pain destroit,
> De char vivent, el ne mangüent.
> Que püent il, se color müent?
> Les dras ronpent, rains les decirent;
> Longuement par Morrois fuїrent.
> Chascun d'eus soffre paine elgal,
> Qar l'un por l'autre ne sent mal.
>   (vv. 1644-50)

It is therefore appropriate that thoughts of their former life return when the potion's power diminishes and they are able to sense the devastation caused by its former strength.

Tristan:
> Et poise moi de la roïne,
> Qui je doins loge por cortine;
> En bois est, et si peüst estre
> En beles chanbres, o son estre,
> Portendues de dras de soie.
>   (vv. 2179-83)[5]

Iseut:
>   . . .
> En bois estes com autre serve,
> Petit trovez qui ci vos serve.
> Je sui roïne, mais le non
> En ai perdu par ma poison
> Que nos beümes en la mer. . . .
> Les damoiseles des anors,
> Les filles as frans vavasors,
> Deüse ensenble o moi tenir
> En mes chanbres, por moi servir,
> Et les deüse marїer
> Et as seignors por bien doner.
>   (vv. 2203-207, 2211-16)

Tristan is ashamed of his recreantise.

> Oubliё ai chevalerie,
> A seure cort et baronie;
> Ge sui essilliё du païs,
> Tot m'est falli et vair et gris.
>   (vv. 2165-68)

His functions as knight run parallel to Iseut's as queen (vv. 2173-78).

The return from Morois figures principally as reestablishment in suitable costume, as Rigolot has shown. Ogrin purchases rich clothing for the queen (vv. 2733-44).[6] Even Marc is now taking pity on her: "Trop a mal trait en sa

jovente" (v. 2644), and Dinas is back to assure correct
conduct, including the forthcoming escondit. Dinas sees to
her dress, both when Iseut is returned to Marc (vv. 2880-888;
especially: "Riche ert la robe et gent le cors: Les eulz
out vers, les cheveus sors"), and when she is at the Mal Pas
(vv. 3868-72). And Marc's largesse is extended to Tristan by
means of the same motif: "Molt par li a a bandon mis Or et
argent et vair et gris" (vv. 2921-22). Iseut's clothing is
in fact so fine that it can be placed on a church altar and
made into a chasuble "still" in the church (vv. 2984-95).
Her dress for the ambiguous oath is equally regal (vv. 3903-
11). In fact it sets the stage for one of the most dramatic
moments in the poem: Tristan disguised as a leper bearing
her on his back across the marsh so that her dress will be
unsullied during the oath.

The oath is thus a counterpart to the earlier "flour on
the floor" episode in which Iseut was denied her right to
exculpation. For the escondit, Marc has recovered his fran-
chise (vv. 2658-59); Iseut's dress no longer contrasts with
her lot, but rather underscores the position that by rights,
before God and men, she swears to be hers. There is no
impropriety, no ignoble conduct during her oath, as had been
the case because of Marc's villainy earlier.[7] The only
ladres is Tristan himself (vv. 3299, 3662, 3684, etc.).

Marc's vacillations in Beroul's Tristan--"Li rois n'a
pas coraige entier, Senpres est ci et senpres la" (vv. 3432-
33)--account for his inconsistency in refusing on one occasion to grant the escondit, and then allowing it later. But
it also touches on a fundamental feature of Beroul's art:
his abrupt interventions to interject new but essential
material into the narrative.

> Seignors, du vin de qoi il burent
> Avez oï, por qoi il furent
> En si grant paine lonctens mis;
> Mais ne savez, ce m'est avis,
> A conbien fu determinez
> Li lovendrins, li vin herbez. . . .
>   (vv. 2133-38)

Similar are the arbitrary announcement, just before Tristan
springs from his bed to Iseut's, that he had been wounded
that very day by a boar, and that the wound was not bound
(vv. 716-20); as well as the puzzling but brief episode
about Marc's horse ears. The "Senpres est ci et senpres la"
is literally true for the whole romance! The structural
principle for such abrupt juxtaposition of discrete episodic
material is parataxis, as Vàrvaro remarks "il carattere
quasi autonomo della singola scena che fin da principio si
presenta appunto come irrelata, ma non nel senso che essa
esca dalla nebbia dell'imprecisione: al contrario, essa
appare come se fosse nota da sempre. Ogni capoverso del
racconto è un inizio in medias res."[8] Parataxis is notable
in the chansons de geste, and is perhaps most evident in so-
called contradictory laisses like those giving Roland's two
responses to Ganelon's designating him to command the rearguard: "Sire parastre, mult vos dei aveir cher" and "Ahi
culvert, malvais hom de put aire." They represent bifurcated
developments from a single motif, what Eugène Vinaver has
called the "esthétique du miroir."[9] The problem with such
passages is that, as in the Roland episode, the mirrored
reflection inverts the object so that the two do not coincide: apparently simultaneous, each development from the
same motif seems, upon reflection, to exclude the other.
However, they are not for all that uncomplementary.[10] There
are always three felons, no matter how many may be slain or
what their names may be! The cohesion of these elements derives from what Rigolot terms the "disponibilité fonction-
nelle" of the motif, which, like Iseut's dress, makes them
conducive to meaningful narrative behind sequential incon-
gruities or contradictions.[11] The repetition, essentially
rhetorical despite its relative simplicity, is fundamental
to the poem's narrative cohesion, to those aspects of composition that bind sometimes disparate and even contradictory
developments together into a meaningful narrative. Paul
Zumthor has termed such motifs "désignatifs concrets"; they
are especially prominent in Beroul.[12]

The two visits to Ogrin are two bifurcating developments of the same motif, but the differences are made credible by the artificial interjection of the diminution in the
strength of the potion after three years. An equally probing
example of artificial bifurcation, with concomitant concentration and simplification of the narrative, is contained
in the "Saut Tristan" sequence. The clash resounds sharply
within v. 986: "Eschapé sui!" Tristan exclaims exultantly,
then, abruptly: "Yseut, l'en t'art!" Oblivious heretofore
to Iseut's fate, heedless of the fact that she is to be
thrown into the fire--Iseut can hardly leap from the
chapel!--Tristan dashed away headlong. When safe with
Governal there occurs the sudden reversal in v. 986:
Tristan wishes he were dead! For Iseut is going to die,
and he cannot save her. "Certes, por noient eschapai:
En l'art por moi, por li morrai" (vv. 987-988).

There is of course enhanced intensity in such juxta-
positions. Tristan's two parallel, but discrete reactions
to the consciousness of his escape are in fact complementary
elaborations of two possible reactions to the fire; like
Roland's two responses to Ganelon, the juxtaposition and
separation are typical of paratactic bifurcation.[13] Each
segment of the bifurcated response concentrates, narrows
the focus to such an extent that all other considerations
are blotted out of the mind, or rather temporarily set aside
by the author. Like Tristan long after the spectacular jump
from the chapel and running from the sea alongside a stream,
we still hear with him the fire that caused his panicked
flight even before he had seen it: "Molt par ot bien le feu
qui bruit" (v. 962). And, like him, we forget Iseut alone
before the fire. But when Tristan's immediate peril has
passed, Beroul turns abruptly to Iseut, and in effect begins
anew (reprise bifurquée): "Senpres est ci et senpres la"!

The pattern of sudden, unexpected intervention destroy-
ing a stasis lies at the very core of Beroul's romance. The
love potion upset the established hierarchy of king and queen
under God, who govern their subjects according to their rank.

After the potion God is in league with the lovers, cogently
expressed in the ambiguous oath realizing Ogrin's "bel
mentir," but against the king and his suspicious felons.
The diminution of the potion does not take away the problem,
however. Since the love endures (vv. 2686-88), as "fine
amour" (v. 2722), the disbalance in the hierarchy persists.
Hence the tragic death, so unusual in courtly romance. Not
even Thomas and the prose romances could suppress that,
despite their alterations in other constants of the legend;
Chrétien de Troyes did--but Cligés is not Tristan! Sudden
adventure is, of course, characteristic of medieval romance.
But in Beroul the sudden event is not placed in a plot
structured by an all-embracing motif like, say, the quest in
Chrétien. Rather, the motif in Beroul is introduced arbi-
trarily at a suitable juncture, without any apparent relation
to other episodes and in diversified contexts. Beroul's
motifs are consistent, but his narrative is not unified.

The combination of new narrative material with recurrent motifs is peculiar to Beroul's arrangement of episodes,
insofar as one can perceive from the manuscript fragment; as
Jean Frappier describes his compositional manner: "Il est
vrai que la structure du Tristan [of Beroul], dominé par deux
ou trois thèmes aux retours fréquents, offre un caractère
plus musical que logique et discursif."[14] Each configuration
is a different development. The structure juxtaposes discrete clusters of variant episodes emanating from like
motifs. The original paratactic structure is worthy of some
of the best examples among chansons de geste still being
written in Beroul's time (for example, the fine paratactic
juxtaposition of parallel motifs in succeeding laisses as
structural unities in the Prise d'Orange).

Rather than strive for abstraction and narrative unity
through internal consistency,[15] or even some form of inter-
lace, Beroul prefers the freedom to locate a significant
motif at critical junctures, thereby pulling the material
into a cluster much like iron filings about magnets of
various shapes. His vision may be narrower than Thomas',

but it avoids dissipation and diffusion of interest in favor
of the concentration essential to the dramatic impact of
each narrative cluster (motif + narrative amplification).[16]
The repetition acquires thereby an incremental affective
value, particularly when, as in the case of Iseut's dress,
it has significance prior to its use in the narrative. This
is not amplification as practiced in most courtly romances
and derived from the rhetorical tradition of the schools,
where abstraction and dissipation of interest are the source
of elegance and a certain normative analysis - as in Thomas'
version. For one thing, Beroul's descriptions are too brief,
too material, and too formulaic. But amplification is a
feature of oral tradition.[17] The episodes, formally distinct
in the horizontal linearity of the narrative, are placed together as blocks of unequal size. The motif is inserted at
selected moments in the narrative, and each recurrence recalls and counterpoints the previous instances. For example,
Tristan is at the beginning of Beroul's fragment a knight
errant without armor.

> N'en merré armes ne cheval
> Ne conpaignon fors Governal.
> Ha! [Dex], d'ome desatorné!
> Petit fait om de lui cherté!
> Qant je serai en autre terre,
> S'oi chevalier parler de gerre,
> Ge n'en oserai mot soner:
> Hom nu n'a nul leu de parler.
>   (vv. 241-48)[18]

A subsequent adaptation adroitly elicits ironic contrast
when Tristan refuses Marc's offer of clothing before the
separation from Iseut (vv. 2919-26). But the irony is even
more complex; Tristan has no intention of departing either
time: the three years are not up in the first episode,
and Iseut needs his help in the second.

     Characteristic of romance is the frame holding together
and giving direction to one or more adventures. The quest
motif in Arthurian romance regularly serves to link otherwise disparate episodes often arising themselves from a

contrived context.[19] In Thomas' _Tristan_ the largest frame
is provided by the love potion symbolizing the love, as
Frappier has demonstrated. In Beroul this possibility is
rejected in favor of looser but more compact episodes. The
rejection is evident in the very fragmentation of the potion
motif patent in the abrupt introduction of new information
on its duration ("Mais ne savez, ce m'est avis . . .").
Beroul has compressed the frame into a recurrent motif within
the discrete episodic adventure, thus concentrating less on
what binds the adventures together, than on the juxtaposition
of motif and adventure _within_ the adventure. He eliminates
thereby the need for broader but more dissipated narrative
sweep and consistency. It is necessary in the unique episodic adventures that the motif retain its fundamental
epithetic use, varied in form and content perhaps, but of
unvarying significance. Thus Iseut's clothing may change
from episode to episode, but it does not change the fact that
she is queen and does deserve the clothing, surroundings,
treatment that are her due and that we know to be her due
whether she has them or not. Iseut is to be burned without
benefit of _escondit_; suddenly we see a queen before the fire.
The vision has an immediate, direct impact. The reappearance
of Iseut in the forest in torn clothing revitalizes the same
motif. The function is eminently rhetorical in its repeti-
tive quality. But the technique is paratactic. The impact
derives from the artful ("artificial") placing of the motif.

Le Gentil has described Beroul as follows: "Devant
nous . . . s'affirme une sensibilité exceptionnellement vive,
tout entière dominée par l'impression du moment. Nous
sommes en présence d'un art très direct, très spontané, mais
aussi fragmentaire."[20] What Le Gentil elsewhere calls
Beroul's "vision très directe du monde contemporain"[21]
detects unerringly those objects of great affective value
that he may place at critical narrative junctures; by
repetition in sharply diversified developments, even in
contradictory episodes, they produce a cumulative affective
chain interlocking the episodic fragments of narrative

abutting sharply against one another. Beroul himself caught
the uniformity and the caprice characteristic of his art in
the words "Senpres est ci et senpres la": plus cela change
plus c'est la même chose!

Notes

1. Citations from Beroul, The Romance of Tristran, ed.
A. Ewert (Oxford 1939). On the surrender of Iseut to the
lepers, see Pierre Jonin, Les Personnages féminins dans les
romans français de Tristan au XIIe siècle (Aix-en-Provence,
1958), pp. 134-38. Tristan is beaten like a "lazre" in
Thomas d'Angleterre; see Bartina H. Wind, ed. Les Fragments
du roman de Tristan (Leyden, 1950); 2nd ed., TLF (Geneva-
Paris, 1960), Douce 501-582, and Joseph Bédier, Le Roman de
Tristan, 2 vols. SATF (Paris 1902-1905), II, 275-76.

2. "Valeur figurative du vêtement dans le Tristan de
Béroul," CCM, 10 (1967), 453. Rigolot seems aware of the
a priori significance elsewhere: "Le poète avait besoin
d'un objet simple et naturel, emprunté au monde du réalisme
quotidien, et qui cependant lui permît d'exploiter un
potentiel figuratif latent" (p. 449). Cf. Jonin, p. 59.

3. The enormity of the act is demonstrated by Jonin,
pp. 67-73. Episodes here correspond to the divisions set
forth in Alberto Vàrvaro, Il 'Roman de Tristran' di Béroul
(Turin, 1963), p. 40, n. 9.

4. A la recherche d'une poétique médiévale (Paris,
1970), pp. 87-90.

5. Sentiments a far cry from those expressed in vv.
1404-406: "Mex aim o li estre mendis Et vivre d'erbes et
de glan Q'avoir le reigne au roi Otran," pronounced while
Tristan was still under the domination of the potion. The
diminution in the potion's strength brings the lovers back
to their senses--and their clothing; see Erich Köhler, Ideal
und Wirklichkeit in der höfischen Epik, 2nd ed. (Tübingen,
1970), pp. 154-55. But it is doubtful that their love is
a sin as such; see Janet Caulkins, "The Meaning of pechié
in the Romance of Tristran by Béroul," RomN, 13 (1971-1972),
545-49. The return to proper dress is anticipated by Marc's
"investiture" of the lovers when he discovers them alone
in the woods and suspects their innocence; see Jean Marx,
"Observations sur un épisode de la légende de Tristan,"
Recueil Clovis Brunel, 2 vols. (Paris, 1955), II, 265-73.
Cf. also Vinaver, Tristan et Iseut à travers le temps
(Brussels 1961), pp. 23-24; and Alan Fedrick, "A Note on
the Folie Tristan de Berne," MAE, 32 (1963), 126-27.

6. "Que richement vest la roïne," v. 2744; not only
"richly," but also "nobly" (see von Wartburg, FEW, s.v.
rîki, XVI, 712-15).

7. Philippe Ménard, Le Rire et le sourire dans le roman courtois en France au moyen âge (Geneva, 1969), pp. 362-63.

8. Vàrvaro, p. 205.

9. Recherche, p. 82; cf. Pierre Le Gentil, "La Légende de Tristan vue par Béroul et Thomas," RPh, 7 (1953-1954), 111-12.

10. See Vàrvaro, pp. 192-95; Vinaver, Recherche, p. 98; Le Gentil, pp. 113-14.

11. P. 449.

12. Paul Zumthor, Essai de poétique médiévale (Paris, 1972), pp. 352-55. Cf. especially p. 353: "L'action semble s'interrompre, pour faire place à un petit tableau statique, marginal: effet surtout fréquent dans les romans les plus anciens, comme le Tristan de Béroul, où l'enchaînement des unités narratives, pour être moins saccadé que dans la chanson de geste, tient encore de ce modèle. . . . Il s'agit presque toujours d'images clichées ou emblématiques, types d'origines diverses intégrés à la rhétorique du roman." Cf. Vinaver, Recherche, p. 99: "c'est à travers le monde des choses que s'exprime l'essentiel du récit"; also F. X. Baron, "Visual Presentation in Béroul's Tristan," MLQ, 33 (1972), 99-112. The boire d'amour is the most striking example; see Jean Frappier, "Structure et sens du Tristan: version commune, version courtoise," CCM, 6 (1963), 268.

13. Jean Rychner, La Chanson de Geste. Essai sur l'art épique des jongleurs (Geneva-Lille, 1955), pp. 80-82.

14. Frappier, p. 273, n. 74.

15. In the sense in which the Middle Ages most frequently understood "unity," that is narrative with a beginning, middle, and end that cohere without discrepancies; see my "Theory of Composition in Medieval Narrative Poetry and Geoffrey of Vinsauf's Poetria nova," MS, 31 (1969), 123-26.

16. Cf. Vinaver, Recherche, who calls this "un complexe de motifs et de thèmes toujours présents; à la conscience du contexte immédiat s'ajoute et parfois se substitue celle d'un contexte thématique" (p. 85).

17. Albert B. Lord, The Singer of Tales (New York, 1968), pp. 23-26.

18. Later disguised as a ladre, he still carries the knight's sword under the costume (vv. 3568-76). The irony derives from recall of and reflection on the recurrent motif in the narrative; see Norris J. Lacy, "Irony and Distance in Béroul's Tristan," FR, 45, Special Issue 3 (1971), 21-29.

19. See my "La Forme et le sens de la quête dans l'Erec et Enide de Chrétien de Troyes," Rom, 92 (1971), 342-43.

20. Le Gentil, p. 111.

21. Le Gentil, p. 117.

DU SANG SUR LA NEIGE:
NATURE ET FONCTION DE L'IMAGE DANS LE CONTE DU GRAAL

Daniel Poirion

Perceval, appuyé sur sa lance, reste à regarder, pensif, trois gouttes de sang tombées sur la neige, dont les fraîches couleurs lui rappellent celles d'un visage aimé: la scène construite autour de cette belle attitude du héros a été souvent commentée.[1] Sa qualité poétique s'allie à une signification assez claire si l'on étudie le passage dans sa relation avec le reste du récit. Tous les éléments qui entrent dans la composition de ces quelque 450 vers (4141-4602), éd. Roach; 4121-4576, éd. Lecoy) ont un rapport avec les aventures du jeune héros qui va maintenant rejoindre la cour d'Arthur. Se révélant supérieur à la force désordonnée de Sagremor et à la brutalité insolente de Keu, il égale au moins, il surpasse peut-être la courtoisie de Gauvain. Ainsi se vérifie le sens donné par le "sot" au rire prophétique de la pucelle:[2] il est reconnu comme le meilleur chevalier du monde.

La relative simplicité de cette interprétation pousse la critique à s'interroger plus subtilement sur le "symbole" contemplé par Perceval. Récemment Pierre Gallais y a vu un rapport établi entre l'amour humain et l'amour divin, les couleurs du sang sur la neige pouvant se référer aussi bien au cortège du Graal qu'au teint de Blanchefleur.[3] Ainsi les études consacrées aux "structures anthropologiques de l'imaginaire" sont venues enrichir des spéculations plus anciennes sur le "symbolisme médiéval," et l'analyse littéraire exploite avec bonheur le savoir recueilli dans des lectures psychologiques ou philosophiques. Néanmoins la question se pose de savoir si les images littéraires peuvent être assimilées aux images iconographiques. L'évocation par le langage est indirecte. Dans un texte nous n'avons pas

143

affaire directement au monde "imaginaire," mais seulement
à la fabrication des images, par un vocabulaire, des procédés de grammaire et de rhétorique, des formules. Il n'y
d'image, à proprement parler, que dans la pensée du
lecteur ou de l'auditeur. Image au second degré, provoquée
par une certaine technique de l'écriture (descriptive, par
exemple, ou allégorique).

Il faudrait donc se rappeler ce décalage essentiel
quand on cherche à expliquer l'imagination poétique ou
romanesque en fonction des structures et des significations
d'un système dit "symbolique." Un tel système appartient
au contexte, non pas au texte. Son intervention dans
l'explication de la littérature doit rester subordonnée au
problème plus général de la relation possible ou probable
entre un texte et ses divers contextes. Faute de quoi on
retombe toujours dans les mêmes approximations et les mêmes
confusions. Et l'on comprend le malaise et la méfiance de
Peter Haidu devant les exégèses de S. Bayrav, de Reto
Bezzola ou de D. W. Robertson.[4] Il souligne à juste titre
l'écart entre les prétendues typologies symboliques et la
fonction poétique des images dans le roman. Mais il n'a
sans doute pas raison de chercher dans cet écart un effet
d'ironie, comme si celle-ci était la seule différence
possible entre l'imagination littéraire et l'imaginaire
figuratif.[5] Et il a certainement tort de présenter comme
une alternative la différence entre le symbole et l'allégorie, en rouvrant avec Jean Frappier une vieille discussion à propos de l'oie blessée et du sang répandu sur la
neige.[6] Car les deux notions impliquent deux perspectives
différentes sur l'activité de l'imagination: l'une, le
symbole, part de la figure, l'autre, l'allégorie, du langage,
la figure devenant allégorique par référence à un discours
qui la commente, et le langage symbolique par allusion à une
image figurative qui pourra se substituer à lui.

L'image suggérée par Chrétien de Troyes, à partir
d'un récit nous décrivant la chasse au faucon, et les traces
laissées sur la neige, nous permet de comprendre le jeu

complexe auquel se livre le roman poétique quand il semble
rivaliser avec les arts figuratifs. Elle nous invite surtout à chercher le lien établi par la rêverie romanesque
entre le langage et le--ou plutôt--les mondes imaginaires.
L'herméneutique littéraire ne doit pas être une sorte de
prestidigitation, feignant de lire dans le texte ce qu'elle
va, en fait, chercher dans d'autres discours: livres
d'historiens, de théologiens, de sociologues, de psych-
analystes. Tout ce savoir, souvent hypothétique, générale-
ment probable, rarement certain, il importe de le convoquer
au secours de l'oeuvre étudiée, mais en prenant soin de
signaler, et si l'on peut, de justifier son intervention.
Plus que jamais tributaire des sciences humaines la critique
littéraire doit faire une cure d'humilité: son rôle est de
repérer dans l'oeuvre les divers modes de communication, les
diverses relations qui s'y établissent entre des réalités
dont l'exploration dépasse sa compétence. Mais ce repérage
nous met sur la voie de la signification. Humilité n'est
pas timidité.

*
* *

Au milieu d'un récit d'aventure, dont le support est
en quelque sorte le registre chevaleresque, avec ses che-
vauchées, ses rencontres, ses batailles alimentant notre
rêve d'actions héroïques, voici que se prépare une scène
mettant en oeuvre une forme d'imagination plus dense et plus
riche. Ce changement se traduit par un ralentissement du
récit, par une certaine redondance des références aux cir-
constances, au décor, à quelques détails pittoresques:

> La _nuit_, an une _praerie_,
> lez une forest sont _logié_.
> Cele _nuit_ ot il bien _negié_,
> que mout _froide_ estoit la contree,
> et Percevax la _matinee_
> fu levez si com il soloit,
> qui querre et ancontrer voloit
> avanture et chevalerie,
> et vint droit an la _praerie_
> ou l'oz le roi estoit _logiee_,
> qui fu _gelee_ et _annegiee_.
>   (4140-150)

Il s'agit ici d'une transition, avant un passage plus
descriptif. Mais la répétition des mêmes mots, ou d'autres
apparentés, commence à imposer quelques thèmes imagés: nuit,
matinée, prairie, neige. Cette dernière image, reprise par
le nom nois/noif (vv. 4153, 4175, 4177b), alternera avec le
mot blanc (vv. 4168, 4182, 4184), en contraste implicite
avec la nuit, mais en opposition explicite avec le sanc (vv.
4167, 4177b, 4183), que reprend le nom vermauz (4182).
L'apparition du thème du sang rouge est préparée par la
narration des vers 4152-69, expliquant comment l'oie,
blessée par le faucon, a pu laisser une trace sanglante
sur la neige.

Ces motifs imagés sont présentés dans le récit comme
saisis par le regard de Perceval qui voit et qui esgarde
(vv. 4154, 4165, 4174, 4177, 4185, 4187), le spectacle
tendant à se schématiser sous ce regard de plus en plus
sélectif et actif, si bien que l'image perçue et contemplée
par le personnage n'est plus désignée que par l'expression
les gotes de sang, ou les (trois) gotes (vv. 4183, 4189,
4268, 4304, 4403, 4427). Cette condensation de l'image
regardée par Perceval coïncide avec une certaine immobili-
sation du héros dans cette attitude pensive qui frappe
l'imagination du lecteur. En somme celui-ci imagine un
personnage qui lui-même regarde et imagine quelque chose.
C'est dire combien l'apparence concrète de ce fameux symbole
nous est difficile à voir, contrairement à ce qui se passe
quand nous étudions la peinture ou la sculpture de l'époque.

Mais le texte nous a donné un certain nombre d'indications à partir desquelles on peut tenter de reconstituer
l'image contemplée. Il y a, peut-être, comme cadre et support, l'empreinte de l'oie qui a foulé la neige: "et Perce-
vax vit defolee/la noif qui soz la gente jut" (vv. 4174-75);
une sorte de cercle ou d'ovale (car il faut sans doute lire,
au vers 4176, "et le sanc qui ancor parut," plutôt que
"entor," comme dans l'édition Roach). Tel est le schème
abstrait à partir duquel la pensée de Perceval retrouve un
visage. Construction savante, ou naïve? Baltrusaïtis et

P. Francastel nous ont appris à regarder les chapiteaux et
les tympans: les scènes et les figures n'y sont pas pro-
jetées dans notre espace en perspective, mais soumis à la
contrainte géométrique et technique du cadre et du support.[7]
Le schématisme des gouttes de sang nous fait songer à cette
esthétique où le fantastique apparaît comme une interprétation de la structure abstraite qu'il faut décorer. Entre
l'image concrète et le support abstrait il peut y avoir un
rapport naturel ou symbolique, la symétrie devenant par
exemple un affrontement. Dans l'image qui nous intéresse
s'il y a un rapport intellectuel, il tient au nombre trois;
on a eu du mal à comprendre, dès le XIIIe siècle, ce qu'il
représente, puisque dans son Parzival (livre VI) Wolfram von
Eschenbach essaie de préciser: "Le héros regarda comment
les gouttes de sang étaient disposées: deux d'entre elles
figuraient à ses yeux les joues de Condwiramour, et la
troisième son menton."[8] Mais on peut plus vraisemblablement
attribuer cette troisième tache de couleur rouge à la bouche,
à quoi font souvent allusion les descriptions poétiques de
la femme.

En dehors de ce nombre trois, sur lequel il sera
tentant de spéculer, compte tenu de son rôle dans divers
codes symboliques, le schématisme de l'image consiste
essentiellement en un contraste entre le blanc et le rouge.
Certains, comme Martín de Riquer, cherchent à le réduire,
conformément à l'esthétique moderne, et à la pratique de la
peinture à l'huile qui aimera mélanger le rouge avec le
blanc pour faire une sorte de rose. Le texte nous dit que
les trois gouttes espandirent sur le blanc (v. 4168), que
le vermeil est sur le blanc assis (vv. 4182, 4404), que ces
gouttes anluminoient le blanc (v. 4428). Aucun de ces
verbes n'exprime l'idée de mélange; c'est le contraste qui
"enlumine" le blanc. Les deux couleurs sont juxtaposées
comme dans la composition d'un blason. C'est d'ailleurs
à la technique héraldique que faisait allusion le portrait
de Blanchefleur à qui pense Perceval, selon toute probabilité:

> et mialz li avenoit el vis
> li vermauz sor le blanc asis
> que li sinoples sor l'argent. [9]

En fait l'analogie entre l'image et le visage consiste
justement dans ce contraste entre le blanc et le rouge,
celui-ci se répartissant en trois taches. Le portrait
littéraire de la jeune fille et l'image tracée sur la
neige se réduisent donc à un idéogramme que le langage
poétique le plus sobre, le plus abstrait, était capable
d'évoquer. D'une part le mécanisme de la mémoire est ainsi
parfaitement expliqué par une double transformation, de la
scène en un blason, et du blason en portrait. D'autre part
le schématisme de l'image est assez simple pour être aisé-
ment exprimé par un langage qui ne peut prétendre décrire
dans tous ses détails une scène de la nature.

Mais la présentation même de cet idéogramme dans le
cours du récit nous permet de mieux comprendre le fonction-
nement de l'analogie, de la samblance. Elle n'est au fond
saisie que par Perceval. Pour les spectateurs lointains,
les gens de la cour, que surprend l'attitude du chevalier
pensif, mais aussi pour ceux qui se rapprochent comme
Sagremor, Keu et Gauvain lui-même, il est difficile de
deviner ce que Perceval regarde et imagine. Les plus
vulgaires interprètent son immobilité comme une sorte de
sommeil. Le plus courtois suppose qu'il a dû perdre un
être cher, que sa bien aimée lui a été enlevée (vv. 4336-
39); mais il ne voit pas l'image qui commence à s'effacer au
moment où il s'approche; la semblance est brouillée. La
trace sensible disparaissant, Perceval à son tour laisse
s'évanouir le souvenir. On ne pouvait mieux suggérer la
relation entre la mémoire et la sensation. Cette relation
passe par l'intelligence, la pensée rationnelle que résume
le schéma abstrait. Ce qui est conforme à la physiologie
de l'époque, et à la théorie des trois cellules cérébrales:
1. imaginatio et sensus communis; 2. cogitatio; 3. memoria. [10]
L'idéogramme, support de la cogitatio, est l'élément commun
à la perception-imagination et au souvenir. Avec notre

idéogramme le langage et l'image se rejoignent pour serrer
au plus près le contenu de la pensée. Il est probable que
cette pensée, ainsi condensée, était là pour provoquer la
glose. Mais avant d'envisager cette glose il convient de
situer la démarche du romancier, dans ce passage, par
rapport aux procédés de création littéraire.

*
* *

Il faut se garder de deux excès, quand on étudie les
images chez Chrétien de Troyes. L'un serait de chercher chez
lui une mimésis de la réalité. Les auteurs du Moyen Age ont
bien conscience de l'impossibilité où se trouve leur langage
de traduire dans toute sa richesse le spectacle de la nature
ou la beauté d'une personne. Le topos qui formule habituel-
lement cette impossibilité n'est pas seulement un trait de
modestie ou une prétérition: c'est une vérité élémentaire.
On peut louer les descriptions de villes qui déploient les
formes variées d'activité sous le regard d'un voyageur.[11]
Mais le romancier ne cherche pas à faire un tableau; il
énumère les métiers et les objets fabriqués par les artisans.
Sa description est une liste de mots mise en forme par la
rhétorique. Inversement il ne faut pas chercher à réduire
l'art de Chrétien de Troyes à la rhétorique, car s'il la
connaît et la pratique, il s'en sert librement en essayant
d'agir sur le lecteur autrement que par la persuasion ou le
conformisme littéraire. Ainsi la technique traditionnelle
du portrait, reconnue chez lui par nos stylisticiens comme
Alice Colby,[12] est révisée en fonction de l'emblème qui va
suggérer le sens de la beauté. Cette démarche est particu-
lièrement évidente dans Cligès, où le portrait traditionnel
de Soredamors se trouve suivre l'image d'une flèche, qui
évoque à la fois le trait de désir suscité par la beauté et
le rayon de lumière traversant les yeux, verrière du coeur.
La vocation esthétique et érotique de la beauté est alors
indiquée par ce signe, cet idéogramme de la flèche, qui per-
turbe l'ordre traditionnel de la description. Dans le Conte
du Graal l'idéogramme n'est pas donné en même temps que le
portrait proprement dit (vv. 1793-1827). Il y est simple-

ment préparé par le contraste des couleurs qui résume ce
portrait; et ce que nous donne la scène du sang-sur-la-
neige c'est, avec l'analogon, la semblance, l'équivalent
de la flèche signant la beauté de Soredamors. Mais on a
changé de signature, et l'on a cette fois affaire à un
idéogramme plus complexe.

   La fabrication de cet idéogramme n'est cependant pas
sans rapport avec l'art poétique traditionnel. En fait de
symbole, la semblance relève plutôt de ce qu'on pourrait
appeler une esthétique de la comparaison. Dans tout notre
passage l'auteur multiplie les expressions caractéristiques
de la comparaison: "la fresche color li resanble/qui est an
la face s'amie" (vv. 4178-79); "ausins estoit, an son avis"
(v. 4181); "li ert avis" (v. 4186; "an l'esgarder m'estoit
avis" (v. 4429). Perceval n'a donc pas cette mentalité sym-
boliste dont on nous explique qu'elle caractérise la vision
du monde au XIIe siècle. Il parle au contraire en homme qui
sait la différence entre le langage poétique et la réalité
des choses.

   La semblance est l'envers de la comparaison poétique,
celle que nous trouvons dans l'éloge de la dame par les
troubadours, comme celle que nous proposent les traités de
Mathieu de Vendôme ou de Geoffroy de Vinsauf d'après la
poésie latine: la blancheur du corps y est traditionnelle-
ment comparée à celle de la neige, la couleur des joues à
celle de la rose ou de l'aurore, comparaison parfois poussée
jusqu'à l'hyperbole, quand par exemple Bernard de Ventadour
dit que la neige paraît brune et obscure à côté du corps de
sa dame (A tantas bonas. . .). Et c'est bien à cette rhétorique de la comparaison hyperbolique que se rattache la
démonstration de courtoisie à quoi se livre Perceval dans
tout cet épisode, et qui va mériter le certificat délivré
par Gauvain:

          Certes, fet mes sire Gauvains,
          cil pansers n'estoit pas vilains,
          ençois estoit cortois et dolz . . .
              (4433-35)

Mérite qu'illustrent encore l'éloge dont Perceval salue la
reine (vv. 4563-67) et les offres de service présentées à
la demoiselle-qui-rit (vv. 4575-77).

Nul doute que la comparaison est bien un procédé de
langage, le procédé poétique par excellence, interprétation
littéraire de ces similitudes que traduiront différemment
d'autres techniques d'expression, notamment les art figuratifs. Ainsi la littérature met l'accent sur la logique, sur
l'articulation même d'un rapprochement entre deux choses,
tandis que l'art figuratif met l'accent sur les termes mêmes,
sur les objets qu'il peut juxtaposer, mais non comparer. Or
si l'on considère la structure des romans de Chrétien de
Troyes on voit l'importance de la comparaison aussi bien dans
la composition d'ensemble que dans la rédaction des détails
descriptifs et narratifs. Le lecteur est sans cesse invité
à rapprocher des scènes et des épisodes pour en saisir les
nuances, les différences, chargées d'une signification
esthétique ou morale. La bipartition des romans favorise ce
genre de réflexion sur comparaison, soit qu'une première
partie propose un certain type d'aventure que va reprendre
et perfectionner le héros de la seconde partie (Erec, Cligès,
Yvain), soit que deux héros poursuivent parallèlement des
aventures, l'un se distinguant de l'autre par une certaine
manière d'affronter les difficultés (Lancelot et Gauvain).
Le Conte du Graal combine ces deux principes de composition,
la seconde partie opposant les deux quêtes, celle de Perceval
et celle de Gauvain.

Dans le détail de la composition, la comparaison des
scènes, successives ou éloignées, justifie ce qui nous semble
parfois simple répétition ou fastidieuse variation. Ainsi le
thème des couleurs retient notre attention dans les tournois
qui opposent Cligès à Sagremor, en noir, à Lancelot, en vert,
à Perceval, en rouge, à Gauvain, en blanc. Sans faire appel
à un dictionnaire des symboles on sent bien que cette méta-
morphose du noir au vert, au rouge, enfin au blanc doit avoir
un sens, au moins en relation avec la personnalité des pro-
tagonistes. Une telle conception du roman implique une

lecture attentive, une mémoire fidèle (il ne faut rien
oublier), un mélange de rêverie et de réflexion. Et l'in-
sertion de l'image, dans une telle rêverie, est prévue pour
servir au jeu de ces comparaisons.

C'est ainsi que les critiques ont bien raison de chercher, au delà de l'épisode où elle figure, l'annonce ou le
rappel de cette image des trois gouttes de sang sur la
neige. Car sa fonction n'est pas de signifier isolément,
ni d'être commentée en tant que symbole au gré de notre
fantaisie ou de notre culture, mais de jalonner la série
discontinue des scènes où l'aventure logique et linéaire
du chevalier fait place à la rencontre du merveilleux.

Ce que nous enseigne notre roman, c'est la stricte
discipline de la comparaison à quoi le langage romanesque
soumet l'imagination. Comparaison ouverte, exemplaire,
expliquée par Perceval lui-même entre le spectacle naturel
et la beauté de l'aimée. Comparaison muette entre ce même
spectacle et la scène surnaturelle du Graal, dont on vient
de parler et dont on va encore parler en des termes qui
sont justement choisis pour faciliter la comparaison,
puisqu'on fait allusion à la lance blanche et à la goutte
de sang qui sort de la pointe et qui coule jusqu'à la main
du valet. En effet, 600 vers avant notre épisode, la
cousine de Perceval lui demandait:

> or me dites se vos veïstes
> la lance don la pointe sainne
> (3534-35)

Et 200 vers après notre épisode la Demoiselle à la mule
lui reprochera:

> que tu ne poïs demander
> por coi cele gote de sanc
> saut par la pointe del fer blanc!
> (4632-34)

Cette fois l'analogie n'est plus dans la seule couleur,
mais dans la substance. Elle se situe à un autre niveau de
la composition, car elle relie l'épisode des gouttes de sang

à l'ensemble du roman, au lieu de clore avec lui l'éducation
courtoise de Perceval. Elle suggère un approfondissement du
sens, qu'elle oblige à chercher, non pas, encore une fois,
dans l'interprétation de l'objet isolé comme un symbole, mais
dans tout le système des images évoquées par le Conte du
Graal. Et même s'il faut bien, nous allons y arriver, sortir
du texte pour interpréter les scènes par référence à la
culture savante ou populaire, chrétienne ou celtique, il
convient d'abord de saisir les liens, les rapports, les
rappels que le retour des mots (faisant image) inscrit dans
le texte.

Mais, dira-t-on, et si ces rencontres, ces analogies
que nous croyons saisir à l'intérieur de l'oeuvre étaient
l'effet du hasard? Chrétien de Troyes a-t-il vraiment cal-
culé tous ces effets? Il est exact qu'en cherchant un sens
derrière tous les détails on prend un risque, comme prend un
risque le psychologue qui cherche un sens derrière tout comportement, toute communication humaine. On songe à la
naïveté de ceux qui voient un signe dans chaque phénomène de
la nature. Mais l'homme n'est pas la nature; a fortiori le
langage humain n'est pas un phénomène comme les autres: il
implique une signification. La question pourrait être de
savoir si ce sens que nous cherchons, si ces relations, ces
échos furent consciemment ménagés ou non. Question impor-
tante s'il s'agit de juger l'homme, Chrétien de Troyes;
beaucoup moins s'il s'agit de comprendre l'oeuvre, car nous
savons bien que dans la création littéraire, plus encore
que dans toute activité humaine, tout n'est pas conscient.
Il y a même une part évidente d'automatisme. Mais l'inconscient et l'automatisme ne sont pas le hasard. Au contraire,
c'est là que s'exercent les déterminations les plus chargées
de sens. De plus, le recours à l'image atteste le souci de
laisser parler l'oeuvre au delà du récit, du dialogue en
forme, du discours rationnel. Le Moyen Age ne connaît pas
l'inconscient freudien. Mais il connaît le rêve, l'extase,
et ce qu'il appelle l'entr'oubli. On ne peut refuser à
l'auteur ce qu'il accorde à Lancelot, à Yvain, à Perceval:

un type de pensée qui se laisse envahir par l'imagination.
La poétique de Chrétien de Troyes ici a l'art de nous faire
rêver. Elle nous propose un texte, un langage, des mots
qui suscitent en nous des images. Il nous faut donc sortir
du texte pour étudier ce monde des images avec lequel il
semble vouloir nous mettre en relation. Et c'est là que
les vraies difficultés commencent.

*

*   *

On ne peut plus nier la nécessité où nous sommes de
rechercher dans un certain contexte culturel la signification des figures, des formes et des objets figuratifs auxquels notre roman fait allusion en les mêlant à l'aventure.
P. Francastel était justement très sévère pour Edmond Faral
qui refusait de suivre Jean Marx dans son explication du
roman à partir des mythes celtiques.[13] Entre le nom et la
chose dont il évoque l'image, il n'y a pas une relation
directe et définitive comme le pensait Faral. Les sociologues et les ethnologues nous montrent le sens pris par les
objets et leur figure dans les différentes civilisations.
Les uns mettent l'accent sur la permanence de certaines
significations (cette tendance caractérise surtout l'anthro-
pologie structuraliste de Gilbert Durand); d'autres sou-
lignent la relation singulière qui s'établit avec l'époque
et le milieu, le groupe humain. De toute façon ils nous
aident à comprendre qu'une lance n'est pas simplement l'arme
commune à tant de sociétés diverses, et encore moins s'il
s'agit d'une lance qui saigne! Mais faut-il y voir un
symbole celtique ou un symbole chrétien?

Revenons à nos gouttes de sang. Depuis 1913, nous
rappelait Martín de Riquer, on a retrouvé le motif de celui
qui souhaite une femme rouge comme le sang, blanche comme
la neige, noire comme le corbeau dans tous les folklores
d'Europe. Une très ancienne légende irlandaise en donne
une version inversée: c'est une jeune fille qui, voyant
un corbeau boire du sang sur la neige, dit qu'elle aimera
un jeune homme qui aura les cheveux noirs comme le corbeau,
les joues rouges comme le sang, le corps blanc comme la

neige.[14] Le roman gallois de Peredur rétablira le motif tel
que nous le trouvons dans notre Perceval, mais en gardant
l'image du corbeau, absente de notre conte (le noir y étant
repoussé à la périphérie du portrait, avec le manteau de
Blanchefleur, et en prologue de la scène sur la neige, avec
la nuit qui précède l'éblouissement par la blancheur
matinale). Notre idéogramme des gouttes de sang confirme
l'ouverture du roman sur ce type d'imagination qui caractérise les contes folkloriques. Plus riche de suggestion que
la comparaison littéraire, notamment par la scène de chasse
qui justifie l'image, le motif folklorique est moins dense,
moins complexe qu'un thème mythique. Le sang sur la neige
n'est pas un mythe. Son interprétation est plus immédiate.
Et l'auteur a dû le mettre là d'abord pour nous permettre de
mesurer le degré d'initiation auquel Perceval est déjà
parvenu: il déchiffre cette devinette, lui qui n'a pas su
comprendre l'énigme du Graal.

Or justement le cortège du Graal est une scène d'une
autre nature. Elle comporte encore des éléments qu'on retrouve dans le folklore (le repas où il faut/où il ne faut
pas poser de question).[15] Mais sa composition ressemble
plutôt à un rituel: cet étrange défilé accompagne en effet
la cérémonie d'un repas, en même temps qu'il se propose
comme une énigme, une épreuve pour le visiteur. Au moins
deux rites se superposent, si l'on veut y prêter attention.
L'un est exceptionnel: il consiste dans l'attribution de
l'épée destinée à Perceval. L'autre doit se répéter,
puisqu'il semble correspondre au repas habituel du vieux
roi. La superposition des deux rituels tend à rapprocher
dans notre imagination l'épée et la lance. C'est un élément important pour interpréter la scène; une sorte de lien
est établi entre les aventures de Perceval et le destin
mystérieux dont la lance à-la-goutte-de-sang apparaît comme
la relique.

On se demande alors quel est le mythe de ce rite. Et
les critiques ont pensé à quelque mythe celtique. D'autres
ont pensé à l'orient. Enfin nombreux sont ceux qui recon-
naissent là des éléments chrétiens, avec les premiers

imitateurs et continuateurs du roman. Pourtant il est probable que ce rituel a été imaginé, inventé par Chrétien de Troyes. Non certes à partir de rien. Il a dû s'inspirer des légendes, qui elles-mêmes gardaient les vestiges de vieux mythes, plus ou moins transformés. C'est ainsi que les légendes chrétiennes ont déjà utilisé des mythes plus anciens. Mais le génie de l'auteur est d'avoir, en construisant son rituel, suscité le mirage d'un mythe où convergent les divers héritages culturels qui ont modelé l'homme occidental. Car c'est cela, le mythe qu'il faut chercher: non pas une source ancienne, mais le miroir d'une unité spirituelle apparaissant derrière les contes et dans les livres. Mais l'auteur n'a-t-il donné aucune indication sur le récit mythique qui expliquerait le rituel du Graal? C'est ici que nos gouttes de sang peuvent encore nous servir.

En effet l'image même tracée sur la neige, que Perceval s'attarde à contempler, nous a été expliquée par un récit nous rapportant la chasse dont l'oie a failli être victime. Ce récit joue, par rapport à l'image folklorique, le rôle du mythe par rapport au rite. A cette analogie de fonction littéraire doit s'ajouter une ressemblance dans la signification. C'est-à-dire que la violence dont les trois gouttes de sang sont la trace peut être une allusion à la violence dont la lance-qui-saigne est le signe. Il est intéressant de noter que le pseudo-prologue que constitue l'Elucidation nous raconte un mythe répondant au même schéma: la prospérité du royaume de Logres a été détruite quand le roi Amançon eut fait violence à l'une des fées qui offraient aux voyageurs les nourritures qu'ils désiraient. La punition du roi Pêcheur et la lance-qui-saigne peuvent donc s'expliquer par un crime sexuel. On rejoindrait ainsi, en lui donnant un sens, la belle reconstitution faite par Jean Marx de la légende celtique; de plus nous pourrions expliquer ainsi la raison du coup felon donné par l'épée ou la lance, l'instrument du châtiment ou l'instrument du crime. Mais pour cela il faut retrouver le mythe archaïque derrière la légende. La structure d'un mythe réunit plusieurs significations superposées correspondant à divers codes, à divers points de

vue sur une culture: cosmologie, alimentation, sexualité,
type de société, objets symboliques. On pourrait rassembler
en un schéma narratif élémentaire quelques éléments de mythe
présents dans le conte du Graal; son inachèvement accroît
les incertitudes, surtout en ce qui concerne le thème
positif qui doit redresser le thème négatif donné dans la
première partie du roman:[16]

Narration :	Faute : Punition	/ Réparation	: Récompense
Aventure	silence : échec	/ (question)	: (succès)
cosmologie	hiver : stérilité	/ (été)	: (fécondité)
alimentation	chasse	/ pêche	
sexualité	viol : blessure	/	
société	inceste : infirmité	/	
symboles	lance : sang	/ graal	: nourriture

Il faut demander aux anthropologues s'ils peuvent, à
partir de ces vestiges, reconstruire le mythe archaïque, ce
qu'a cru faire Jean Marx, mais en nous proposant en fait
une légende d'allure beaucoup plus récente, d'autant plus
qu'il tenait compte de récits du XIIIe siècle. Avant toute
chose on s'interrogera sur la relation, il faut bien dire,
mystérieuse qui semble s'établir entre un roman du XIIe
siècle et un mythe préhistorique, sans doute quelque sombre
histoire d'inceste.[17] Car enfin ce ne sont pas les seules
légendes celtiques, telles que nous les connaissons, ni
d'autre part les légendes et histoires chrétiennes, qui peuvent expliquer comment Chrétien de Troyes a pu retrouver un
mythe plus ancien qu'elles, et qui leur est commun. Les
critiques ont bien vu, parfois, le parallélisme entre
d'éventuelles sources païennes et chrétiennes expliquant la
scène du Graal.[18] Parlons plutôt de convergence rassemblant
autour d'une table et d'un autel les symboles de la nourri-
ture et du sacrifice. Cette convergence, certains auraient
aujourd'hui tendance à l'expliquer par quelque obscure
affiliation à une doctrine ésotérique, d'autres (ou les
mêmes) par l'effet de cette bizarre mémoire génétique qui

garderait en chacun d'entre nous le souvenir de l'homme
préhistorique. Ce que la scène des gouttes de sang nous
fait d'abord comprendre, c'est qu'un romancier comme Chrétien
de Troyes, par le biais du folklore, auquel il emprunte tel
ou tel motif imagé, nous ramène à un type de pensée archaïque,
où l'on communique par objets symboliques. Car le folklore
est un mythe dégradé, appauvri, réduit à un récit linéaire
et à une signification simplifiée, bref au merveilleux qui
remplace la magie. Mais l'imagination folkorique est, par
rapport à la pensée rationnelle, régressive. Elle nous
ramène, sur le chemin du mythe, à ce langage précédent
l'écriture dont les anciens pictogrammes ont conservé la
trace. Nos trois gouttes de sang sur la neige sont comme
un pictogramme dont on peut se servir pour déchiffrer la
scène rituelle du cortège. Elles peuvent nous aider à
combler les lacunes d'un conte par une glose analogue à
celle dont Marie de France sentait la nécessité devant
l'obscurité des récits anciens.[19]

*

*   *

Ce qui cependant étonne, dans le Conte du Graal, et
renforce l'impression mythique laissée par le récit, c'est
la prépondérance de l'image, la signification des scènes
les plus fascinantes semblant déborder largement celle que
nous apportent les discours et les analyses. Un équilibre
qui caractérisait notre auteur dans les oeuvres antérieures
semble ici rompu. On est submergé par les images. Est-ce
parce que le roman est inachevé? Mais les dernières aventures de Gauvain confirment cette suprématie des séquences
imagées sur le récit logique et le discours analytique.
Chrétien est-il finalement à ce point séduit par le merveilleux folklorique qu'il en prenne le style pour "rimoier
le meillor conte . . . qui soit contez an cort real"? C'est
ici qu'il faudrait, à notre avis, faire intervenir un autre
élément que le folkore pour expliquer la relation entre la
rêverie romanesque et l'imagination mythique: nous voulons
parler de l'expérience du rêve.

En effet les symboles ou les archétypes, que depuis
Jessie Weston jusqu'à Pierre Gallais, en passant par Emma
Jung et Jean Györy, on croit reconnaître dans notre conte,
ne peuvent se justifier par une sorte de tradition occulte
et continue. Mais tout être humain a l'expérience des rêves,
et les hommes du Moyen Age ont cherché à les interpréter à
partir des images qui les hantent. Le romancier-poète a
trouvé là sinon le modèle exact, du moins le principe de ces
séquences imagées dont la logique nous échappe d'abord, et
qui gardent un caractère énigmatique. Ainsi il est remarqu-
able que le franchissement du pont de l'épée par Lancelot
reproduise un thème de rêve présent dans des civilisations
très diverses.[20] Et bien sûr l'auteur a pu le trouver dans
une légende, mais sa structure et sa signification ont dû
s'imposer à lui comme se traduisant en un langage que chacun
d'entre nous parle une partie de sa vie, la nuit, en songe.
De ce point de vue on ne peut manquer de souligner le
caractère onirique de la scène du Graal, dont le château
est apparu subitement et disparu de même, sans laisser de
trace dans la topographie locale: le merveilleux de cette
aventure, souligné par la cousine de Perceval (vv. 3452-68)
est un compromis entre le rêve et la réalité. On peut comprendre alors l'apparition du roi Pêcheur comme une apparition de rêve, avec éventuellement le transfert de personnalité (par rapport au père), le dédoublement de personnages,
que nous savons être loi courante dans un rêve. L'aventure
de Gauvain à la Roche de Canguin, où l'on a vu une visite
au séjour des morts, fait d'abord penser à un songe du même
type, où les parents morts apparaissent tout naturellement
au dormeur. En d'autres termes dans son traitement du
merveilleux Chrétien de Troyes reste en deçà des structures
mythiques, au delà des formes folkloriques, mais très près
des thèmes oniriques. Ainsi la scène du cortège du Graal
pourrait se comprendre en lui appliquant les lois de transfert, de condensation, de dédoublement que les psychologues
attribuent au rêve, et que l'écrivain peut reconstituer à
partir des deux procédés de la rhétorique: la métonymie et

la métaphore. Comme exemple bien connu de déplacement
métonymique on peut donner la blessure aux jambes, qui
figure la castration, et comme exemple de métaphore, la
lance-qui-saigne, figurant le sexe viril.

Malgré l'exemple des rêves on hésitera, il est vrai, à
reconnaître dans les objets et les personnages du Graal les
symboles d'un drame à dominante sexuelle. Les querelles
entre psychanalistes suffiraient à rendre prudents les pro-
fanes. Néanmoins sans pousser très loin notre oniromancie
on peut trouver quelques indications dans le texte, si l'on
veut bien ne pas les chercher dans les seuls symboles,
toujours équivoques, mais dans les séquences dramatiques,
elles, chargées de sens. C'est ainsi que notre image des
gouttes de sang est précédée d'une sorte de glose narrative
assez explicite. L'attaque de l'oie par un faucon, la
manière dont elle est frappée et abattue contre terre, le
renoncement à une étreinte plus précise ("lïer ne joindre")
se situent au carrefour des vocabulaires guerrier et sexuel.

La suggestion sexuelle se précise si l'on rapproche
cet épisode de la première expérience féminine vécue par
Perceval quand il a quitté sa mère. La scène a pour décor
la tente mi-partie de couleur vermeille, et décorée d'un
aigle doré et brillant, au milieu d'une prairie. Là une
demoiselle est restée seule:

> el lit tote sole gisoit
> une dameisele andormie,
> tote seule sanz conpaignie;
> alees erent ses puceles. . . .
>   (668-71)

La même tentation s'offre au faucon:

> tant c'une an trova a bandon
> qu'ert d'antre les altres sevree. . . .
>   (4158-59)

L'attaque du jeune homme est aussi brutale que celle de
l'oiseau:

```
         que li vaslez an un randon
         la beisa, volsist ele ou non. . . .
               (705-706)

         por un faucon qui vint bruiant
         aprés eles de grant randon. . . .
               (4156-57)
```

Mais dans les deux cas l'agresseur ne va pas jusqu'au bout
de son acte. Le faucon est reparti, pour une raison mal
expliquée: "trop fu main," dit l'édition Roach; "trop fu
tart," l'édition Lecoy. En fait le dénouement reste énigmatique, parce qu'il figure ce qui est arrivé à Perceval:
il a été retenu par l'interdit maternel, qui a eu en lui un
trop grant retentissement:

```
         De pucele a mout qui la beise;
         s'ele le beisier vos consant,
         le soreplus vos an desfant,
         se lessier le volez por moi.
               (544-47)
```

Et l'on sait que Perceval prendra bien soin d'affirmer à
l'ami de la demoiselle qu'il n'a pas été plus loin que le
baiser.

Voilà donc nos gouttes de sang nous renvoyant à la
fois à la Demoiselle de la tente et à Blanchefleur. Quel
rapport entre ces deux demoiselles? N'est-ce pas qu'avec
la seconde Perceval a quitté la partie avant d'aller
jusqu'au bout? Certes les deux amoureux ont dormi "boche
a boche, braz a braz," mais, qui sait? peut-être ne
s'est-il rien passé de plus que les baisers. En tout cas
Perceval est parti malgré elle:

```
         et si fu soie tote quite,
         et la terre, s'il li pleüst
         que son coraige aillors n'eüst.
               (2912-14)
```

Resterait à savoir si cette non consommation de l'acte
sexuel a quelque rapport de sens avec la scène énigmatique
du Graal.

Il faut dès lors demander à la psychologie du rêve, à
la psychanalyse, si la blessure du père, "par mi les janbes
navrez" (v. 434), si l'infirmité du roi Pêcheur "feruz d'un
javelot/par mi les hances amedos" (vv. 3498-99), si l'épée
traîtresse qui "volera an pieces" quand Perceval viendra à
la bataille (vv. 3648-49) n'expriment pas la même hantise,
la même peur de l'impuissance. De toute façon la signification de ces éléments mystérieux passe par l'histoire et
la personnalité de Perceval: le roman psychologique,
racontant tous les événements dans la perspective du héros,
fait de celui-ci la clé de toutes les énigmes. Et c'est
sans doute pourquoi, proposant à son lecteur l'image d'une
énigme vivante, l'auteur a recours tout naturellement au
langage du rêve, renouvelant ainsi la structure mythique
qui dormait dans de vieilles légendes.

*
* *

On a depuis longtemps remarqué chez Chrétien de Troyes
une certaine opposition entre la matière légendaire dont il
semble s'inspirer et le sens qu'il donne aux aventures. Il
ne s'agit pas d'une opposition entre le paganisme et le
christianisme: il est peu vraisemblable que l'auteur ait
hésité sur ce plan religieux au point de faire de cette
hésitation le thème de ses romans. D'autre part il ne
s'agit pas d'un contraste purement formel entre deux
manières de conter, l'une, de tradition orale, faisant plus
grande la part du merveilleux, l'autre, formée par la tradition latine, obéissant davantage à la rhétorique et à la
logique rationnelle. Quelque chose est en jeu dans cette
lutte entre le _mythos_ et le _logos_, dont l'équilibre varie
de _Cligès_ au _Conte_ _du_ _Graal_.

Le langage imagé est à étudier avec soin, dans cette
perspective, car il se trouve au coeur d'une contradiction à
la fois technique et idéologique. Technique, car il s'agit
de garder ouverte la communication avec cette humanité plus
archaïque qui s'exprime dans le rêve, le folklore et le
mythe, tout en s'adressant à des lecteurs "plus sutil de

sens," et rompus à la glose qui ne veut pas laisser "tres-
passer" les idées intermédiares. [21] Idéologique parce qu'il
convient, pour l'écrivain, de contrôler ces pulsions qui
travaillent la pensée sauvage, et de construire la loi des
hommes sur des idées claires et pures. Ce double souci
caractérise l'idéal courtois qui exerce sa censure à la fois
sur les manières et sur le langage, épurant l'expression du
désir, notamment dans la poésie. Un siècle plus trad, se
révoltant contre la loi courtoise, Jean de Meun sera conduit
à braver simultanément l'euphémisme traditionnel et l'idéal
de chasteté, ce qu'il fera notamment en parlant de la
castration de Saturne. [22]

En songeant à cette révolte ultérieure, qui prouve
malgré tout qu'on n'a pas attendu la psychologie moderne
pour établir un rapport précis entre la sexualité et le
langage, on peut s'interroger sur le parallélisme, marqué
par Chrétien de Troyes, entre le mutisme de Perceval devant
la scène énigmatique, et la série d'actes manqués qui jalon-
nent au moins la première partie de ses aventures. Que la
sexualité soit en cause, c'est évident en raison des inter-
dits complémentaires formulés par la mère et par Gornemans.
Et que ce double tabou soit à mettre en relation avec
l'idéologie courtoise semble probable, puisque l'auteur se
préoccupe de morale chevaleresque dans tous ses romans. La
courtoisie, censurant à la fois le sexe et la parole, n'est-
elle pas remise en cause dans ce roman? On se pose générale-
ment la question en partant d'une hypothèse suggérée par les
continuations et les imitations du Conte du Graal: on suppose que la courtoisie à laquelle Perceval est parvenu, au
moment de son retour près d'Arthur, était faite pour être
dépassée pour atteindre à un état qu'on imagine plus religieux, et même plus chaste encore.

Mais nous ignorons les intentions de l'auteur touchant
la fin du roman. On peut remarquer que ses dénouements ne
sont pas toujours très convaincants. Chrétien de Troyes
semble plus habile à définir les problèmes qu'à trouver des
solutions. Or ce qui fascine dans le Conte du Graal c'est

le caractère obsessif et angoissé des images comme celle du
sang sur la neige. Le discours rationnel de l'oncle ermite
n'en dissipera pas tout à fait le cauchemar. La morale
pratique n'a pas raison du rêve. Cette impuissance de la
raison, que souligne l'inachèvement de l'oeuvre par hasard
ou non, confirme l'importance de l'échec dans l'histoire de
Perceval: on est tenté d'y voir le signe d'un désaccord
profond de Chrétien de Troyes avec la loi courtoise, mais
parce que celle-ci exerce sur le désir une fatale contrainte
au détriment de la naturelle joie d'amour.

Ici on peut éventuellement commencer une enquête de
"psychocritique," en explorant le chemin de l'inconscient:
elle doit nous ramener à quelques thèmes de la psychanalyse,
touchant notamment l'obsession de la castration. Mais de
toute façon il convient d'étudier systématiquement le langage
des images, dont la série discontinue dit certainement autre
chose que le discours rationnel, le dialogue courtois ou
chrétien, le récit chevaleresque auxquels elle est mêlée.
Cet écart entre le thème imagé et la thèse idéologique ne
doit pas être réduit par notre esprit de système: c'est
pour le vivre, au besoin dans la contradiction, qu'on a
écrit et qu'on lit encore ces histoires qui nous rendent
"pensifs" et entretiennent notre rêverie.

Notes

1. Citons notamment: Martín de Riquer, "Perceval y
las gotas de sangre en la nieve," RFE, 39 (1955), 186-219;
Jean Frappier, Chrétien de Troyes et le Mythe du Graal:
Etude sur Perceval ou le Conte du Graal (Paris: SEDES,
1972), pp. 130-41; Pierre Gallais, Perceval et l'initiation
(Paris: Sirac, 1972); Joël Grisward, "Com ces trois goutes
de sanc furent, qui sor le blance noif parurent: Note sur
un motif littéraire," dans Etudes de Langue et de Littérature
du Moyen Age offertes à Félix Lecoy (Paris, 1973), pp.
157-64.

2. Vv. 1031-1060. Nos citations sont faites d'après:
Les Romans de Chrétien de Troyes, V, Le Conte du Graal
(Perceval), éd. Félix Lecoy, CFMA (Paris: Champion), 1973.

3. Perceval et l'initiation, pp. 97-8, 139, 144-5,
etc. (voir l'index).

4. Peter Haidu, Lion-queue-coupée: L'Ecart symbolique chez Chrétien de Troyes (Genève: Droz), 1972, pp. 11-15.

5. Peter Haidu, Aesthetic Distance in Chrétien de Troyes: Irony and Comedy in Cligès and Perceval (Genève: Droz, 1968).

6. Frappier, Chr. de Tr. et le mythe, p. 140, n. 73.

7. J. Baltrusaïtis, La Stylistique ornementale dans la sculpture romane (Paris, 1931); P. Francastel, L'Humanisme roman: Critique des théories sur l'art du XIe siècle en France (Paris, 1942).

8. Livre VI, Parzival, trad. Ernest Tonnelat (Paris, 1934), I, 246.

9. Vv. 1821-23. Sinople indique alors la couleur rouge. Noter que l'édition Lecoy met au v. 2910 Belissant au lieu de Blancheflor.

10. Cf. J. R. Smeets, "François Villon, De laatste strofen van Le Lais: lyriek en wetenschap," Non-Conformisten, Wassenaar, 1971, pp. 63-96.

11. Vv. 5692-716.

12. Alice Colby, The Portrait in Twelfth Century French Literature (Genève: Droz, 1965); compte-rendu par Charles Méla, RPh, 24 (1971), 529-34.

13. Pierre Francastel, La Réalité figurative (Paris: Gonthier, 1965), p. 103.

14. Cf. Frappier, Chr. de Tr. et le Mythe . . . , p. 134.

15. Cette remarque nous a été faite par Madame Le Rider, qui prépare une thèse sur Chrétien de Troyes.

16. Claude Lévi-Strauss parle du travail du romancier devant les éléments du mythe disloqué: "Il recueille ces matériaux épars et les remploie comme ils se présentent, non sans percevoir confusément qu'ils proviennent d'un autre édifice." (Mythologiques, III: L'Origine des manières de table [Paris, 1968], p. 106).

17. D. Poirion, "L'Ombre mythique de Perceval dans le Conte du Graal," CCM, 16 (1973), 191-98.

18. Frappier, Chr. de Tr. et le Mythe, p. 209.

19. "Assez oscurement diseient . . . ," "Prologue," v. 12, Les Lais, éd. Rychner, CFMA (Paris: Champion, 1966).

20. Cf. Géza Roheim, Les Portes du rêve, trad. M. Manin et Fl. Verne (Paris: Payot, 1973), pp. 271-77.

21. Ces expressions sont de Marie de France, "Prologue," éd. cit., vv. 20 et 22.

22. D. Poirion, "Les Mots et les Choses selon Jean de Meun," IL, 26:1 (1974), 7-11.

Part IV

Bower/Masque

STUDIES IN OLD FRENCH DRAMATIC LITERATURE

THE UNCOURTLINESS OF NICOLETTE

Nathaniel B. Smith

In the history of courtly literature <u>Aucassin</u> <u>et</u> <u>Nicolette</u> represents a new and iconoclastic attitude. The <u>chanson</u> <u>de</u> <u>geste</u> had been satirized before, and the idyllic novel bore the seeds of its own degeneration, but the aristocratic and moralistic tradition of the <u>roman</u> <u>courtois</u> established by Chrétien de Troyes found a clever and telling mockery of itself in the seemingly innocent little <u>chantefable</u> <u>Aucassin</u>.[1]

<u>Aucassin</u> <u>et</u> <u>Nicolette</u> has been described as "a sort of thirteenth-century anti-novel," Aucassin himself as "a veritable anti-hero," and the <u>chantefable</u> as an "anti-genre";[2] but Nicolette herself has not had the critical attention which, as motivating force of the story's action and as its chief exemplar of the feminine ethic, she undoubtedly deserves.

According to A. Robert Harden, <u>Aucassin</u> has traditionally been considered as "the purest example imaginable of characters motivated by idyllic love."[3] Certainly the tone was set by La Curne de Sainte-Palaye's choice of the title <u>Les</u> <u>amours</u> <u>du</u> <u>bon</u> <u>vieux</u> <u>temps</u>: <u>on</u> <u>n'aime</u> <u>plus</u> <u>comme</u> <u>on</u> <u>aimait</u> <u>jadis</u> under which to publish the first non-periodical edition of <u>Aucassin</u> in 1756;[4] and Nicolette herself has been generally taken as fairly "straight." For this heroine who is so much more appealing than her clumsy, do-nothing lover, some critics have even seemed to nourish a secret admiration.

Thus Albert Pauphilet writes that: "Les charmes de Nicolette sont parmi les choses dont cet auteur ne rit pas," and that the enumeration of Nicolette's attributes by Aucassin "n'est pas autre chose . . . qu'un essai d'analyse de ce qui chez certaines femmes est inhérent à tous leurs

169

gestes, et qu'on appelle le charme." Nicolette, says
Pauphilet, shows that "c'était un des aboutissements de
la courtoisie, que de remettre aux femmes une espèce de
suprématie";[5] and she is "bien de ce temps où la poésie
lyrique établit la royauté de la femme."[6]

Such a Nicolette seems to unite the qualities of the
medieval courtly lady and of what Goethe mysteriously called
"das Ewig-weibliche."[7] And other critics, while occasionally
seeing a bit of exaggeration or satire in Nicolette, have
tended to regard her as a fine, upstanding model of thirteenth-century womanhood.[8]

However, I believe that the author, with subtlety but
clarity, wished to portray a far earthier Nicolette than
usually imagined. One of the most striking stylistic characteristics of the work, the regular and thematic use of
certain registers of physical terms, makes lexical frequency
the most appropriate point to enter the Spitzerian "philo-
logical circle" of Nicolette.[9] It will be seen that the
author's choice of terms and epithets for Nicolette,
Aucassin's references to her, and her own utterances, depict
with unanimity a Nicolette who is a sort of definition by
negation of the traditional courtly heroine.

It is a valid question whether in Nicolette we really
have a changed heroine or just a changed perception of the
heroine of courtly romance. If it were only Aucassin who
perceives her in a new, down-to-earth manner, this might
reflect more on his character than on hers; but all images
of her--those furnished by Aucassin, by the author, by
Nicolette herself, even by Aucassin's mother (as will be
seen)--coincide in pointing to a heroine who is hopelessly
and forever at odds with the world of Laudine and Enide.

Evidence of Nicolette's "true nature" abounds. It can
be no coincidence that, when Aucassin finds himself close
upon Nicolette's trail, the word cors, "body," occurs four
times in one eighteen-line laisse (XXIII), thrice in the
expression gent cors referring to Nicolette's "nice" or
"beautiful" body, and once in telling us that the shepherds'

news of Aucassin's "amie o le gent cors" enters directly
into his own <u>cors</u> (XXIII, 1-3)--suggesting a more body-to-
body than heart-to-heart relationship.

The word <u>cors</u> occurs nine other times in <u>Aucassin</u>,
four with the more general meaning of "person"[10] and five
as "body," including two more characterizations of
Nicolette's <u>cors</u> as <u>gens</u> (III, 15; V, 6).[11] Nicolette's
other stock attribute is also physical: her "bright face"
(<u>cler</u> <u>vis</u> or <u>face</u> <u>clere</u>), referred to twelve times.

This physically-oriented vocabulary is not due merely to
Aucassin's perception of Nicolette; the major description of
her, in his absence, is as notable by its sensuality as by
its detail, beginning with the blond curly hair, the bright,
laughing eyes, the well-shaped face,[12] the lips redder than
cherry or rose in the summertime, and the dainty white teeth.

Barbara Nelson Sargent has quite rightly called attention to the unconventional position of this portrait, which
comes long after Nicolette's first appearance in the story.
Sargent also writes: "The portrait of the heroine has no
affective function; she is quite alone as she makes her way
across the garden," hence showing the author's independence
from or even rejection of the convention that the heroine
should first be described as she first inspires the hero
with love.[13]

It can also be added that the description does have a
certain affective function which concerns not the hero but
the audience: by giving us a private glimpse of her alone,
the author brings us closer to Nicolette, and catches us up
skillfully in his narrative. Hence the postponement of the
portrait is not merely a rejection of convention, but also
a positive trait of some originality.

Proceeding downward with the description, the author
presents Nicolette's "firm breasts which lifted up her
clothing as if they were two walnuts," and her waist, so
"slender that you could enclose it in your two hands." By
these details, and particularly by passing into the second
person, the author practically invites us--or rather his

medieval audience, presumably mostly male and middle to
lower-middle class[14]--to reach out and seize the desirable
young lady in our hands.

The _mameletes_-walnuts comparison is unique to my knowledge; the graphic description of Nicolette's waist is quite
unusual;[15] and another surprising detail is that "the daisies
which she broke with the toes of her feet and which lay upon
the top of her foot were completely black compared to her
feet and her legs, so white the girl was."[16]

Now, legs, feet, and toes are not normally described
for a lady, only for males and monsters.[17] But Nicolette's
feet are mentioned three times (including once her _menuisse
du pié_, "instep") and her legs and toes once, whereas "these
parts of the body were ordinarily covered by clothing and
. . . the portraits were often not detailed enough to
include them," in the twelfth-century romance at least.[18]
In the "lower" genres, particularly in the _pastourelle_
tradition, we do find references to feminine legs, feet,
and rarely toes,[19] which merely confirm that the inclusion
of these details would not be appropriate to a courtly
description. The mention of Nicolette's toes is perhaps
particularly significant, since Aucassin soon informs us
that the love of a woman is planted, among other places,
in her toe (XIV, 21).

Nicolette, then, has allowed herself to be sketched,
as it were, in a most improper pose--as more of an Ingres
Odalisque, perhaps, than a Madame Récamier of David.
Nicolette, let us recall, has just in rather unladylike
fashion taken flight from her prison by shinnying down a
rope made of sheets and towels knotted together. She is
shown dressed only in "un bliaut de drap de soie que ele
avoit molt bon." This silk tunic, though of good quality
and apparently fairly long, since she must hold it up with
both hands to keep it from the dew, seems at least for the
purposes of this description to be her only article of
clothing, of which the upper section is the _corset_ which
the shepherds later in the day remember her as wearing

(XXI, 8). Her simplicity of attire contrasts to the complex
costumes of many other literary heroines of the twelfth and
thirteenth centuries, whose bliaut, chemise, manches,
mantel, and adornments of various sorts are often described
in some detail.[20]

Whether it is with intent or from oversight that the
author does not here mention the mantel in which Nicolette
is seen at Aucassin's prison (XII, 33; XVI, 5), the point
here is that while crossing the garden Nicolette is depicted
barefoot and in scanty clothing, thus permitting the intimate physical detail of the description. Nor is this the
first time that Nicolette has been so immodest as to lift
up her clothing to reveal more of herself, since Aucassin
has just told us of the sick pilgrim who was made healthier
than ever by the sight of Nicolette's ganbete, her "dainty
leg" (XI, 12-31). This satire of a saintly miracle or of
the powers of true love has often been commented on. For
our purposes let us retain only Nicolette's apparent exhi-
bitionism, in what one critic has delightfully called
"descrizione al rallentatore del pudico spogliarello";[21] the
fact that Aucassin thinks primarily of her physical attributes when lamenting his absent lady, whose earliest characterization, let us recall, is as "Nicole le bien faite"
(III, 3); and the similarity to the message Nicolette leaves
with the shepherds, indicating to Aucassin the fabulous
value of even one "member" of the "beat" (Nicolette) who
will cure him of his ills (XVIII, 17-31; XXII, 34-37).

The imprisoned Aucassin's tribute to Nicolette is
worth a closer look. After pronouncing the stock epithets
flors de lis and douce amie o le cler vis (XI, 12-13), he
proceeds to say:

> 'plus es douce que roisins
> ne que soupe en maserin,'
>   (XI, 14-15)

hence comparing the evidently unspiritual pleasures of his
douce amie to those of grapes and of wine-soaked bread in a

bowl. Then comes the pilgrim story, and finally a series
of parallel terms of rather special significance:

> 'Douce amie, flors de lis,
> biax alers et biax venirs,
> biax jouers et biax bordirs,
> biax parlers et biax delis,
> dox baisiers et dox sentirs,
> nus ne vous poroit haïr.'
>   (XI, 32-37)

The parodic aspect is clear from the repetition, in reversed
order, of most of the same pairs of attributes as in
Aucassin's previous lament (VII, 12-16). Now, all the words
in both "catalogues" are exclusively physical, and most of
them have even more particular associations, such that indeed "no man could hate" Nicolette (XI, 37).

For example, jouer in Old French frequently suggests
that the jeu d'amour and can be a euphemism for coïr.[22]
Bordir or border (as in VII, 15), literally "to talk, gossip,
mock, joke; have fun, play," readily calls to mind the word
bordel, which in the twelfth century began to take on its
present meaning of "maison de prostitution,"[23] and its
derivatives bordeler, bordelage, bordelerie, etc.

The next quality Aucassin attributes to Nicolette is
biax delis, or biax deduis in VII, 14. Delit, "entertain-
ment, pleasure, delight," often refers to sexual pleasure,
as when a straightforward poet tells us:

> Lou jeu d'amors sens atendre
> Li fix per delit;[24]

and the same is true of deduit, "amusement, sport, love-
making, pleasure."[25]

The next term, dox baisiers, certainly fits in the
same series, and recalls Aucassin's demand that in return
for entering the battle, he be allowed to see Nicolette
"tant . . . que j'aie deus paroles u trois a li parlees
et que je l'aie une seule fois baisie" (VIII, 36).[26]

Finally, Aucassin associates with Nicolette <u>dox</u> <u>sentirs</u>; a physical rather then mental "feeling" is implied by the corresponding term in the earlier passage: <u>biax</u> <u>acolers</u>, "happy embracing" (VII, 16). Indeed, <u>sentir</u> as "fleischlich geniessen" is well attested.[27]

It is particularly revealing that the same suggestive words and roots are often associated in other Old French allusions to sexual love. We find <u>jeus</u>, <u>beisier</u>, and <u>santir</u> together describing Lancelot and Guenièvre in bed, and a few lines later <u>delitable</u> and <u>deduit</u>.[28] Examples from other authors associate <u>desirier</u>, <u>acoler</u>, <u>baisier</u>, <u>sentir</u>, and <u>delis</u>; and <u>deliter</u>, <u>baisier</u>, and <u>jüer</u>.[29] What we have, then, in Old French, is a complex of words suggesting physical love, used by our author in these two parallel passages to show what the absent Nicolette really means to Aucassin.

That this physical vocabulary signals a major theme of the <u>chantefable</u> is shown by the occurrence of five of these words, outside of our two passages, a total of twenty-one times (<u>baisier</u> 11, <u>acoler</u> 5, <u>deduis</u> 3, <u>delis</u> 1, and <u>sentir</u> in the physical sense 1).

Nicolette herself uses this vocabulary to describe her feelings toward Aucassin:

> 'Quant mes dox amis m'<u>acole</u>
> et il me <u>sent</u> grasse et mole,
> dont sui jou a tele escole,
> baus ne tresce ne carole,
> harpe, gigle ne viole,
> ne <u>deduis</u> de la nimpole
> n'i vauroit mie.'
>   (XXXIII, 4-10)

Thus, the delights of all these things are nothing compared to the delights of being <u>acole</u> and <u>sentie</u> by Aucassin and of living with him in Torelore in great <u>aise</u> and <u>deduit</u>, an expression used twice, for good measure, in successive sentences (XXXIV, 2-4).

Later, separated from Aucassin by the Carthaginians, Nicolette becomes even more explicit about her desire for him:

            'Vos douces amors me hastent
            et semonent et travaillent.
            Ce doinst Dix l'esperitables
            c'oncor vous tiengne en me brace,
            et que vos baissiés me face
            et me bouce et mon visage. . . .'
                            (XXXVII, 12-17)

    Is there inconsistency betweeen the expression grasse
et mole and the previous description of Nicolette's slender
waist (XII, 24-25)?   In XXVII, according to Barbara Nelson
Sargent, "the young girl's extreme slenderness is . . .
denied by the girl herself."[30] But surely an author who has
given us a detailed physical description of the heroine and
whose hero claims that a women's love resides, in part, "en
son le cateron de sa mamele" (XIV, 20), can have fallen into
no confusion here. Nicolette is simply slender where she
should be, and grasse e mole, "plump and soft," where she
should be, just as the pastoral Robin, having embraced
Marion, says:

            'Je cuidai tenir un froumage,
            Si te senti je tenre et mole'[31]

There is hence no contradiction at all; and Colby shows
that "medieval ladies were expected to be pleasingly plump
and slender at the same time" (graile and grasse).[32]
    The foregoing observations help justify other details
of the chantefable which have often been found puzzling.
For example, the Viscount, Nicolette's stepfather, gets
right to the heart of the matter when he asks Aucassin: "Que
cuideriés vous avoir gaegnié se vous l'aviés asognentee ne
mise a vo lit?" (VI, 19-21). Far from denying any such
intention, Aucassin immediately accepts it and its consequences, launching into his famous discourse on the advantages of hell over heaven.
    Later, Aucassin finds the Viscount's phraseology so
appropriate that he uses it to tell Nicolette from his prison
that the chief reason he will regret her departure is that
the first man who saw her "vos meteroit a son lit, si vos

asoignenteroit" (XIV, 4-6). Then, only suicide would
remain for him since, as he twice says, "vos ariiés jut
en lit a home, s'el mien non" (XIV, 6-7, 13-14). In this
light, it is perhaps significant that the word lit occurs
10 times in Aucassin, gésir 11, drap (de lit) 4, and dormir
and endormir 4.[33]

Our Nicolette, then, is much closer in spirit, like
the words used to characterize her, to the shepherdess
Marion and her companions of the pastourelle than to the
distinguished ladies of the roman courtois. As unladylike
as her means of escaping from imprisonment in Beaucaire is
her eventual return disguised, in male clothing, as a
jongleur; and it has often been observed that Nicolette
takes on conventionally male attributes and initiatives by
directing the action, in a way one might expect of a Lunette
but never of a Laudine.

Certainly, Aucassin's parents have a low opinion of
this adventuress; and Aucassin's mother exhorts him:

> 'Di va! faus, que vex tu faire?
> Nicolete est cointe et gaie;
> jetee fu de Cartage,
> acatee fu d'un Saisne;
> puis qu'a moullié te vix traire,
> pren femme de haut parage.'
> (III, 7-12)

The characterization "cointe et gaie" has been a
slight mystery. Since it is unlikely that Aucassin's
mother would describe Nicolette flatteringly, this verse
8 was "mis par d'anciens éditeurs dans la bouche d'Aucassin
comme une première réponse à sa mère," but according to
Roques, who translates cointe and gaie as "gracieuse" and
"gentille,"[34] "c'est plutôt une constation faite par celle-
ci, une concession à l'évidence, qui n'affaiblit pas l'objection suivante."[35]

However, cointe and gaie, like many of the other words
we have ssen applied to Nicolette, can have an unfavorable
side. Cointe, though usually complimentary, in the sense

of "knowledgeable, intelligent, clever, handsome, joyful,"
etc., also carries the less positive meanings of "crafty,
sly" and "high-handed, arrogant."[36]

Nor does _gai_ always have positive connotations; it
can mean _unbekümmert_ ("carefree; careless"), as in Wace's
description of the Danes:

> La gent de Danemarche . . .
> Fiere fu e preisant [?], _gaie_ e luxurïeuse,
> Nuls hom ne se teneit a une femme espusee;[37]

the association here with "lascivious" is particularly
interesting, but let us give Nicolette the benefit of the
doubt and translate _gai_ as "vivacious," or perhaps
"frivolous."

Aucassin's protective mother, realizing all too well
what attracts her once-innocent son to Nicolette, is essentially saying to him: "You fool! What are you doing? That
Nicolette is a crafty, frivolous little thing; she was taken
(thrown?) out of Carthage and bought from a Moor; if you
really want to get married, find a woman of high birth" (i.e.,
one whose charms are more respectable than Nicolette's).

But the good Countess's warnings are in vain, for
"no one can detach him from the shapely Nicolette" (III,
3-4); and at the end, we find the two becoming married at
last, and

> puis vesquirent il mains dis
> et menerent lor _delis_.
> Or a sa _joie_ Aucassins
> et Nicholete autresi.
>   (XLI, 20-23)

The words _joie_, suggesting the _joie d'amour_,[38] and _delis_,
whose connotations we have already seen, thus continue up
to the very end the theme of physical love--not _too_ sensual,
but adolescent, a bit in the style of Manon Lescaut and even
with a touch of innocence, but none the less far from the
heroines of Chrétien de Troyes.

In this respect, the chantefable ends where it began,
without the evolution of characters and roles which would
have shown a purpose other than satire and amusement.
Aucassin and Nicolette continue to contradict the stereo-
typed world of romance and its conventional male and female
roles. As Aucassin is anti-hero, so Nicolette is anti-
heroine. The satire Aucassin et Nicolette shows how broadly
French taste had changed since the last years of the twelfth
century. According to whether we choose for the time of
composition an early or a late date within the first half of
the thirteenth century,[39] Aucassin et Nicolette will appear
either as a sort of intermediate stage between the waning
courtly romance and the rising genre of the fabliau,[40] or
else as a refined and consciously archaizing corruption of
the courtly tradition with elements of the idyllic novel and
the fabliau--in either case the work of an author of genius,
too early or too late and above all a bit too subtle to be
appreciated as much by his times as by our own.

Notes

1. This paper was read at the First Triennial Congress
of the International Courtly Literature Society (Philadelphia, May 6-7, 1974), to whose participants I am grateful
for suggestions and encouragement, particularly Raymond J.
Cormier, organizer of the Congress and producer of an admirable and harmonious dramatic version of Aucassin, Reto R.
Bezzola, James J. Wilhelm, my former professor Louis F.
Solano, and Mireille Guillet-Rydell, whose paper on "The
Image of the Forward Female in Selected Epics and Romances,"
including the seductive Saracen princess, reinforced my
interpretation of Nicolette. For their advice, I am also
grateful to Joseph Snow and Susanna Peters Coy of the Depart-
ment of Romance Languages, University of Georgia, and to Sara
Sturm of the Department of French and Italian, University of
Massachusetts, Amherst.

2. Barbara Nelson Sargent, "Parody in Aucassin et
Nicolette: Some Further Considerations," FR, 43 (1970),
605. A. Robert Harden, "Aucassin et Nicolette as Parody,"
SP, 63 (1966), 6. Mariantonia Liborio, "Aucassin et
Nicolette: I limiti di una parodia," CN, 30 (1970), 159.

3. Harden, art. cit., p. 1.

4. Chez Duchesne: Vaucluse and Paris; a second work,
La Châtelaine de Saint-Gilles, is included under the same
title.

5. Albert Pauphilet, Le Legs du moyen âge: Etudes
de littérature médiévale (Melun, 1950), pp. 246-47.

6. Art., "Aucassin et Nicolette" in Dictionnaire des
lettres françaises, ed. Cardinal Georges Grente et al.,
Robert Bossuat et al.: Le Moyen âge (Paris, 1964), p. 86.

7. Faust, line 12110 (second-to-last line of Part II).

8. Cf., e.g., Omer Jodogne, "La Parodie et le pastiche
dans Aucassin et Nicolette," CAIEF, no. 12 (1960), 56-57.

9. The importance of language and vocabulary in
Aucassin has been discussed by the articles mentioned in
note 2 and more particularly by Eugene Vance, "The Word at
Heart: Aucassin et Nicolette as a Medieval Comedy of Language," YFS, 45 (1970), 33-51, which considers various linguistic aspects other than the problem of Nicolette, and by
Simone Monsonégo, Etude stylo-statistique du vocabulaire
des vers et de la prose dans la chantefable "Aucassin et
Nicolette" (Paris, 1966), which, concentrating on the linguistic contrasts between the verse and the prose passages
and between the first and second portions of Aucassin, does
not provide statistical analyses bearing on the question
at hand.

10. Cf. Aucassin et Nicolette, ed. Mario Roques. 2nd
ed., CFMA (Paris, 1963 [1929]), glossary, p. 63, art. cors;
all our textual references are to this edition, with indication of laisse and line numbers.

11. The same expression is used, among other examples,
by the prowling chevalier to describe the desirable shepherdess at the beginning of Adam le Bossu, Le Jeu de Robin
et Marion, ed. Ernest Langlois, CFMA (Paris, 1966 [1924]),
1. 10.

12. Translating traitice with Alice M. Colby, The
Portrait in Twelfth-Century French Literature (Geneva,
1965), pp. 29-30, against "elongate," as in Roques'
glossary, p. 100.

13. Sargent, "Parody . . . ," pp. 603-605.

14. On this question, cf. Edelgard E. du Bruck, "The
Audience of Aucassin et Nicolette: Confidant, Accomplice
and Judge of Its Author," MichA, 5 (1972), 193-201.

15. The waist, in Colby's research, "is very rarely
described" (p. 60), and then only vaguely (as graisle,
etc.). For several mamelettes-pomettes comparisons cf.
Colby, pp. 59-60; Adam le Bossu, Le Jeu de la feuillée, ed.
Ernest Langlois. 2nd ed., CFMA (Paris, 1951 [1917]), 1. 152
and n.; Karl Rogger, "Etude descriptive de la chantefable
Aucassin et Nicolette," ZRP, 67 (1951), 409-457, and 70
(1954), 1-57, p. 15. The latter, unjustifiably in my view,
considers the portrait of Nicolette to be "celui qui court
l'Europe au moyen âge," and not at all original. Similarly,
Sargent, "Parody . . . ," p. 602; June Hall Martin, Love's

Fools: Aucassin, Troilus, Calisto and the Parody of the
Courtly Lover (London, 1972), p. 30; Joan B. Williamson,
"Naming as a Source of Irony in Aucassin et Nicolette,"
SF, N.S. 51 (1973), 401-409 (405: "a paragon of virtue,"
etc.).

16. Mescinete, it might be worth noting, can mean not
only "kleines Mägdlein," but also "Konkubine"; see Adolf
Tobler and Erhard Lommatzsch, Altfransösisches Wörterbuch,
8 vols. complete to date (Wiesbaden, 1925-), V, art.
meschinete, cols. 1593-94.

17. Colby, pp. 62-63, 69, 83, 84, 93.

18. Colby, p. 96.

19. Cf. Rodolfo Renier, Il Tipo estetico della donna
nel medio evo (Ancona, 1885), pp. 31 (Moniot de Paris, pastourelle), 36 (Adam de la Halle, Le Jeu de la Feuillée, 147-
49), 39 (anon.); also Amadas et Ydoine, 148 (MS V, 168);
etc.

20. For examples, cf. Eunice R. Goddard, Women's
Costume in French Texts of the Eleventh and Twelfth Centuries (Baltimore, 1927), pp. 49-55, etc.

21. Liborio, art. cit., p. 165, n. 41.

22. Cf. Tobler-Lommatzsch, IV, art. jöer, col. 1969.

23. Albert Dauzat et al., Nouveau dictionnaire étymologique et historique (Paris, 1964), art. borde, pp. 97-98;
Walther von Wartburg, ed., Französisches etymologisches
Wörterbuch, 21 vols. (Tübingen, 1922-), art. bord, I, 439,
gives the thirteenth century for this meaning. The two
roots, though apparently unrelated (cf. FEW, I, 441, art.
*borda), were no doubt easily subject to confusion.

24. For this and other examples, cf. Tobler-Lommatzach,
art. delit, II, 1333-34.

25. Kenneth Urwin, A Short Old French Dictionary for
Students (Oxford, 1967), p. 16; cf. Tobler-Lommatzsch, art.
deduit, II, 1269.

26. With the latter passage would fit the stronger
meaning of baiser of today's French; it is not clear when
the primary meaning of kissing gave rise to the meaning of
sexual intercourse, but the second meaning is attested
already in Old Provençal; cf. FEW, art. basiare, I, 269.

27. Cf. Tobler-Lommatzsch, art. sentir, IX, 480-481.

28. Chrétien de Troyes, Le Chevalier de la charrete,
ed. Mario Roques, CFMA (Paris, 1958), vv. 4674-75, 4683-85.

29. Tobler-Lommatzsch, art. sentir, IX, 481; art.
jöer, IV, 1969.

30. Sargent, art. cit., p. 603.

31. Adam le Bossu, Le Jeu de Robin et Marion, ed.
cit., 11. 551-52.

32. Colby, p. 66; cf. Tobler-Lommatzsch, art. _cras_, II, 1015.

33. Cf. Roques' glossary.

34. Cf. his glossary, pp. 62, 75.

35. Roques, p. 42, III, 8n.; note that Roques' explanation would really require _mais_ at the beginning of line 9.

36. Tobler-Lommatzsch, art. _cointe_, II, 542: "schlau; hochfahrend, stolz"; in one example "les enchantemenz cuintes" translates "incantationes callidas."

37. Cf. Tobler-Lommatzsch, art. _gai_, IV, 38-39, for this and other examples.

38. Tobler-Lommatzsch, art _joie_: the chief definition is "Freude (auch Liebesfreude)" (IV, 1716). Examples include _joie_ associated with _deport_ or _deduit_ (col. 1716); the expression _joie d'amor_ (col. 1717, 16); and a metonymic meaning "Gegenstand der Liebe, Geliebte" (col. 1718, 1729); cf. also IV, 1713, 9-10. _Joi_, of course, is a key word of the troubadours' love vocabulary. For _fille de joie_, etc., cf. FEW, art. _gaudium_, IV, 81.

39. On dating cf. Roques, pp. xiii-xv.

40. On the _fabliau_ aspects of _Aucassin_, cf. Harden, art. cit., pp. 7, 8; on the dating of the _fabliau_, Per Nykrog, _Les Fabliaux: Etude d'histoire littéraire et de stylistique médiévale._ 2nd ed. (Copenhagen, 1973), p. 4, etc.

PREFIGURATION AND LITERARY CREATIVITY IN THE
SACRIFICE D'ABRAHAM OF THE MISTERE DU VIEL TESTAMENT

Barbara M. Craig

John R. Elliott, Junior, in his article "The Sacrifice of
Isaac as Comedy and Tragedy" (Studies in Philology, 66
[1969], 36-59) has pointed out that the plot of medieval
plays dealing with the Abraham and Isaac story have a ritual
basis derived from the Mass and Easter liturgy.[1] Like the
Mass and the Easter plays which conclude with the Resurrec-
tion, so the story of Abraham has its movement from tristia
to gaudium.[2] The interpretation of the story as a prefiguration of the Crucifixion had been provided by the church
fathers and preserved in the Glossa ordinaria.[3] Thus the
medieval playwrights who presented the story together with
its figurative meaning were merely conveying to the stage
church doctrine well known at the time. The success of
their plays was almost assured by the fact that their
subject-matter offered in allegorical terms the central
events of the Christian faith.

While agreeing with Elliott's assessment of the nature
and significance of the Abraham plays, I feel that in order
to explain fully the popularity of these works one needs
to give further consideration to their literary impact.
Although Elliott speaks in passing of various literary
devices used by authors to enhance their works his major
preoccupation is to prove that these plays are comedies.
This he does conclusively. He has not, however, provided a
systematic study of any one of the plays as literature. To
complement Elliott's work and in an effort to measure the
contribution of literary excellence to the lasting popularity
of at least one medieval Abraham and Isaac play, I propose
to examine the Sacrifice d'Abraham, lines 9365-10598 of the
Mistére du Viel Testament.[4] By a study of the literary

183

attributes of this play I hope to determine the relative
importance of the religious significance and the literary
merit of the work in its vigorous survival.

In preparing the story of Abraham and Isaac for the
stage the unknown author of the Sacrifice d'Abraham had to
transmit to his audience at least three possible levels of
understanding. The "literal" level, that is the direct
transposition into drama of the Biblical account (Genesis
xxii.1-19), offered few problems. To be sure, it involved
showing on the stage angelic appearances, travel, the
climbing of a mountain, and a burnt offering. All this,
however, was simple for any medieval playwright to envisage
on the stage. This mechanical aspect of the dramatist's
work will not, therefore, concern us further.

A more vital level of comprehension to be imparted was
that of the mystical interpretation of the story as a prefiguration of the salvation of man by the death of Christ.
To convey this figurative significance our playwright turned
first to the device of the procès de paradis, borrowed,
probably, from a Passion play.[5] In the Sacrifice d'Abraham
the procès involves only three speakers, God and two of his
allegorical daughters, Miséricorde and Justice. The debate
among these three elucidates the prefigurative implications
of the events dramatized.

The intention of portraying Isaac as a figure of Christ
is furthered by the way the author builds up the character of
Isaac. In Genesis xxii Isaac is represented by only a few
words.[6] In the play he is fully developed. Emphasis is
given to the remarkable circumstances of his birth to Sarah
in her old age, as by a miracle. This amplification was
undoubtedly intended to suggest an analogy between Isaac's
birth and that of Jesus. Later, when Abraham and Isaac
arrive at the mount, the fact that Isaac joyfully carries
the wood for the burnt offering is likewise given prominence; this picture evokes the image of Christ carrying the
cross. The analogy continues when Isaac learns God's
message. Like Christ in the Garden of Gethsemane, Isaac

would rather be spared the ordeal that confronts him. Three
times he asks whether his father will indeed act against
human nature and offer up his son (ll. 10108-113; 10126-29,
10151-54). Like Christ, too, Isaac ultimately brings himself to accept God's will; he becomes "jusque a la mort
obedient . . ." (l. 10192). Just as Christ pardons those who
have tormented him, so Isaac prays that God may comfort and
strengthen Abraham (ll. 10358-63, 13371-73). This careful
development of the constancy of the boy is evidently the
playwright's method of illuminating the fact that Isaac is a
figure of Christ. In this work, then, the prefigurative
significance of the story is not only explained from without,
in the procès, but made an essential part of the work itself.

A third task of the playwright is to interpret the
Biblical narrative in such a way that the fifteenth-century
audience will find the story credible and moving. He must
enable the spectators to see their own experiences reflected
in the situation and characters of the play. This require-
ment makes the greatest demands on the literary creativity of
the author. He goes about achieving his goal chiefly by
humanizing his personages. The Old Testament patriarch is
conceived not only as a figure of God but also as a man.
While realizing that the audience knows that Abraham will be
submissive to God's will, the dramatist develops the anguish
felt by the father on being told he must sacrifice his son.
Abraham's dismay is shown in the first words he utters upon
receiving God's message:

> O quelle nouvelle
> D'une part belle
> Et bonne, en tant qu'elle
> Procéde des cieulx,
> De l'autre cruelle. . . .
> (ll. 9753-57)

The inner struggle waged in Abraham's heart is poignantly
revealed throughout the play. It is clear, for example,
in an early prayer:

> Beau sire Dieu, conseille moy
> De cela que faire doy.
> Doy je mon enfant mettre a mort?
> Ouÿ. Non fais. Si fais. Pourquoy?
> (11. 9880-884)

In this last line, with the words "non fais," Abraham seems
about to rebel. However, he stops immediately and submits
once more with "Si fais." Each wave of emotion that sweeps
over Abraham is followed by a reminder that God's will must
be observed. In the moment of supreme testing Abraham stands
firm. He gives his son a parting kiss and raises his sword
to strike down the boy. Only then does the angel intervene
to stop the stroke.

We have seen that the character of Isaac is mainly
developed in such a way as to assure his identification as
a figure of Christ. Yet the playwright also paints him as
a carefree child, unaware of his destiny. In the opening
lines of the play Isaac asks for his mother's permission to
join the shepherds in the fields (11. 9534-36). There he
plays games with his companions (11. 9559-67). He is
delighted to accompany his father on his journey to the
mount. His subsequent horror on learning that he himself is
to be the sacrificial victim (11. 10102-10107) is natural
and human. His eventual submission to God's will becomes
credible only because by this time the spectators realize
that Isaac is a Christ figure.

Isaac's mother, Sarah (Sarra), does not appear in the
verses of Genesis that are the source of the play. Our
dramatist has chosen to include her and in so doing he makes
of her the feminine complement of the two male protagonists.
Father and son overcome their instinctive unwillingness to
fulfill God's command. They control their natural emotions
with the help of their reason (their realization that obedience to God must take precedence over human inclination).
Both Abraham and Isaac, however, make it clear that they do
not believe Sarah capable of such disciplined conduct. When
Abraham first receives God's message he wonders whether he
should share it with his wife. He soon decides she is too

weak (fragille, 1. 9789) to cope with the problem. Her
mother-love might drive her to oppose Abraham's actions
(11. 9790-94). Even as he moves forward to consummate his
task Abraham fears he may cause Sarah to die of grief
(11. 10030-10035). Isaac also prays that his mother may
not be led to sin against God:

> Ne que de rien ne tempeste ou tormente,
> Dont contre toy puisse commettre offence.
> (11. 10382-383)

When Abraham and Isaac, their mission completed, finally
return home and tell Sarah what has taken place, her reaction reveals just how well-founded were their apprehensions.
Sarah declares that she would never have allowed Isaac to
go with his father had she known the purpose of the journey
(11. 10565-566). Sarah becomes, then, a typical example of
the concept of woman revealed in most non-courtly literature
of the middle ages. She is a creature of sentiment who
might have caused the ruin of her husband and their progeny,
just as Eve did in the story of the Fall.

In addition to creating realistic and moving protagonists our dramatist used many other literary devices to
enrich his work. One of the most frequently encountered is
dramatic irony. Irony is inherent in the story, for Abraham
and the audience have heard God's message but Isaac and
Sarah do not share the knowledge. Thus Abraham can say:

> O doullente, quant tu m'as dit
> Que ton enfant au mont menasse
> Tu ne pensoyes pas l'esdit
> Qu'il falloit que je le tuasse
> Et que je le sacrifiasse.
> (11. 9821-25)

Ironic asides are often muttered by Abraham, as in his
answer to Isaac's request to go with his father to witness
the sacrifice:

> Hellas! ouy,
> Mon amy; c'est de ton trespas
> Que tu es ainsi resjouÿ.
>   (ll. 9975-77)

The playwright resorts to irony to help the audience share
in the pathos of the moment.

Still another literary process is used by the author
to add to the musical quality of his text. This is the introduction of variety in verse form. Although octosyllabic
couplets prevail, as in all medieval French drama, several
passages in the Sacrifice d'Abraham have different rhymes
and metres. In the opening lines of the prologue (ll. 9365-
400), three and four-syllable lines alternate with six- and
ten-syllable lines.[7] The same procedure is repeated later,
within the play proper (ll. 9729-40). The rich rhyme and
irregular metre of these lines prepare the audience for the
conflicting emotions that will arise as the play progresses.
Elsewhere short lines are similarly used to reflect either
trepidation (ll. 9753-66), or sorrow (ll. 10030-10037), or
elation (ll. 10514-518). One rondeau is inserted (ll. 10273-
280) when father and son take leave of one another. This
forme fixe allows the repetition in the refrain of the
pathetic farewells:

> Abraham
> A Dieu, mon filz.
>   Isaac
>   A Dieu, mon pére.
> Bendé suys; de bref je mourray.
>   (ll. 10273-274; 10276; 10279-280)

Passages in decasyllables help to establish a tone of
solemnity. Thus early in the play (ll. 9741-52) the angel,
Ceraphin, uses ten-syllable lines to instruct Abraham in the
nature of the sacrifice he must make. Again, close to his
death, Isaac voices his final prayer in four stanzas of
decasyllabic verse, rhyming aab aab bb cc (ll. 10358-397).
After the angel withholds the sword (ll. 10502-513) Abraham
gives thanks to God in a twelve-line stanza of decasyllables,

rhyming <u>aab</u> <u>aab</u> <u>bbc</u> <u>bbc</u>. The last lines of this hymn of
praise lead into a short song of joy, written in five-
syllable lines:

> Doy je chanter, crier, plorer, ou braire
> Pour mieulx louer la puissance de Dieu?
>   O povre vieillart,
>   Tu seras gaillart,
>   Le Dieu triumphant
>   Dessus ton enfant
>   A eu son regart.
>   (ll. 10512-518)

This last is an excellent example of how a shift in metre
corresponds to a change in the mood of the speaker.

One other literary technique used with good effect in
the play is the division of lines between speakers. Examples are too numerous to cite but a glance at the text
will show that the breaking-up of the lines lightens the
dialogue and makes it more realistic.

While all the traits mentioned thus far bear witness
to the author's desire to make of his play a work of art,
his literary concern is probably best demonstrated in the
structure of the play. By his arrangement of the well-known
material the playwright has achieved a remarkably close-
knit, balanced drama. If one excludes short passages which
may be considered as prologue (ll. 9365-434) and epilogue
(ll. 10527-598), the play proper falls into three divisions
which, for the sake of convenience, may be called "acts."[8]
Act I (ll. 9435-712) leads up to, but does not include, the
delivery of God's message to Abraham. Act II (ll. 9713-
10282) brings Ceraphin before the patriarch. When Abraham
hears God's command he laments but none the less sets about
obeying. Act III (ll. 10283-10526) presents Isaac's deli-
verance and the sacrifice of the lamb in his stead. A more
detailed analysis of the structure of these three acts
follows.

Act I (ll. 9435-712)

Scene 1 (ll. 9435-515) <u>Procès de paradis</u>. God announces
He will arrange a prefiguration of
the Crucifixion, using Abraham and
Isaac to represent God and Christ.
Miséricorde protests.

Scene 2 (ll. 9516-33) Abraham sends his shepherds into
the fields.

Scene 3 (ll. 9534-49) Isaac asks permission to go with
the shepherds.

Scene 4 (ll. 9550-567) Isaac plays games with the shepherds.

Scene 5 (ll. 9568-609) Abraham is overcome with sleep.

Scene 6 (ll. 9610-712) <u>Procès de paradis</u>. Details of the
sacrifice are given. God wishes
Abraham to offer his child "de
courage franc" (l. 9681).

In Act I the heavenly scenes frame those set on earth.
The themes of prophecy and prefiguration dominate the act.
Miséricorde, in her traditional role of advocate of humanity,
protests against God's decision, stating that He is asking
too much of Abraham's obedience:

> Ce luy sera ung trop grant dueil
> Se Isaac, qui est son enfant seul,
> A livrer a mort commendez.
>   (ll. 9496-498)

Thus already in the heavenly scenes of Act I the struggle
between the opposing forces of the play, God's command and
man's response (the expression of his human nature), is
established.[9] As yet the two lines of action, heavenly and
earthly, though projected, do not meet. The audience knows
what is about to happen but Abraham is shown in his humanity,
still ignorant of his fate. Abraham's unnatural drowsiness
shown in Scene 5 suggests that he will soon perceive a
vision. The audience's anticipation of the imminent crisis
mounts at this point.

Act II (11. 9713-10282)

Scene 1 (11. 9713-800)   God's messenger descends to
                              Abraham.

Scene 2 (11. 9801-828)   Abraham laments but prepares to
                              carry out God's order.

Scene 3 (11. 9829-879)   Procès de paradis. God demands
                              that Isaac, like his father,
                              agree willingly to be offered
                              in sacrifice.

Scene 5 (11. 9936-10022)   The journey begins.

Scene 6 (11. 10023-10062)   Abraham and Isaac climb the
                              mountain.

Scene 7 (11. 10063-10087)   The altar is raised.

Scene 8 (11. 10088-10097)   Isaac is told God's will.

Scene 9 (11. 10098-10168)   Isaac protests.

Scene 10 (11. 10169-10282)   Isaac submits to God's command.

     The structure of Act II is very different from that of
Act I but just as closely knit. Scene 1 is related to every
other scene because all action, both spiritual and physical,
results from it. The union is, however, particularly close
between Scene 1 (where God's command is delivered) and
Scene 2 (where, after hesitation, Abraham sets out to do
God's will); between Scene 1 and Scene 8 (where Abraham im-
parts God's message to Isaac); and between Scene 3 (where
God makes the condition that Isaac must die willingly) and
Scene 10 (where Isaac acts in accordance with this condition). The dominant theme of Act II is the fulfillment of
the prophecies given in the procès de paradis of Act I.
Although both father and son hesitate before submitting to
divine will, they nonetheless reluctantly advance toward the
moment where they will carry out the command. This movement
toward reconciliation with God is visually presented by the
journey toward the mount, the raising of the altar, and
Abraham's binding of his son for sacrifice. With temporary
fluctuations, the dramatic interest rises throughout Act II
until, in Scene 10, Isaac bows in obedience to God's will.

Act III (11. 10283-10526)

Scene 1 (11. 10283-10357)   Procès de paradis. God decides
                             to provide a lamb for the
                             burnt offering.

Scene 2 (11. 10358-10441)   Isaac prays. Abraham laments.

Scene 3 (11. 10442-10455)   Angel descends to save Isaac.

Scene 4 (11. 10456-10495)   The lamb given by God is dis-
                             covered and sacrificed.

Scene 5 (11. 10496-10526)   Abraham and Isaac rejoice and
                             prepare to go home.

        Act III presents what at first appears to be a hurried
conclusion to the play, since few lines of text are involved.
Yet the act contains three scenes that are dramatically and
spiritually important: the appearance of the angel to save
Isaac; the discovery of the lamb furnished by God; and the
burnt offering. Taking into account the stage effects that
would undoubtedly accompany these happenings one realizes
that the paucity of text is an inaccurate measure of the
dramatic effectiveness of the concluding act.

        Scenes 1 and 3 of Act III are closely linked to all
that has gone before in the play. They represent the result
of the prophecies set forth in Acts I and II. In Scene 1
of Act III dramatic anticipation begins to drop when God
declares Himself satisfied. It is completely released in
Scene 3 with God's message of mercy. Between these two
mystical scenes there is an interlude presumably introduced
to maintain some tension and also for a practical purpose,
to occupy the time it would take Ceraphin to descend and
come before Abraham. With the second appearance of the
angel the sequence of events set in motion by his first
coming is brought to an end. The tragic mood dissolves,
giving place to one of rejoicing.[10] The sacrifice of the
lamb and the burnt offering introduce a new rise in dramatic
interest. They also complete the plot and climax the
spiritual significance of the play. The sacrifice of the
lamb symbolizes the Crucifixion. The burnt offering suggests

purification by fire and the flames associated with the
coming of the Holy Spirit. It also provides a parallel
to the Eucharist. In Act III the spiritual and the dramatic
coincide. The last lines of Act III form a link between
the spiritual exaltation of the events just portrayed and
the return of the protagonists to everyday life. (Prologue,
ll. 9365-434 and Epilogue, ll. 10527-598.)

Thus far prologue and epilogue have been omitted from
our discussion. They stand outside the drama proper and
function structurally as framework. Yet as such they have
literary importance. The prologue establishes the earthly
situation of the play and introduces the characters. The
epilogue brings Abraham and Isaac back to the real world
and to the physical starting-point of the drama. In the
epilogue Abraham and Isaac rejoin the shepherds, travel
home, and relate their experiences to Sarah. Because of
this return in the epilogue to the scene of the prologue the
structure of the play could well be considered circular.
The playwright feels a need to round out the events dramatized, to bring his travelers back home. From a theological
point of view, however, the ending must be judged differ-
ently. Although Abraham and Isaac on their return appear
outwardly unchanged, they are, in fact, spiritually en-
lightened. They have stood the test, proven their devotion,
and received a sign of God's favor. They now have the
mission of proclaiming God's mercy. Thus, although the
external structure of the play is circular, from the point
of view of its didactic and dramatic content the end of the
play marks a new beginning rather than a return to the
starting-point.

In considering, now, the structure of the whole
Sacrifice d'Abraham the accompanying diagram may be helpful.

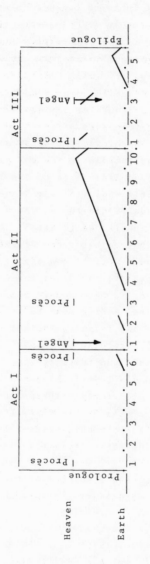

Rising lines indicate a rise in dramatic interest, falling lines a fall in
dramatic interest. The prologue counts 99 lines; Act I, 277 lines; Act II,
569 lines; Act III, 243 lines; and the epilogue, 71 lines.

The chart shows immediately many elements of balance and
symmetry in the structure of the play. The prologue matches
the epilogue. Each act contains two scenes at the heavenly
level of action or related to it. In Act I the two passages
of the procès de paradis frame the earthly scenes. In
Acts II and III the heavenly scenes form a different pattern.
In Act II the message from God sets in motion the human
problem presented by the play. It is quickly followed by
a scene in heaven. In Act III the process is reversed: a
supernatural scene is followed by the descent of God's
messenger to solve the crisis induced by the first appearance of the angel. The two pronouncements from God balance
each other. Isaac's acceptance of God's will at the end of
Act II corresponds to Abraham's acceptance early in the
same act. The journey to the mount in Act II parallels the
return journey in Act III and the epilogue.

From the point of view of interweaving themes the
structure of the play is more complex. The prologue and
Act I offer a glimpse of the human side of Abraham and his
family. They are as yet unaware that they will be summoned
to undergo special testing. One might call this theme of
"humanity" theme A. In Act I, also, and running parallel
to theme A, are the two scenes in the Court of Heaven. They
introduce three more themes: that of God's will (B); that
of the allegorical significance of the story (C); and that
of the struggle in the hearts of Abraham and Isaac, which we
may call AB, for it arises from the collision of A with B.
Theme C is revealed only to the audience. Themes A, B, and
AB are mingled in varying patterns in Act II, depending upon
the speakers and their moods. By the end of Act II themes A
and AB have yielded to theme B which remains dominant in
Act III until Scene 3, when it is replaced by joy. Joy in
its turn is caught up in thankgiving with the burnt offering.
This thanksgiving brings together all the themes that have
appeared previously in the play.

The student of medieval art and literature will recognize the characteristics of balance, symmetry, and the
interweaving of themes as traits long associated with the

medieval concept of structure.[11] The fact that they are so
abundant in the Sacrifice d'Abraham indicates that our dramatist took considerable pains to provide them for his play.
Evidently he knew that his carefully developed structure .
would be admired by his contemporaries as a mark of literary
excellence.

In conclusion, our study of the literary qualities of
the Sacrifice d'Abraham of the MVT shows that the playwright,
while remaining faithful to his Biblical source and the
teachings of the exegetes, used great literary skill in
preparing his play. He interpreted his characters with
sensitivity to make them comprehensible, contemporary, and
appealing to his spectators. He added a Sarah who is the
personification of the "realistic" medieval view of woman
and thus provided a contrast to the divinely directed male
characters. He embellished his work with irony, pathos,
ane variety in verse form. Finally he devised for his play
a firm structure in which balance is struck between heavenly
forces and human response. The multiple themes are entwined
and finally fused in the burnt offering in the last act of
the play. After a reconciliation between God's will and
man's nature has been achieved, the drama closes with a
ritual thanksgiving. The spiritual nature of the whole
work reflects the religious devotion of the author. The
effectiveness of the play as drama, however, is due to the
skill of the playwright in transforming Biblical history and
exegesis into dramatic literature.

A further point must be added. The Sacrifice d'Abraham,
although probably written about the mid-fifteenth century,[12]
was popular enough in the sixteenth to be printed several
times between 1500 and 1550. There remain to-day three
prints of the MVT dating from approximately 1500, 1520, and
1542.[13] As an independent play partial versions of the
Sacrifice d'Abraham dating from 1510 to 1520 are still
extant.[14] An expanded revision was put out by at least
two printers in 1539.[15] If one agrees that Théodore de Bèze
based his Abraham sacrifiant (1550) on the Sacrifice

d'Abraham this would extend the influence of the medieval
play to the end of the century and beyond.[16] Elliott,
noting the enduring popularity of the Sacrifice d'Abraham
in France at a time when the Abraham plays disappeared in
England, explains that the Reformation in England "brought
a virtual end to the dramatization of Biblical subjects"
(Elliott, p. 53). I do not believe that the lesser impact
of the Reformation in France than in England is in itself a
satisfactory explanation of the persistence of the French
play. I submit that it was the literary excellence of the
Sacrifice d'Abraham that caused it to survive. The play
was respected as a model by later playwrights. Each new
remanieur adapted the material to his particular point of
view but left the skeleton of the work, its structure and
its poetry, essentially unchanged. The continuance of the
tradition of the Sacrifice d'Abraham was no doubt due in
part to the religious significance of the story but even
more to the literary qualities of the play as it appeared
in the MVT.

Notes

1. See also O. B. Hardison, Junior, Christian Rite
and Christian Drama (Baltimore: Johns Hopkins Press,
1965), pp. 35-79.

2. Hardison, pp. 284-85.

3. First compiled in the tenth century, the Glossa
ordinaria remained popular into the Renaissance; see PL,
113-14 (wrongly attributed to Walafrid Strabo). See Emile
Mâle, The Gothic Image: Religious Art in France of the
Thirteenth Century, trans. D. Nussey from the 3rd French
edition (1913; rpt. New York: Harper, 1958), p. 138.

4. Le Mistére du Viel Testament, ed. J. de Rothschild.
SATF, 6 vols. (Paris: Didot, 1878-1891). Le Sacrifice
d'Abraham is found in II, 1-79. Hereafter the Mistére du
Viel Testament will be referred to as the MVT.

5. The procès de paradis had already been used with
success by Mercadé and Greban.

6. In the King James' version, Genesis xxii.7 reads:
"And Isaac spake unto Abraham, his father, and said, My
father: and he said, Here am I, my son. And he said,
Behold the fire and the wood: but where is the lamb for a
burnt offering?"

7. It is possible that these lines were intended to be sung.

8. In his discussion of the Sacrifice d'Abraham Elliott (p. 54) treats ll. 9365-712 as a prologue similar to those found in many English Abraham plays. In ll. 9435-712, however, the two major themes of the play are presented, to be developed in the rest of the play. Thus, in my opinion, only ll. 9365-434 should be considered as prologue and ll. 9435-712 as Act I.

9. Elliott (p. 55) sees this protest as occurring first in the 1539 version (see infra, n. 15). It is, however, already present in the MVT version in these lines spoken by Miséricorde.

10. This is the moment where the movement from tristia to gaudium, mentioned above, takes place.

11. On structure in the medieval drama see Moshé Lazar's article, "Dramatisation de la matière biblique dans le Mistère du Viel Testament [Joseph et ses frères]" in Mélanges Rita Lejeune (Gembloux: Duculot, 1969), II, 1435-51. See also on microfilm the unpublished doctoral dissertation of Carol J. Terrill, "The Conflict between Good and Evil as a Structural Influence in Medieval French Drama," DAI, 34 (1974), 3359A-60A (Kan.).

12. For probable date of the earliest plays of the MVT see my critical edition of the first three parts of the MVT: 'La Creacion,' 'La Transgression,' and 'l'Expulsion' of the 'Mistère du Viel Testament,' ed. B. M. Craig. Univ. of Kansas Humanistic Studies, 37 (Lawrence, 1968) p. 1, n. 3.

13. Rothschild I, pp. xxi, xxiv, and xxvi.

14. See Le Recueil Trepperel, facsimilé des trente-cinq pièces de l'original, ed. E. Droz (Geneva: Slatkine Reprints), p. 14, and Rothschild VI, 231-39.

15. Rothschild I, xxx and II, xlix. The fact that so many prints of the Sacrifice d'Abraham have survived suggests many more existed.

16. I tend to agree with the editors of the most recent edition of the Abraham Sacrifiant that Bèze may have been inspired by the Sacrifice d'Abraham but did not base his text on it. See Abraham sacrifiant, ed. K. Cameron, K. M. Hall, and F. Higman (Geneva: Droz, 1967), p. 13.

Part V

Conscience

STUDIES IN MODERN FRENCH LITERATURE

ROMANTIC HEROISM IN STENDHAL'S LE ROUGE ET LE NOIR: A VICTORY OVER THE "MACHINE"

James F. Hamilton

Two major theses dominate the history of criticism on Le Rouge et le Noir. The most widely accepted interpretation, that the story of Julien Sorel is the victory of the true self over the artificial self, emphasizes the moral dimension of the hero's struggle.[1] The other view contends that Le Rouge is a political novel, as promised by its subtitle-- Chronique du XIXe siècle--which dramatizes class conflict during the reactionary Restoration.[2] The contradictory truths of romantic heroism and social realism converge in certain motifs. The best known, that of "walls," combines the ideas of social division and estrangement.[3] Another motif, one which has not received sufficient attention, is the "machine." It sets the tone at the beginning and end of the novel, from the textile and saw mills to the guillotine. The motif and related theme of automatism provide an objective way of choosing between the two major theses and a balanced approach to the novel as a whole by corresponding more closely to the author's presentation of opposing forces. They pit material reality against heroism.

The Rouge opens with a brief, picturesque description of Verrières which quickly gives way, in the second paragraph, to an account of its industrial activity. Textile mills powered by mountain torrents have brought prosperity to the town "depuis la chute de Napoléon."[4] Instead of supplying additional information as to the historical moment, Stendhal devotes the entire third paragraph to one particular machine. It dominates Verrières with an overpowering din:

> A peine entre-t-on dans la ville que l'on est étourdi
> par le fracas d'une machine bruyante et terrible en
> apparence. Vingt marteaux pesants, et retombant avec

201

un bruit qui fait trembler le pavé, sont élevés par
une roue que l'eau du torrent fait mouvoir. Chacum
de ces marteaux fabrique, chaque jour, je ne sais
combien de milliers de clous. (p. 4)

The long passage (half of which is quoted above) not only
introduces the owner, M. de Rênal; it symbolizes the reign-
ing mentality of the Restoration which demanded conformity
to utilitarian modes of thought and behavior. The rapport
between M. de Rênal and his machine is made clear by the
Mayor's mechanical way of thinking. Despite his hatred of
Father Chélan, he decides to engage his protégé, Julien
Sorel, as a tutor. The young man had studied theology for
three years with the intention of entering the seminary,
and M. de Rênal concludes: "Il n'est donc pas libéral, et
il est latiniste" (p. 13).

Another machine sets the stage for the first view of
Julien Sorel, and it is also described in detail: "Une
scie à eau se compose d'un hangar au bord d'un ruisseau.
. . . . C'est une roue mise en mouvement par le ruisseau
qui fait aller ce double mécanisme; celui de la scie qui
monte et descend, et celui qui pousse doucement la pièce
de bois vers la scie, qui la débite en planches" (p. 16).
The saw represents the romantic destiny of Julien which
is "put into motion" by the Mayor's visit to Sorel's mill.
When the boy is knocked down from the rafters by his envious, conniving father and barely spared from falling
to a sure death, the reader is made aware that Julien Sorel
is marked for a violent end.

When the two machines are juxtaposed, they offer
different, competing views of life. In order to ascertain
the particular character of Le Rouge et le Noir, one must
decide which of them prevails. To grant precedence to
M. de Rênal's hammer machine is to emphasize the socio-
economic determinism of the historical moment. From this
perspective, Le Rouge is read as an historical novel about
the conflicts between the Ultras and the Liberals, the
Jansenists and the Jesuits in post-revolutionary France;

and Julien Sorel is regarded as a plebeian who fails in his
revolt against arbitrary authority and social injustice.[5]

If, on the other hand, one regards the hazardous situation of Julien perched above the saw as typifying the novel
(in the tradition of René seated on the edge of a volcano),
it becomes the story of a personal destiny which transcends
the contending political forces, the struggle of a superior
individual to achieve personal identity.[6] I maintain that
Julien Sorel liberates himself from the Restoration by surmounting the "machines" of society--its social and moral
codes--and by overcoming automatism--a conduct conditioned
by the Napoleonic code of glory and fortune--so as to attain
full stature as a Romantic Hero. The concept is fundamental
to romanticism.[7] It illuminates the moral elevation of
Julien at the end of Le Rouge et le Noir, which testifies
to his victory over the mediocrity and materialism of
France in 1830.

Julien's romantic heroism consists at first of a
potential; he has a superior intelligence and an acute
sensitivity. His ambition, although motivated by an heroic
ideal of Napoleonic conquest, is tainted by a profound sense
of inferiority and self-contempt. An automatic way of thinking governs his being. He judges everything on the basis of
his three major reading experiences--the Mémorial de Sainte-
Hélène, the imperial army bulletins, and the Confessions.
For example, he is revolted by the idea of becoming a tutor
in the Mayor's household because of Rousseau's repugnance to
eating with servants (p. 20) and Napoleonic glory leads him
to regard women in terms of "an heroic duty" to dominate
them (p. 55). His ideas are transformed into a code which
becomes a second nature to the detriment of his real self.
Out of necessity, he memorizes the Gospel; adopts a mask,
the black suit of a seminarian; employs deceit in order to
succeed, as in the slander of Elisa. Thus, the moral distance between Julien Sorel and M. Valenod, the superinten-
dent of the Verrières workhouse, is initially insignificant.
Each compensates for his humble origins, plans to humiliate

the Mayor by making Mme de Rênal a mistress, is ready to
destroy others in order to achieve success.

Julien avoids the corruption of M. Valenod and the
stereotype of M. de Rênal, "cet automate de mari," through
the uplifting grace of romantic love (p. 114). Although
intending to seduce Mme de Rênal as a test of his courage,
Julien's pride submits to the beauty of love. It opens up
a new world for him in which victory is mutual and obtained
through surrender, and it creates a spiritual need on his
part which is never fulfilled by his future advancements.
The harmony between Julien and Mme de Rênal is foreshadowed
soon after their arrival at Vergy, the country estate, where
they literally construct their own "way" in life, a little
gravel path around the orchard and under the walnut trees
(p. 48). Planned and completed without the approval of
M. de Rênal, the path negates his Cours de la Fidélité
through its spontaneity and promise of freedom.

The love of Mme de Rênal and Julien verifies the
novel's romantic character. Its energy liberates Mme de
Rênal from the confining roles of mother and obedient,
passive wife. She is reborn in the spring setting of Vergy.
Her impulsive, daring conduct belies the image imposed upon
her by the Mayor, a little "machine" vulnerable to disrepair
because of its weakness (p. 47). Such automatic reasoning,
whether that of an Ultra or Julien's military ethic, proves
to be inapplicable in the realization of romantic love.
Despite the nocturnal garden scene where Julien grabs her
hand as the clock strikes ten, he succeeds in seducing Mme
de Rênal not through his schemes but because of his spontaneous submission to her anger: "En effet, il devait à
l'amour qu'il avait inspiré et à l'impression imprévue
qu' avaient produite sur lui des charmes séduisants, une
victoire à laquelle ne l'eût pas conduit toute son adresse
si maladroite" (p. 86).

Paradoxically, it is Julien's lucidity and courage,
those qualities considered to be prerequisite for success
in the political world, which make him fear love and render

him incapable of achieving its perfection: "Au lieu d'être
attentif aux transports qu'il faisait naître, et aux remords
qui en relevaient la vivacité, l'idée du devoir ne cessa
jamais d'être présente à ses yeux. Il craignait un remords
affreux et un ridicule éternel, s'il s'écartait du modèle
idéal qu'il se proposait de suivre" (p. 86). When Julien is
finally convinced that Mme de Rênal no longer regards him as
an inferior, he responds to love and appreciates its spiritual quality; but, this change does not occur until Julien
transcends reason. His self-doubts disappear, and he experiences a life outside of the historical moment with its
political rivalries: "Je ne suis pas auprès d'elle un
valet de chambre chargé des fonctions d'amant. Cette crainte
éloignée, Julien tomba dans toutes les folies de l'amour,
dans ses incertitudes mortelles. . . . Au milieu de ces
alternatives d'amour, de remords et de plaisir, les journées
passaient pour eux avec la rapidité de l'éclair. Julien
perdit l'habitude de réfléchir" (pp. 116-17).

The love of Mme de Rênal and Julien proves to be im-
perfect for it is prone to regress into mechanical modes
of thought and conduct. Metaphorically, the tensions of
Verrières threaten to overwhelm the harmony of Vergy. For
example, after returning from the country, Julien delivers
an enthusiastic eulogy of Napoleon, "l'homme envoyé de Dieu
pour les jeunes Français," and he takes offense at Mme de
Rênal's cold disapproval (p. 93). Overreacting in an
interior monologue, he rages in terms so totalitarian that
they surpass the arbitrary actions of his rivals:

> Que deviendraient-ils ces nobles, s'il nous était
> donné de les combattre à armes égales! Moi, par
> exemple, maire de Verrières, bien intentionné,
> honnête homme comme l'est au fond M. de Rênal!
> comme j'enlèverais le vicaire, M. Valenod et toutes
> leurs friponneries! comme la justice triompherait
> dans Verrières! Ce ne sont pas leurs talents qui
> me feraient obstacle (p. 94).

Similarly, Mme de Rênal retreats to her habitual pattern of
thinking when the youngest of her children, Stanislas, be-

comes seriously ill. Like Julien, she continues to be subject to her formative experiences, a convent education, and
she interprets the illness as God's punishment for her in-
fidelity (p. 113). Thus, Mme de Rênal and Julien do not
immediately attain the romantic's freedom from convention.

The fear of damnation is overcome by the immediate
danger posed by an anonymous letter to her husband. It
inspires great courage and brilliant diplomacy on her part,
which surprises Julien (p. 134). Free of ideology and
unconscious of her wealth, Mme de Rênal derives more self-
understanding from love initially than Julien: "Mme de
Rênal eut un instant l'illusion que Julien pourrait accepter
les offres de M. Valenod et rester à Verrières. Mais ce
n'était plus cette femme simple et timide de l'année précé-
dente; sa fatale passion, ses remords l'avaient éclairée"
(p. 156). She suffers more than Julien from the necessity
of his departure for the seminary in Besançon and she
attains heroism first. Although realizing her need of
Julien, she sacrifices herself by thinking first of his
fate--the resurgence of his idée fixe which degrades his
real character: "Loin de moi, Julien va retomber dans ses
projets d'ambition si naturels quand on n'a rien" (p. 156).

While Julien remains far less lucid as to the meaning
of love in his life, he does realize that a radical change
has taken place in his view of the world. Although accus-
tomed to scorning his peasant father and brothers, who hate
him in turn, he is surprised at his reaction to M. Valenod's
dinner party. He is disgusted by the host's flaunting of
luxury and the pretentions to learning on the part of the
guests, rich liberals (pp. 139-41). Julien's manners have
been refined in the noble society of M. de Rênal and his
sentiments have achieved an acute délicatesse through love.
Hence, he feels for the first time like an aristocrat: "Il
se trouvait tout aristocrate en ce moment, lui qui pendant
longtemps avait été tellement choqué du sourire dédaigneux
et de la supériorité hautaine qu'il découvrait au fond de
toutes les politesses qu'on lui adressait chez M. de Rênal"

(p. 142). His sense of superiority continues in Besançon,
where he feels contempt and then pity for the ignorant,
loutish seminarians whose idea of happiness consisted of
a good diet, suit of clothes, and exemption from manual
labor (p. 182).

Julien's disdain approaches the misanthropy of René,
who renounced society. It is noticed by M. de La Mole:
"Les autres provinciaux qui arrivent à Paris admirent tout,
pensait le marquis; celui-ce hait tout" (pp. 273-74). Consequently, Julien scorns all segments of society and rises
above the traditional conflict of classes. Through a heroic
self-concept, delicate sensitivity, and refined taste, he
gains membership in the natural elite of intelligence and
heart. His superiority attracts Mathilde de La Mole in
spite of herself, and she compares him to Robespierre,
Danton, Roland, and Boniface de La Mole. Similarly, Father
Pirard and M. de La Mole, being unable to account for his
spirit, suspect that Julien is of noble blood (pp. 233, 275).

The rapid advancement of Julien is made possible by the
heroic demands of love, whose intrigues unfold in two circumstances of archetypal meaning. They hold the key to his
success in surmounting the fixed forms of society (class distinction, roles, and decorum) and prepare the novel's conclusion. First of all, happiness is associated with crime
in Le Rouge et le Noir. When Mme de Rênal interprets the
illness of Stanislas as a punishment for her adultery, this
feeling of sin taints the innocence of love but exalts its
passion to the point of becoming deformed:

> Leur bonheur était désormais d'une nature bien
> supérieure, la flamme qui les dévorait fut plus
> intense. Ils avaient des transports pleins de
> folie. Leur bonheur eût paru plus grand aux yeux
> du monde. Mais ils ne retrouvèrent plus la sérénité
> délicieuse, la félicité sans nuages, le bonheur
> facile des premières époques de leurs amours, quand
> la seule crainte de Mme de Rênal était de n'être
> pas assez aimée de Julien. Leur bonheur avait
> quelquefois la physionomie du crime (p. 117).

By disregarding convention, romantic love assumes the aspect of a crime against society. In its extreme form, this violent outcome is sought as an end in itself, a release from boredom: "S'exposer au danger élève l'âme et la sauve de l'ennui" (p. 308). Because Julien Sorel and Mathilde de La Mole feel oppressed by the monotonous Parisian salons, where opinions political and religious are forbidden, they are attracted to one another by their potential for unpredictable action. Julien is fascinated by Mathilde's M Machiavellian duplicity and spontaneity: "Alors, pour achever le charme, il la croyait une Catherine de Médicis. Rien n'était trop profond ou scélérat, pour le caractère qu'il lui prêtait" (pp. 318-19). For Mathilde, only the sentence of death confers honor on a man; and she sees this potential in Julien (p. 285).

Such heroic ideals harness the energy provided by love to political purposes and foster a relationship prone to self-destructive violence. For example, Julien raises a dagger against Mathilde during his first visit to her room (p. 341) and he later re-establishes their intimacy by threatening her with a medieval sword taken from the library wall (p. 347). This dark side of romanticism is given vent at the ball where Julien eulogizes crime for its own sake: "Tant pis! dit Julien; du moins, quand on fait des crimes, faut-il les faire avec plaisir: ils n'ont que cela de bon, et l'on ne peut même les justifier un peu que par cette raison" (p. 293). Thus, when passion is divorced from the moral content of romantic love, it becomes nihilistic.

From the early nineteenth-century perspective of Stendhal, the association of love and crime makes sense. In a society characterized by hypocrisy and false distinctions, the natural inclination of love becomes frustrated by the demands of corrupt institutions such as the marriage of convenience. A literary precedent exists in Rousseau's La Nouvelle Héloïse, which is used as a guide to love by Julien (pp. 164, 340) and Mathilde (p. 309). As the dominant moral link of man with the pre-political "state of

nature," love offers the would-be revolutionary some hope
for change. It is alone capable of releasing the primitive
forces of passion which dare to defy the relentless "machine"
of society. For example, the demands of the heart compel
Mme de Rênal and Mathilde de La Mole to betray the interests
of their families and class.

Paradoxically, such "crimes" have the potential of
restoring the balance between the internal and external
worlds as witnessed by the second archetypal situation of
Julien's first "imprisonment." After his nocturnal visit
with Mme de Rênal upon leaving the seminary for his new
post in Paris, he spends the day in one of his mistress'
bedrooms as her contented "prisoner" (p. 233). The rapport
between prison and happiness is verified subsequently during
Julien's mission to England. He seeks out the English
philosopher, Philip Vane, who is finishing his seventh year
of imprisonment by the aristocracy, and is astonished by the
prisoner's happiness: "Julien le trouva gaillard; la rage
de l'aristocratie le désennuyait. Voilà, se dit Julien en
sortant de prison, le seul homme gai que j'aie vu en
Angleterre" (p. 276).

Stendhal's romantic portrayal of love through the
related themes of crime and imprisonment is moderated by
the realistic portrayal of its potentially destructive
effects. Julien's identity is imperiled by Mathilde de
La Mole, who imposes upon him a courtly code of conduct
which subjugates his will and undermines his self-confi-
dence. At one point, he is tempted to fall on his knees
and to beg for mercy (p. 350). His suffering elicits no
pity for it affords Mathilde an immense enjoyment (p. 351).
The threat to Julien's self-esteem reaches a climax in
Strasbourg during a diplomatic mission. Absorbed in
thoughts of Mathilde and her rejection of him, he foresees
only failure in life (p. 390). Unable to exert his will, he
submits to the plan of his friend, Korasoff, and follows the
mechanical procedure of sending prepared love letters to Mme
de Fervaques in order to make Mathilde jealous. It appears
to succeed.

Material success does not restore Julien's romantic
identity. With the granting of a title and a commission
in the hussars, Julien devotes himself to maintaining the
trappings of his new station (p. 447). His change of roles,
from the black suit of a seminarian to the red uniform of
the military, entails a further deterioration of his moral
life. Passionate love yields to thoughts of a son who will
continue his new name as if he had given up his dreams of
personal glory. In fact, Julien feels that his romantic
destiny has run its course: "Après tout, pensait-il, mon
roman est fini, et à moi seul tout le mérite. J'ai su me
faire aimer de ce monstre d'orgeuil, ajoutait-il en re-
gardant Mathilde; son père ne peut vivre sans elle et elle
sans moi" (p. 444). Because his heart is silenced by cal-
culation, Julien does not realize the price of his success--
the loss of self. Fortunately, he is saved from a spiritual
death by a violent crime, the attempted assassination of Mme
de Rênal. His imprisonment substantiates the romantic
character of Le Rouge et le Noir.

To regard Julien as a "might-have-been" or as a martyr
(interpretations which he rejects) is to exaggerate the
political significance of his condemnation (p. 487). For
example, in his speech to the jury, Julien defends not so
much a political truth as a personal one by confessing his
plebeian origins which had formerly caused him shame. He
succeeds not only in freeing himself from caste complexes
but released briefly the provincial citizenry from its
material concerns through a high level of emotion. In contrast to the novel's opening scene, the pounding of machines
is replaced by the beating of hearts. Even the jurors, who
had been described by M. de Frilair as "des machines,"
return a verdict which contradicts his orders (italics
Stendhal's; p. 476).

Julien's real crime transcends Article 1342 of the
Penal Code, the conflict of classes, and the animosity of
M. Valenod. He feels "justly condemned" because of his
offense against Mme de Rênal and their love (p. 484).

His only hope for salvation depends upon the existence of
Fénelon's God, who will perhaps forgive him because he has
loved (p. 485). As a believer in love, Julien's last
efforts are dedicated to preserving his personal existence
against the clergy's desire to make him a martyr through a
false conversion, the charge of jealousy as the motive for
his crime, and the attempt to politicize his love by
those who encouraged Mme de Rênal to beg the King for
clemency. The moral force of Julien's passion derives from
the fact that it eludes the conventional contexts of religion
and politics:

> Votre âge, reprit gravement le janséniste, la figure
> intéressante que vous tenez de la Providence, le motif
> même de votre crime, qui reste inexplicable, les dé-
> marches héroïques que Mlle de La Mole prodigue en
> votre faveur, tout enfin, jusqu'à l'étonnante amitié
> que montre pour vous votre victime, tout a contribué
> à vous faire le héros des jeunes femmes de Besançon.
> Elles ont tout oublié pour vous, même la politique . . .
> (p. 505).

Julien's final struggle transcends political intrigues
and petty rivalries. He is forced to face the idea of death,
which is rendered terrible by the guillotine, a machine used
by society in order to humiliate the condemned through fear.
His first thought after being arrested is of the guillotine,
and he contemplates suicide as a means of avoiding the in-
dignity of a public spectacle (pp. 451, 457). During his
imprisonment, Julien exerts a constant effort to maintain
enough courage for the final test. A particularly difficult
moment follows the visit of Father Chélan, rendered depen-
dent by age, and Julien is seized by the fear of death which
he attempts to dispel by objectifying the guillotine:

> Il n'y avait plus rien de rude et grandiose en lui,
> plus de vertu romaine; la mort lui apparaissait à une
> plus grande hauteur, et comme chose moins facile. Ce
> sera là mon thermomètre, se dit-il. Ce soir je suis
> à dix degrés au-dessous du courage qui me conduit de
> niveau à la guillotine. Ce matin, je l'avais ce
> courage. Au reste, qu'importe! pourvu qu'il me

revienne au moment nécessaire. Cette idée de thermo-
mètre l'amusa, et enfin parvint à le distraire (p. 459).

After his condemnation by the jury, Julien calms his
nerves also by thinking of Danton's supposed observation
as to the impossibility of conjugating the berb _guillotiner_
in all of the past tenses (p. 485). However, unlike the
revolutionary, he cannot go to the guillotine consoled by
the idea of having made a significant contribution to his
country. Julien must look elsewhere for confirmation of his
personal worth and dignity. He succeeds. On the day of his
execution, the guillotine disappears from Julien's mind. No
reference is made of it. His courage remains firm. Moreover, bathed in a strong sunlight, he experiences the ecstasy
of romantic elevation, total detachment from the world
through immersion in the souvenirs of his love at Vergy:
"Jamais cette tête n'avait été aussi poétique qu'au moment
où elle allait tomber. Les plus doux moments qu'il avait
trouvés jadis dans les bois de Vergy revenaient en foule à
sa pensée et avec une extrême énergie" (p. 506).

In order to appreciate the ending to Le _Rouge_ et le
Noir, one must regard Julien as being happy at the moment of
his death and one must be happy for him. Even though the
novel ends with the burial procession in which the mechanical forms of thought and sentiment reassert themselves,
through religious ceremony and Mathilde's histrionics, their
meaning derives primarily by contrast with Julien's final
naturalness. They verify his identity as a man superior to
his fate, a misunderstood genius. Through a reversal of
values, politics is shown to be the realm of illusion while
truth is found in romantic love. The latter ceases to be a
game played by Julien in order to test his will power and to
reaffirm his purpose. It becomes his reason for being and
that of Mme de Rênal, who dies from heartbreak. Conversely,
politics becomes a game in which Julien declines to play
the role assigned to him, that of a repentant upstart. His
refusal exposes the corrupt Restoration "stage" and the
ignoble vindictiveness of its strutting actors.[8]

To conclude, Stendhal's Le Rouge et le Noir shows
itself to be an anti-political novel, a rejection of the
author's era in favor of imagination, energy for its own
sake, and the cult of passionate love. The romantic identity of the hero is verified, in my opinion, by his victory
over automatism. Limited at first to sporadic moments of
nervous release, Julien's detachment and moral superiority
are transformed into a complete state of mind and world view
at the novel's end. He overcomes the Restoration principle
of materialism, as represented by M. de Rênals' hammer
machine, through the ideal of love, and he transcends his
fate, as previewed by his near fall in the sawmill, by
accepting full responsibility for his actions. Similarly,
the heroic codes of conduct, the self-imposed one of Napoleon
and that of Mathilde de La Mole, give way to confidence in
his own goodness. Undaunted before the guillotine, Julien
attains the only distinction valued by the Romantic Hero--
"la noblesse du coeur" (p. 497).

Notes

1. See Francine Albérès, Le Naturel chez Stendhal
(Paris: Nizet, 1956), p. 415; Victor Brombert, Stendhal
et la voie oblique (Paris: Presses universitaires, 1954),
pp. 134-47; Michael Wood, Stendhal (Ithaca: Cornell Univ.
Press, 1971), p. 91.

2. See Maurice Bardèche, Stendhal Romancier (Paris:
La Table Ronde, 1947), p. 187; H.-F. Imbert, Les Métamor-
phoses de la liberté (Paris: Corti, 1967), p. 572.

3. See Martin Turnell, "Le Rouge et le noir," in
Stendhal, ed. Victor Brombert (New Jersey: Prentice-Hall,
1962), pp. 16-21.

4. Stendhal, Le Rouge et le Noir, ed. Martineau
(Paris: Garnier, 1960), p. 3. All references are to
this edition.

5. This view is represented by Bardèche, p. 220,
and F. W. J. Hemmings, Stendhal (Oxford: Univ. Press,
1964), p. 56.

6. See Pierre-Georges Castex, Stendhal: Le Rouge
et le Noir (Paris: C.D.U., 1967), p. 110, who contends
that Stendhal is primarily interested in portraying
individuals rather than the society of his day.

7.   See Richard B. Grant, "A Dilemma of the French Romantics: Myth and Sentiment," _Symposium_ (Fall-Winter 1969), p. 255, who theorizes that romanticism is best defined by the Romantic Hero.

8.   Stendhal refers most often to _Macbeth_ in his 1827 defense of Shakespeare. See _Racine et Shakespeare_ (Paris: Garnier-Flammarion, 1970), pp. 54, 56, 57, 76, 95.

ALTERED STATES OF CONSCIOUSNESS IN FLAUBERT'S
MADAME BOVARY AND KAFKA'S A COUNTRY DOCTOR

Leo Weinstein

The serious investigation of Altered States of Consciousness (ASC) has been pursued for only a relatively short
time; in fact, Charles T. Tart states categorically:
"Formal psychology in this century simply has not dealt
with ASCs, especially positive ASCs, to any reasonable
extent, considering their potential importance."[1]

While such vague terms as trance, hypnosis, dream,
and ecstacy have been used to describe such states, Tart
defines ASC as follows: "An altered state of consciousness for a given individual is one in which he clearly
feels a qualitative shift in his pattern of mental func-
tioning, that is, he feels not just a quantitative shift
(more or less visual imagery, sharper or duller, etc.)
but also that some quality or qualities of his mental
processes are different. Mental functions operate that
do not operate at all ordinarily, perceptual qualities
appear that have no normal counterparts, and so forth."[2]
Among the general characteristics of ASCs Arnold M. Ludwig
lists: alterations in thinking; disturbed time sense;
loss of control; change in emotional expression; body
image change; perceptual distortions; change in meaning
or significance; feelings of rejuvenation; and hyper-
suggestibility.[3]

In their work, much of which has dealt with the
effects of psychedelic drugs and mystical experiences, the
ASC researchers have largely neglected the testimony of
writers and artists whom Taine had been eager to consult
in his study of hallucinations.[4] On the other hand, their
experiments on the hypnagogic state, on dream consciousness, meditation, hypnosis, and the psychophysiology of

215

some ASCs offer fruitful instruments that may be applied
(with due caution) to the study of literary subjects.[5]

The purpose of this paper is three-fold: (1) to
examine whether recent findings concerning ASCs shed any
new light on phenomena described in Gustave Flaubert's
Madame Bovary and Franz Kafka's Ein Landarzt (A Country
Doctor), that is to say, whether or to what extent the
intuitions and observations of these two authors correspond
with experimentally observed states of consciousness; (2) to
compare the manner in which the two writers utilized ASCs in
their narratives; and (3) to evaluate the influence a
passage in Flaubert's Madame Bovary may have had on Kafka's
short story.

The passage in Madame Bovary opens chapter 2 of
Part I. Following are the pertinent parts of the section:

> Une nuit, vers onze heures, ils furent réveillés
> par le bruit d'un cheval qui s'arrêta juste à la porte.
> La bonne ouvrit la lucarne du grenier et parlementa
> quelque temps avec un homme resté en bas, dans la rue.
> Il venait chercher le médecin; il avait une lettre.
> Nastasie descendit les marches en grelottant, et alla
> ouvrir la serrure et les verrous, l'un après l'autre.
> L'homme laissa son cheval et, suivant la bonne, entra
> tout à coup derrière elle. Il tira de dedans son bonnet
> de laine à houppes grises une lettre enveloppée dans un
> chiffon, et la présenta délicatement à Charles, qui
> s'accouda sur l'oreiller pour la lire. . . .
>
> Cette lettre, cachetée d'un petit cachet de cire
> bleue, suppliait M. Bovary de se rendre immédiatement
> à la ferme des Bertaux, pour remettre une jambe cassée.
> Or, il y a, de Tostes aux Bertaux, six bonnes lieues de
> traverse, en passant par Longueville et Saint-Victor.
> La nuit était noire. Madame Bovary jeune redoutait les
> accidents pour son mari. Donc, il fut décidé que le
> valet d'écurie prendrait les devants. . . .
>
> Vers quatre heures du matin, Charles, bien enve-
> loppé dans son manteau, se mit en route pour les
> Bertaux. Encore endormi par la chaleur du sommeil, il
> se laissait bercer au troit pacifique de sa bête.
> Quand elle s'arrêtait d'elle-même devant ces trous
> entourés d'épines qu l'on creuse au bord des sillons,
> Charles, se réveillant en sursaut, se rappelait vite la
> jambe cassée, et il tâchait de se remettre en mémoire
> toutes les fractures qu'il savait. La pluie ne tombait
> plus: le jour commençait à venir. . . . Charles, de
> temps à autre, ouvrait les yeux; puis, son esprit se

fatiguant et le sommeil revenant de soi-même, bientôt
il entrait dans une sorte d'assoupissement, où, ses
sensations récentes se confondant avec des souvenirs,
lui-même se percevait double, à la fois étudiant et
marié, couché dans son lit comme tout à l'heure, traversant une salle d'opérés comme autrefois. L'odeur
chaude des cataplasmes se mêlait dans sa tête à la
verte odeur de la rosée; il entendait rouler sur leur
tringle les anneaux de fer des lits et sa femme dormir.
. . . Comme il passait par Vassonville, il aperçut,
au bord du fossé, un jeune garçon assis sur l'herbe.

--Etes-vous le médecin? demanda l'enfant.

Et, sur la réponse de Charles, il prit ses sabots
à ses mains et se mit à courir devant lui.

L'officier de santé, chemin faisant, comprit aux
discours de son guide que M. Rouault devait être un
cultivateur des plus aisés. Il s'était cassé la jambe,
la veille au soir, en revenant de faire les Rois chez
un voisin. Sa femme était morte depuis deux ans. Il
n'avait que sa demoiselle, qui l'aidait pour tenir la
maison.

Les ornières devinrent plus profondes. On appro-
chait des Bertaux. . . . Le cheval glissait sur
l'herbe mouillée; Charles se baissait pour passer sous
les branches. Les chiens de garde à la niche aboyaient
en tirant sur leur chaîne. Quand il entra dans les
Bertaux son cheval eut peur et fit un grand écart.

C'était une ferme de bonne apparence. . . . Une
jeune femme, en robe de mérinos bleu garnie de trois
volants, vint sur le seuil de la maison pour recevoir
M. Bovary, qu'elle fit entrer dans la cuisine, où
flambait un grand feu. Le déjeuner des gens bouil-
lonnait alentour, dans des petits pots de taille
inégale. . . . Le long des murs s'étendait une abon-
dante batterie de cuisine, où miroitait inégalement la
flamme du foyer, jointe aux premières lueurs du soleil
arrivant par les carreaux.

Charles monta, au premier, voir le malade. . . .
La fracture était simple, sans complication d'aucune
espèce. Charles n'eût osé en souhaiter de plus facile.
Alors, se rappelant les allures de ses maîtres auprès
du lit des blessés, il réconforta le patient avec
toutes sortes de bons mots, caresses chirurgicales qui
sont comme l'huile dont on graisse les bistouris. Afin
d'avoir des atteles, on alla chercher, sous la char-
retterie, un paquet de lattes. Charles en choisit une,
la coupa en morceau et la polit avec un éclat de vitre,
tandis que la servante déchirait des draps pour faire
des bandes, et que mademoiselle Emma tâchait à coudre
des coussinets. Comme elle fut longtemps avant de
trouver son étui, son père s'impatienta; elle ne répondit
rien; mais, tout en cousant, elle se piquait les doigts,
qu'elle portait ensuite à sa bouche pour les sucer.

Charles fut surpris de la blancheur de ses
ongles. . . .

Une fois le pansement fait, le médecin fut invité,
par M. Rouault lui-même, à prendre un morceau, avant
de partir.

Charles descendit dans la salle, au rez-de-
chaussée. Deux couverts, avec des timbales d'argent,
y étaient mis sur une petite table, au pied d'un grand
lit à baldaquin revêtu d'une indienne à personnages
représentant des Turcs. . . .

Tout, du reste, alla bien: la guérison s'établit
selon les règles, et, quand, au bout de quarante-six
jours, on vit le père Rouault qui s'essayait à marcher
seul dans sa masure, on commença à considérer M. Bovary
comme un homme de grande capacité. Le père Rouault
disait qu'il n'aurait pas mieux été guéri par les
premiers médecins d'Yvetot ou même de Rouen.[6]

Flaubert supplies us with exact data: the date is
January 7 (Rouault had broken his leg the night before,
while celebrating Epiphany), the distance Charles has to
travel is six leagues, i.e., some eighteen miles, he left
at 4 a.m. and arrived at daybreak, it was raining when he
left but the sun was shining when he arrived at the farm.
Flaubert displays the same precision in the detailed manner
in which he describes Charles' state of mind and his dream
experience during the ride which must have lasted about
three or three and a half hours.[7] Charles, still drowsy,
suffers a disturbed time sense (an ASC characteristic) since
he has no idea of the passage of time, and soon enters into
a hypnagogic state (the period after lying down in which it
would be difficult to say with certainty whether we are
awake or asleep). Flaubert's description of Charles' experiences during this time[8] corresponds strikingly to the findings of psychological studies.

To begin with, the time (between 5 and 8 a.m.) is
propitious for what van Eeden calls lucid dreams in which
"the reintegration of the psychic function is so complete
that the sleeper remembers day-life and his own condition,
reaches a state of perfect awareness, and is able to direct
his attention, and to attempt different acts of free voli-
tion."[9] Furthermore, in his dozing state, Charles sees

himself double, both student and husband. A similar experience of double-image dreaming was recounted by a subject in
a hypnagogic study who reported "seeing a train station on
which was superimposed an image of strawberrries."[10]
Judging from the content of the hypnagogic hallucinations
Flaubert describes, Charles was under the effects of a D
dream, i.e. one that contains implausible, unrealistic,
incoherent, and distorted material and during which the
subject suffers a complete loss of contact with external
reality.[11]

Concerning hypnagogic dreams, the authors differ from
Freud's view that night dreams are instigated by unconscious
wishes. "In the case of D dreams the instigator is the
reduced sensory input, or withdrawal, which produces a
regressed state. Hence unconscious wishes, if present, are
only a secondary result of the regressed state which allows
such everpresent wishes to emerge."[12] However they may be
produced, there are strong indications that unconscious
wishes are present in Charles' dream and a possible interpretation of it is intended to point out the importance of
the passage studied in Flaubert's novel.

At the moment when chapter 2 of Part I opens, Charles,
inarticulate as he may be, is far from happy. Both in his
profession and in his marriage he has been inadequate. As a
medical officer he has not done anything beyond simple
routine work; as a husband he finds himself completely
dominated by his older and unattractive wife chosen by his
mother and for whom he feels no love. It is significant
that, in his D dream, Charles sees himself simultaneously as
a student and husband. The former indicates that he has not
yet achieved mastery in his profession, the latter recalls
recent events in which his wife once more demonstrated her
power over him by insisting that he should not leave immediately. The dream may thus be viewed as the emergence of
an unconscious wish to overcome his inferior position both
as a medical officer and as a husband.[13]

As it turns out, Charles' visit to the Bertaux farm
will constitute a decisive step toward the fulfillment of
his unconscious wish. By healing M. Rouault's broken leg
his reputation changed from that of a student to one of "a
man of great capacity," and by meeting Emma Rouault he will
lay the foundations for a new marriage in which, for a time
at least, he will experience happiness as a husband. Thus,
in the passage discussed, the interrupted sleep and the
hypnagogic dream during the ride describe an incident with
a fortunate outcome and which will lead to one of the high-
points in Charles' life.

Considering the psychological information at Flaubert's
disposal, his detailed description of Charles' hypnagogic
experience is to a remarkable extent supported by current
findings.

Franz Kafka included his short story Ein Landarzt
(A Country Doctor) among the six works he had written that
he felt would stand the test of time.[14] Despite its author's
stamp of approval, the story figures among his most difficult ones to interpret; even so well-known an authority as
Heinz Politzer comforts the frustrated reader who may not
be able to make much sense of it.[15]

Its principal character is a country doctor who has
been called to the bed of a very sick patient but who stands
helplessly in the snow at night because his horse died the
previous night of exhaustion. His servant girl Rosa returns from the village without having found a horse, and
in disgust the doctor kicks at the door of his pigsty which
opens and reveals a man with "an open blue-eyed face" and
two horses. The doctor tells the girl to help saddle the
horses, but the groom seizes her and sinks his teeth into
her cheek. The doctor holds back his anger; but ere he can
take measures to protect Rosa, the horses carry him off in
the carriage and all he can hear is the door of the house
giving way under the onslaught of the groom. "Dann sind
mir Augen und Ohren von einem zu allen Sinnen gleichmässig
dringenden Sausen erfüllt. Aber auch das nur einen

Augenblick, denn, als öffne sich unmittelbar vor meinem
Hoftor der Hof meines Kranken, bin ich schon dort; ruhig
stehen die Pferde; der Schneefall hat aufgehört; Mondlicht
ringsum; die Eltern des Kranken eilen aus dem Haus; seine
Schwester hinter ihnen; man hebt mich fast aus dem Wagen;
den verwirrten Reden entnehme ich nichts."

(Then my eyes and ears are filled by a humming that
was rushing in steady rhythm to fill all my senses. But
that too lasted but a moment, for, as if the yard of my
patient opened up immediately next to my courtyard gate,
I am already there; the horses stand calmly; the snowing
has ceased; moonlight all around; the patient's parents
rush out of the house followed by his sister; I am almost
lifted out of my carriage; I can make no sense out of
their confused chatter.)

The patient is a boy who whispers in his ear: "Doctor,
let me die." The doctor takes out some instruments but puts
them down again. He reflects that in such cases the gods
are helpful by sending all that is needed. Only now the
thought of Rosa returns to his mind. And from this point on
his thoughts begin to wander, divided between the patient,
his desire to return home and save Rosa from the lecherous
groom, and his own situation as a country doctor. Meanwhile
the horses have pushed open the windows and are looking in.
The doctor refuses a proffered glass of rum and finally
listens to the heartbeat of the sick boy. He finds him
healthy and prepares to leave, but the sister shows him a
blood-soaked towel. Perhaps the boy is sick after all? The
doctor takes another look at his patient and discovers an
open wound near his right hip filled with worms. The boy is
past help, he concludes, but the family, seeing the doctor
busying himself, is pleased. In the presence of the village
elders, they undress him and place him in the bed next to
the boy. The doctor assures his patient that his wound is
not really so bad and then prepares his escape. Throwing
his clothes into the carriage, without bothering to dress,
he jumps on one of the horses expecting to return home as

fast as he had traversed the ten miles that separated him
from his patient. But now the horses seem to be crawling
through the snow. And the story ends as the unhappy doctor
bewails his fate. "Nackt, dem Frost dieses unglückseligsten
Zeitalters ausgesetzt, auf irdischem Wagen, unirdischen
Pferden, treibe ich mich alter Mann umher. Mein Pelz hängt
hinten am Wagen, ich kann ihn nichterreichen. . . .
Betrogen! Betrogen! Einmal dem Fehllaüten der Nachtglocke
gefolgt--es ist niemals gutzumachen."

(Naked, exposed to the frost of this most unhappy of
ages, with an earthly vehicle and unearthly horses, an old
man, I stray about. My furcoat is hanging from the back of
my carriage, I cannot reach it. . . . Betrayed! Betrayed!
Once taken in by the false alarm of the night bell--it can
never be remedied.)

It remains to be seen whether ASC studies can throw
any light on this strange story. Kafka's narrative method
offers one advantage over Flaubert's: there are no author's
interventions, since the story is told in the first person
singular, thus giving us a direct insight into the country
doctor's mental processes. On the other hand, Kafka's intent is obviously not limited to presenting a realistic
portrayal of events. One might argue, for example, that
the entire story reproduces a dream and, since all Kafka
interpretations remain necessarily hypothetical, such a view
could be defended. It does, however, not exclude an approach
that takes the story at face value while trying to discern
those portions of it which can be examined in terms of ASC.

As in Madame Bovary, the ride takes place during a
winter night and, like Charles, the Country Doctor has been
awakened from sleep (the night bell); moreover, considering
that his horse has died from over-exhaustion, it may be
assumed that he is in a tired state of mind. There is no
evidence that he slept or dozed during the ten-mile ride
(although this would be not unlikely), but his time sense
has obviously suffered, since the ride appears to him to
last only a moment. By contrast, his attempted return trip

seems painfully slow to the Country Doctor. A disturbed
time sense is listed among ASC characteristics by Ludwig.[16]
In addition, Robert E. Ornstein points out that "we seem
to construct our experience of duration from the filtered
contents of normal consciousness. When these contents
are artificially restricted, as in sensory privation, our
experience of duration shortens. Conversely, multi-dimensional complex experience causes duration experience to
lenghten."[17] On the same subject Ornstein refers to a
study by the psychologist J. J. Harton which found that
intervals containing successful events were estimated as
shorter than those containing failure.[18]

Objectively, the horses may be going at the same pace
during both rides. Besides the distance covered, the change
of weather from snow storm to moonlight would indicate a certain passage of time. How then can we explain the quickened
time sense? Despite his complaints about his job and his
patients, the Country Doctor displays unusual professional
zeal. Why else would he wait in the snow and let out his
frustration by kicking at the door of his pigsty? He is
so dominated by his stubborn determination to get to his
patient that the thought of Rosa disappears from his mind
until after he has arrived at his destination. Hence the
inexplicable appearance of the horses represents for him an
unexpected success in his mission. On the contrary, the
return ride not only occurs after a failure but the escape
is a total failure as well. Thus the success-failure theory
of Harton would offer a possible explanation of the Country
Doctor's disturbed time sense. It is also arguable that the
first ride is marked by sensory deprivation, as witnessed
by the absence of memory concerning immediately preceding
events (hence the shortened sense of duration) while during
the return ride a multi-dimensional complex experience can
be noted (the thought of Rosa, the abandoned patient, the
Country Doctor's nakedness).

The state of consciousness of the Country Doctor during
his medical service is more difficult to determine. He

arrives apparently in a state of numbness or as if just
awakened from sleep (he does not understand what is being
said to him), and the air is heavy in the room until the
horses push the windows open. Once the thought of Rosa
reoccurs to him, he gives signs not so much of absent-
mindedness as of a divided mind in which three concerns
(his medical service, his worry about Rosa, and his reflections about his professional situation) vie simultaneously
for his attention. This increase in emotional stimulus leads
in the Country Doctor to an ASC characterized by alterations
in thinking which, according to Ludwig, produce "subjective
disturbances in concentration, attention, memory, and judgment. . . . The distinction between cause and effect becomes
blurred, and ambivalence may be pronounced whereby incon-
gruities or opposites may coexist without any (psycho)logical
conflict."[19] This helps us understand better the Country
Doctor's lack of attention and concentration in examining
his patient and his passive acceptance of the treatment he
receives from the patient's parents and the village elders.

Whatever other purposes Kafka pursued in his works, it
is clear that he had carefully studied states of consciousness so that those of his characters are not arbitrary but
usually explicable in terms of recent findings.

It is well known that Flaubert figured among the
writers Kafka most admired. Aside from numerous references
to Flaubert in his diaries and letters, Kafka read the
French novelist with enthusiasm. Max Brod reports that he
and his friend read L'Education sentimentale and La
Tentation de Saint Antoine together in the original.[20]
Although I have been unable to find references in Kafka's
diaries to Madame Bovary, he certainly had read Flaubert's
masterpiece; in fact, one can discover enough similarities
in the two narratives studied above to suggest that Kafka
may have consciously used the framework provided by Flaubert
in writing A Country Doctor. To mention only the most
striking resemblances:

1. Both principal characters are in the medical profession, one a medical officer, the other a district doctor,
and both practice in the country. Neither of them seems to
be more than a routine practitioner.

2. Both are disturbed at night in order to care for
a patient.

3. In both narratives a groom, with horses ready,
and the doctor's maid appear. In Flaubert only a momentary
possibility of aggression is suggested ("L'homme laissa son
cheval et, suivant la bonne, entra tout à coup derrière
elle"), while in Kafka the groom first bites the maid's
cheek and then breaks down the door of the house in order
to attack her.

4. Both men start out in inclement weather (rain and
snow storm, respectively), but their arrival is greeted by
sunshine and moonlight, respectively.

5. In both narratives the horse or horses seem to find
their way with a minimum of guidance.

6. Both men are offered a drink. Charles takes his
with Emma while the Country Doctor refuses a glass of rum.

7. For both men the call to medical service represents
a potential opportunity.[21] Charles happens to come upon an
uncomplicated case while the Country Doctor encounters a
more complex one which, nonetheless, seemed not necessarily
beyond his competence, if he had not been rendered inatten-
tive by other preoccupations.

While these resemblances point to a more or less conscious recall by Kafka of the corresponding episode in Madame
Bovary, a major difference between Kafka's short story and
the passage in Flaubert's novel emerges. Whereas Charles'
visit to the Bertaux farm shows only positive results, the
Country Doctor's home visit ends in total failure. One might
be tempted to conclude that Kafka purposely took Flaubert's
basic elements and covered the rosy tints with pitch-black
color.

Notes

1. Charles T. Tart (ed.), <u>Altered States of Conscious-</u><u>ness</u> (New York: Wiley & Sons, 1969), p. 3.

2. Ibid., pp. 1-2.

3. Arnold M. Ludwig, "Altered States of Conscious-ness," in Tart, op. cit., pp. 13ff.

4. See, for example, Flaubert's letter in reply to Taine's questions in Hippolyte Taine, <u>De l'intelligence</u> (Paris: Hachette, 1948), II, 60.

5. In view of the relatively new field of ASC studies, this paper should be considered as experimental and subject to modifications as new evidence becomes available on phenomena examined.

6. One night towards eleven o'clock they were awakened by the noise of a horse pulling up outside their door. The servant opened the garret-window and parleyed for some time with a man in the street below. He was coming for the doctor; he had a letter for him. Nastasie came downstairs shivering and undid the bars and bolts one after the other. The man left his horse, and, following the servant, suddenly entered behind her. He pulled out from his wool cap with grey top-knots a letter wrapped up in a rag and presented it gingerly to Charles, who rested his elbow on the pillow to read it. . . .

This letter, sealed with a small seal in blue wax, begged Monsieur Bovary to come immediately to the farm of the Bertaux to set a broken leg. Now from Tostes to the Bertaux was a good eighteen miles across country by way of Longueville and Saint-Victor. It was a dark night. Madame Bovary junior was afraid of accidents for her husband. So it was decided the stable-boy should go on first. . . .

Towards four o'clock in the morning, Charles, well wrapped up in his cloak, set out for the Bertaux. Still sleepy from the warmth of his bed, he let himself be lulled by the quiet trot of his horse. When it stopped of its own accord in front of those holes surrounded with thorns that are dug on the margin of furrows, Charles awoke with a start, suddenly remembered the broken leg, and tried to call to mind all the fractures he knew. The rain had stopped, day was breaking. . . . Charles from time to time opened his eyes, his mind grew weary, and sleep coming upon him, he soon fell into a doze wherein his recent sensations blending with memories, he became conscious of a double self, at once student and married man, lying in his bed as but now, and crossing the operation theatre as of old. The warm smell of poultices mingled in his brain with the fresh odor of dew; he heard the iron rings rattling along the curtain-rods of the beds and saw his wife sleeping. As he passed Vasson-ville he came upon a boy sitting on the grass at the edge of a ditch.

"Are you the doctor?" asked the child.

And on Charles' answer he took his wooden shoes in his hands and ran in front of him.

The general practitioner, riding along, gathered from his guide's talk that Monsieur Rouault must be one of the well-to-do farmers. He had broken his leg the evening before on his way home from a Twelfth-night feast at a neighbor's. His wife had been dead for two years. There was only his daughter, who helped him to keep house, with him.

The ruts were becoming deeper; they were approaching the Bertaux. . . . The horse slipped on the wet grass; Charles had to stoop to pass under the branches. The watch-dogs in their kennels barked, dragging at their chains. As he entered the Bertaux the horse took fright and shied.

It was a substantial-looking farm. . . . A young woman in a blue merino dress with three flounces came to the thresh-old of the door to receive Monsieur Bovary, whom she led to the kitchen, where a large fire was blazing. The servants' breakfast was boiling beside it in small pots of all sizes. . . . Along the walls hung many pots and pans in which the clear flame of the hearth, mingling with the first rays of the sun coming in through the window, was mirrored fitfully.

Charles went up to the first floor to see the patient. . . . The fracture was a simple one, without any kind of complication. Charles could not have hoped for an easier case. Then calling to mind the devices of his masters at the bedside of patients, he comforted the sufferer with all sorts of kindly remarks, those caresses of the surgeon that are like the oil they put on bistouris. In order to make some splints a bundle of laths was brought up from the cart-house. Charles selected one, cut it into two pieces and planed it with a fragment of window-pane, while the servant tore up sheets to make bandages, and Mademoiselle Emma tried to sew some pads. As she was a long time before she found her workcase, her father grew impatient; she did not answer, but as she sewed she pricked her fingers, which she then put to her mouth to suck them. Charles was surprised at the whiteness of her nails. . . .

The bandaging over, the doctor was invited by Monsieur Rouault himself to take a bite before he left.

Charles went down into the room on the ground-floor. Knives and forks and silver goblets were laid for two on a little table at the foot of a huge bed that had a canopy of printed cotton with figures representing Turks. . . .

Everything, moreover, went well; the patient progressed favorably; and when, at the end of forty-six days, old Rouault was seen trying to walk alone in his "den," Monsieur Bovary began to be looked upon as a man of great capacity. Old Rouault said that he could not have been cured better by the first doctor of Yvetot, or even of Rouen.

--Gustave Flaubert, <u>Madame</u> <u>Bovary</u>, transl. by Eleanor
Marx Aveling (Paris, London & New York: Société des Beaux-
Arts, 1915), pp. 12-17.

7. Cf. Gabrielle Leleu, <u>Madame Bovary</u>: <u>Ebauches</u> <u>et</u>
<u>fragments</u> <u>inédits</u> (Paris: Conard, 1936), I, 56, which
indicates that Charles passed through Vassonville at 7 a.m.

8. Flaubert had studied this phenomenon closely as can
be seen from his letter to Taine: "L'intuition artistique
ressemble en effet aux hallucinations hypnagogiques--par son
caractère de <u>fugacité</u>--ça vous passe devant les yeux,--c'est
alors qu'il faut se jeter dessus avidement." Taine, op.
cit., II, 60.

9. Frederik van Eeden, "A Study of Dreams," in Tart,
op. cit., p. 150. The author recalls that Dante, in <u>Purg</u>.
IX, spoke of the hour when the swallows begin to warble and
our mind is least clogged by the material body.

10. Gerald Vogel, David Foulkes and Harry Trosman,
"Ego Functions and Dreaming during Sleep Onset," in Tart,
op. cit., p. 79.

11. Ibid., p. 81.

12. Ibid., p. 90.

13. Cf. Leleu, op. cit., pp. 53-54, where six versions
of this passage appear, one of which reads: "Et le tout se
mêlant, ne faisant qu'un. Au fond, cherchant quelque chose,
d'un désir inquiet, qui ne pouvait ouvrir ses ailes sur-
montées de plomb, tandis que le souvenir confus tournait en
place, en dessous."

14. Franz Kafka, <u>Tagebücher</u> <u>1910-1923</u>. <u>Gesammelte</u>
<u>Werke</u>. Hrsg. von Max Brod (New York: Schocken Books,
1948-1949), pp. 328-29.

15. Heinz Politzer, <u>Franz</u> <u>Kafka</u>, <u>der</u> <u>Künstler</u> (Berlin &
Frankfurt/M., 1965), p. 142. An excellent treatment of the
story can be found in Walter H. Sokel, <u>Franz Kafka--Tragik</u>
<u>und</u> <u>Ironie</u> (Munich-Vienna: Albert Langen, Georg Müller,
1964), pp. 267-73 and passim.

16. Arnold M. Ludwig, in Tart, op. cit., pp. 13-14.

17. Robert E. Ornstein, <u>The Psychology</u> <u>of</u> <u>Conscious-</u>
<u>ness</u> (New York: Viking Press, 1972), p. 85.

18. Ibid., p. 87.

19. Ludwig, in Tart, op. cit., p. 13. Some further
speculation on the mental state in question which Sokel,
op. cit., p. 299, calls the split will may be advanced.
Although Kafka gives no indication that the Country Doctor
ever enters into a hypnagogic state, his rambling thoughts
and his obvious physical exhaustion make such a hypothesis
possible. An example of dissociation of thought and image
was found in the study of Vogel, Foulkes, and Trosman, in
Tart, op. cit., p. 79, where "one subject reported he was
driving a car and simultaneously thinking about a problem in

linguistics." Presence of a hypnagogic state at an earlier
time is likewise indicated in a description of the Isakower
phenomenon which is closely akin to hypnagogic manifestations. Merton M. Gill and Margaret Brenman, Hypnosis and
Related States (New York: Wiley and Sons, Science Ed.,
1966), p. 109, n. 2, state: "The auditory impression is of
a humming, rustling, babbling, murmuring, or of an unintel-
ligible monotonous speech." This would correspond to the
steady rhythm of humming that filled the Country Doctor's
ears during the ride and his inability to understand what
was being said to him upon his arrival.

     Finally, the entire experience described in Kafka's
short story may be viewed as a fugue in three stages, as
defined by Gill and Brenman, op. cit., pp. 249-59. These
three states are: (1) Under severe emotional stress an individual goes into an ASC dominated by an intense drive
during which he may experience loss of identity. (2) Stage
one is terminated by a massive repressive maneuver and the
individual returns to his normal state with amnesia for stage
one and becomes aware of his loss of identity. (3) This
stage is marked by restoration of personal identity but with
amnesia for the impulse, affect, and behavior of stage one
and usually also for the loss or alteration of personal
identity of stage two. These stages show a certain corre-
spondence with the three parts of The Country Doctor:
(1) The drive to come to the bedside of his patient and the
ride; (2) the medical service and personal reflections of
the Country Doctor; (3) the return ride. A similar pattern
for somnambulism and fugues is outlined by P. Janet, The
Major Symptoms of Hysteria. 2nd ed. (New York: Macmillan,
1920), pp. 55-57.

     20. Max Brod, Uber Franz Kafka (Frankfurt/M.-Hamburg:
Fischer, 1966), pp. 46, nn. 8, 52, 54.

     21. Kafka's universe is, indeed, somber, but it con-
tains rare opportunities of which the characters cannot take
advantage because they are either too tired at the time
(such as K. when he happens to enter Bürgel's room at night,
in The Castle, ch. 18) or, like the Country Doctor, unable
to focus their entire attention on the difficult task to be
accomplished. For a relatively successful attempt, see Leo
Weinstein, "Kafka's Ape: Heel or Hero?" MFS, 8 (1962), 75-
79. Sokel, op. cit., pp. 272-73, points out the opportunity
the Country Doctor had to be a savior.

RELIGION AS A DRAMATIC TARGET IN TWENTIETH-CENTURY FRANCE

Charlotte F. Gerrard

The French theatre of today, marked by stylistic innovation,
conscious theatricality, and even hermeticism, shares with
its immediate past, the very drama it displaced, the theme
of antitheism. Before turning to the technical virtuosi of
the absurd, it is important to see that philosophically they
were really not so different from their predecessors. In the
early 1950s, Paris witnessed an outbreak of plays critical
of religious organizations, political injustice, and social
inequities. Bishop, archbishop, and accursed priest wander
through Sartre's Le Diable et le Bon Dieu; Alde and Benvenuta
are unofficial spokesmen for God in Thierry Maulnier's Le
Profanateur;[1] and Cocteau's Bacchus offers a great ecclesi-
astic in the Cardinal, as well as a mean one in the Bishop.
The theme of atheism, conscious or involuntary, runs through
these plays which have a common debt to Friedrich Nietzsche,
the author of The Birth of Tragedy.

Cocteau's Hans, the Bacchus of the title, and Maulnier's
Wilfrid the Profaner can each be considered a tragic hero
because both are tragically slaughtered by the establish-
ment.[2] However, they do not want to die; they are not burn-
ing for immolation like Polyeucte. Goetz, in Sartre's play,
is heroic like the other two but he is not tragic. What
looks during the forest asceticism like the overtures to
tragedy becomes a strong but slightly didactic ending. The
effect is as exultant as in Les Mouches, but there is too
much lesson, too little lyricism. Not his language but his
actions gain fascinated approval from the audience. In this
respect, Sartre is applying his theories of a "theatre of
situation," closer to Corneille than to Racine. Sartre
claims he wanted to deal with godlessness only in order to

examine today's man caught between the U.S.S.R. and the
U.S.A. in a sort of socialism. "Au seizième siècle, on
retrouve des problèmes analogues, incarnés dans des hommes
qui pensaient à Dieu. J'ai voulu transposer ce problème ·
dans une aventure personelle. Le Diable et le Bon Dieu,
c'est l'histoire d'un individu."[3]

The political question is undoubtedly as important as
the religious one. Probably the finest critic of the play
calls the situation Leninist, not Stalinist; "l'espoir est
dans la jeunesse des révolutions, le maléfice est dans leur
maturité."[4] This brilliant interpreter stresses Nasty's
importance, noting that while Goetz is converted to atheism
and Hilda "reste la conscience lucide de l'échec, de
l'altérité, du malentendu," Nasty is the one who finally
receives Goetz into the company of practical men.[5] Ricoeur
distinguishes between the effect on the reader and the
reaction of the theatergoer. The text focuses on politics
and ethics, while the production stresses the problem of
atheism.[6] For Ricoeur, Goetz may be guilty of bad faith
in the stigmata scene, but he really believes in God when
he is the ascetic talking to Hilda.[7]

It is possible to conclude that Goetz, through Hilda
and Nasty, gains support and conviction in brotherhood, but
not in divinity. It seems significant and fitting that "the
work of Jean-Paul Sartre was placed on the Index at approximately the time of the first performance of Le Diable et le
bon Dieu (Lucifer and the Lord) in 1951."[8] That is why
Sartre's denial of the opposition between his play and
Claudel's Le Soulier de Satin Slipper appears weak. Even if
the philosopher did not set out to write a rebuttal, he does
seem to study the same subject, what has been called "the
historical drama of the Renaissance when the great schism
split asunder the Church and a new civilization was
founded."[9] It is appropriate to add that Sartre, the philosopher of Praxis, surpasses the sombreness of religious
obedience to attain the bright light of a world full of
opportunity for the oppressed.

Cocteau also seeks reform in Bacchus, but the author
of La Machine infernale is true to himself. He wants the
individual to struggle valiantly, but he is sure the gallant
fighter for freedom will fail. The Bacchus legend of an
elected potentate, given carte blanche for a week, smacks of
Cinderella, or of the modern myth: King or Millionaire for
a Day. Yet in the contemporary drama of Western Europe, the
theme could have proven charming and original. The strident
protest of Mauriac and the fact that Le Diable et le Bon
Dieu preceded it by six months changed the reception of
Bacchus, made it a cause célèbre, and caused inevitable comparisons. Then when Maulnier's Le Profanateur reached Paris,
it became obvious that here was the most stage-worthy of the
three controversial plays, for it has a cohesiveness impossible in Sartre's four hours of tale-spinning, as well as a
bravura hero with flair. This man is commanding, utters
brilliant speeches, and the ladies all find him irresistible.

Yet, if Sartre's dramaturgy and diction are inferior,
Le Diable et le Bon Dieu offers a violent hero who is at once
a complex cynic, an illegitimate son, and an evil angel to
rival Maulnier's fascinating profaner. For the pious,
"Goetz's self-mutilation in the church is a desperate and,
because of the context, blasphemous parody of Christ's
stigmata accepted for the redemption of mankind."[10] The
leper's reaction to the kiss and his pleasure at receiving
Tetzel's indulgence "deflate Goetz's pious gesture." This
act and his humble washing of Karl's feet are "abortive."[11]
In short, to certain viewers, Sartre's play is very dis-
tasteful. To others, it is a variegated canvas that can be
called impious and mocking, majestic and rich.[12] The early
Goetz has been characterized "as the incarnation of evil, as
powerful as Lucifer and as convincing as Mephistopheles."[13]

To the religious critic appalled by blasphemy, Goetz
goes from antitheism to atheism, but Sartre goes in reverse.
"There is the only new idea of this play which otherwise is
only a rehash of laborious Sartrian theorems."[14] There are
those, however, who admire the philosophical power of his

drama to so great an extent that they "have not hesitated
to couple his name with that of Voltaire, and to compare his
influence with that of Voltaire in the eighteenth century."[15]
Intellectually, Sartre does appear as important to his time
as Voltaire to the Enlightenment. For sheer depth of
thought, Sartre surpasses the more dexterous Gide, and if
Valéry is as profound, Sartre is more accessible. Even an
unfavorable Catholic critic admits that Sartre has helped
to cure hypocrisy and has inspired the modern brand of
atheists, who can no longer believe simplistically in science,
progress, or Marxism: "The humanism of despair which Sartre
was outlining at that time, was in the air. There was, in
the will of Sartrian lucidity, a real grandeur."[16]

Contemporary atheists differ from their predecessors
by going beyond a mere attack on orthodoxy or ecclesiastical
organization. The dramatists immediately following World
War II call for independent action on the part of individuals. Whether Wilfrid refuses to become involved with
others or Goetz joins his fellow men in an egalitarian cause,
the iconoclastic heroes of postwar France are doing more
than blaming the Church. They are offering moral values
that are free of religious influence but may prove effective
guides to ethical conduct. A glance backward in time shows
an evolution in stage anticlericalism during the twentieth
century. In La Bigote (produced 1909), Jules Renard attributed the disaster of the mayor's marriage to his wife's
piety. Renard's attack was violent, open, but elementary in
that the priest had no chance to confront the mayor. Gide's
Tirésias in Oedipe (produced 1932) is roundly insulted, and
his confrontations with the proud hero are for the most part
very unpleasant. So too are they in Cocteau's La Machine
infernale. In Antigone (1944), Anouilh's man of compromise,
Créon, is a very sympathetic character who seems at least to
have logic on his side. With Les Mouches appears a fair
battle between Jupiter and Oreste; perhaps this is true
because Sartre is a brilliant dialectician.

In the plays here examined, there is always a scène-à-
faire: between Alde and Wilfrid in Le Profanateur, between

Hans and Cardinal Zampi in Bacchus, and between Goetz and
Heinrich. Since the dramatic conflict is sharper and more
complex in the later plays of the century, lovers of theological argument have increasingly been able to feast eyes
and ears. Yet, in these heretical plays of the fifties,
there is still perfect justification for speaking of anticlericalism, for churchmen are criticized. In Le
Profanateur, Alde is not a priest, but, just back from Rome,
he speaks for the Pope. In Le Diable et le Bon Dieu, the
Bishop is compassionate to the people but not to Heinrich;
the Archbishop is more like a temporal than a spiritual
leader; and Heinrich vacillates between commoners and
colleagues. He is pitiful but not praiseworthy. Bacchus,
as has been demonstrated, offers a complex, richly-conceived
Cardinal, but a stupid and narrow Bishop. Irrespective of
decade then, professed antitheists like Camus, Renard, and
Sartre, or ambivalent "Christians" like Cocteau and Gide can
all be called heretics and atheists, terms that are titles
of nobility to many freethinkers.

   Despite the differences noted in philosophical attitudes
and despite the difference in politics of men like Maulnier
and Sartre, there are more parallels than contrasts among the
playwrights of the 1950-1952 controversy in Paris. The common traits are: complete concern for the individual; absolute honesty with oneself; active opposition to bourgeois
values; hatred of charity, comfort, remorse, or penitence;
love of joy and life and the senses; and finally, inability
to believe in a Supernatural Being. All these traits point
to their mutual inspiration: Nietzsche's philosophy of
affirmation and denial of Christian faith. Even when their
anticlerical attacks are occasionally offset by fair and
favorable portraits of certain churchmen, their heroes are
Nietzschean in their fire, violence, and skepticism. In
Cocteau's case there is further evidence in La Machine
infernale; in Sartre's Les Mouches and the philosophical
treatise, L'Etre et le Néant; in Maulnier's Jeanne et les
juges. The orthodox critics who believe they discern a

hidden love of God in the theological preoccupations of
<u>Bacchus</u>, <u>Le Diable et le Bon Dieu</u>, and <u>Le Profanateur</u> are
deluding themselves and engaging in rationalizations.

The honest, serious, and responsible atheism of the
post-war theatre in France differs from the anticlericalism
earlier in the century. The criticisms contained in the
later plays are of a less emotional nature, deeper, and permit some favorable portraits of priests and prelates. The
case for religion is not summarily dismissed but becomes
rather the focus for certain scenes of powerful dramatic intensity. Such a scene is the one between Heinrich and Goetz
near the end of <u>Le Diable et le Bon Dieu</u>, but the scene that
shows clearer Nietzschean influence is the one in which they
make a bet to test whether Good is possible on Earth. As for
the other two plays, the outcome is Nietzschean in each case.
The dynamic Dionysian person is killed either because he
wishes to die free rather than to live, religiously fettered
(as in <u>Bacchus</u>), or because he is too individualistic to
give his support to an organized cause (as in <u>Le Profanateur</u>).

While in the early 1950s celebrated playwrights were
fomenting theological controversy, Eugène Ionesco was
quietly receiving his dramatic baptism. <u>La Cantatrice
chauve</u>, <u>La Leçon</u>, and <u>Les Chaises</u> were all staged between
1950 and 1952 and have become internationally famous.
Ionesco's theatre has been described as theological, a
theatre "où l'Homme est entraîné aux Enfers par le poids du
péché originel et où il essaye de retrouver la lumière, la
grâce, le paradis perdu. Mais, à la théologie de M. Ionesco,
il manque Dieu. Si l'homme se sauve, ce sera seul."[17]
Ionesco himself reproaches the theatre with being "améta-
physique" and clearly wishes to offer more than psychological, social, or even poetic theatre.[18] Like the dramatists discussed earlier, Ionesco makes certain criticisms of
religion: the murder by Christians of pagans and heretics,
the bestial opinion Moslems held of Christians, and the
tendency common to religious and ideological systems to
"donner aux hommes les meilleures raisons de se mépriser
réciproquement et de s'entre-tuer."[19]

In _Tueur sans gages_, Ionesco's hero resembles Sartre's
Roquentin. Bérenger speaks of a tumultuous emptiness which
overcomes him "comme au moment d'une séparation tragique,
intolérable. Les commères sortirent des cours, percèrent
mes tympans de leurs voix criardes, des chiens aboyèrent,
je me sentis abandonné parmi tous ces gens, toutes ces
choses. . . ."[20] Particularly during the third act, the
protagonist's alienation is overpowering. He walks alone
in the cold wind and breaks the silence intermittently by a
monologue which reveals his isolation.[21] Meeting the killer,
the hero discusses Christ's sacrifice and those of the
saints. Having failed to win the killer with charity and
love, Bérenger tries reason, pointing out that the murders
will not profit the killer. The shattering emotionalism
of the monologue reaches its climax when Bérenger confesses
to the killer:

> Moi-même, souvent, je doute de tout. Ne le répéte
> à personne. Je doute de l'utilité de la vie, du sens
> de la vie, de mes valeurs, et de toutes les dialecti-
> ques. Je ne sais plus à quoi m'en tenir, il n'y a
> ni vérité ni charité, peut-être. Mais dans ce cas,
> soyez philosophe: si tout est vanité, le crime aussi
> n'est que vanité. . . .[22]

Despite the possession of two pistols, Bérenger finally
confronts death by the killer's knife. His lyricism is not
inferior to that of Maulnier's _Le Profanateur_:

> . . . que ma force est faible contre ta froide déter-
> mination, contre ta cruauté sans merci. . . . Et que
> peuvent les balles elles-mêmes contre l'énergie
> infinie de ton obstination? . . . Mon Dieu, on ne
> peut rien faire! . . . Que peut-on faire. . . . Que
> peut-on faire. . . .[23]

The play ends on this desperate and hopeless note.

"Essentiellement tragique" is the way Ionesco characterizes the best work of Samuel Beckett, who treats the
totality of man and his multiple dimensions.[24] The plays
that seem particularly pertinent to the present discussion

are Fin de partie and En attendant Godot. In the former,
Clov, Hamm, and Nagg indulge in the Lord's Prayer, which
in Bacchus resulted in Cocteau's condemnation. Also in
Fin de partie, kitchen rats and sugared almonds vie with
God as subjects of conversation. Beckett too could be
attacked for sacrilege as the prayer is interrupted:

> HAMM: Silence! En silence! Un peu de tenue!
>   Allons-y. (Attitudes de prière. Silence.
>   Se décourageant le premier.) Alors?
> CLOV: (rouvrant les yeux). --Je t'en fous! Et toi?
> HAMM: Bernique! (A Nagg.) Et toi?
> NAGG: Attends. (Un temps. Rouvrant les yeux.)
>   Macache!
> HAMM: Le salaud! Il n'existe pas!
> CLOV: Pas encore.
> NAGG: Ma dragée!
> HAMM: Il n'y a plus de dragées.[25]

In Beckett's most famous play, En attendant Godot,
Estragon voices the desperate belief that "Rien ne se passe,
personne ne vient, personne ne s'en va, c'est terrible."[26]
Later, learning that Godot's visit is once again postponed,
Vladimir asks the boy messenger:

>   Il a une barbe, monsieur Godot?
> GARÇON: Oui, monsieur.
> VLADIMIR: Blonde ou . . . (il hésite) . . . ou noire?
> GARÇON: (hésitant). -- Je crois qu'elle est blanche,
>   monsieur.
>   Silence.
> VLADIMIR: Miséríocorde.
>   Silence.
> GARÇON: Qu'est-ce que je dois dire à monsieur?[27]

The gentle sadness of Beckett's tramps is far more pessimistic and despairing than the noisy anger of Sartre's Goetz.
When Estragon diffidently suggests they drop Godot, Vladimir
replies: "Il nous punirait. (Silence. Il regarde l'arbre.)
Seul l'arbre vit."[28] It is the poignancy of complete hope-
lessness, for seemingly nothing gives meaning to life's
monotony.
    If in this play there is no heroic opposition, no overt
challenge to God or his ministry, Adamov's Paolo Paoli is a

different story. There is a distinct note of anticlericalism in the portrait of the Abbot. He appears mild and
sports a holier-than-thou attitude, yet he is prone to
making deals and interfering. One of the chief characters,
an industrialist named Hulot-Vasseur, calls the Abbot "this
cassock-wearer,"[29] while Paolo calls him the capitalist's
"errand-boy, alias Vicar Saulnier" (p. 283). This priest,
believing himself to be right, advises the innocent escapee,
Robert, to return to a Venezuelan prison. However, this
religious rhetorician encounters the outspoken materialist,
Hulot-Vasseur, to whom he pompously says:

> Si donc, surmontant ces douloureuses hésitations,
> j'ai tout de même décidé de m'adresser à vous, dont
> les convictions sont . . . si diamétralement opposées
> aux miennes, c'est . . . (Très vite.) C'est qu'il
> y va du sort d'un homme.
> HULOT-VASSEUR: Vous ne pourriez pas parler comme tout
> le monde? (pp. 84-85)

Adamov's stage directions make clear his anticlerical view-
point: "The ABBOT, decidedly in eloquent fashion. You have
banished God from the schools, Mr. Hulot-Vasseur, but by so
doing you have banished France. He exists, furiously, but
very satisfied with his cliché" (p. 126).

In dealing with other characters, Adamov also demeans
religion, by intentional frivolity of tone. The entrepre-
neurs speak of manufactured bric-à-brac, "of crucifixions
and nativity scenes apparently like ours, but (In a tragic
voice.) low-priced" (p. 220). Towards the end of the play,
the pacifistic ex-convict is arrested through the machina-
tions of the Abbot, who believes smugly that "at the instant
when, on the battlefields, our wounded are calling for help,
it is criminal to allow discordant voices to arise back home"
(p. 281). He is given his comeuppance by the anti-hero, who
grabs the priest by the collar and shouts, "Just a minute,
Buster!" (p. 286). The curtain falls on Paolo's impious gesture of flicking off the priest's skullcap and on the boyish
cry, "Chapeau!" This ending smacks of a student prank rather
than of a respectful acceptance of clerical advice.

It has been demonstrated, though briefly, that Ionesco,
Beckett, and Adamov seem to treat some of the same themes as
did the heretical dramatists of 1950-1952; lack of faith; a
tendency to demean, diminish, or discredit organized religion; and sympathy for the individual's desire for freedom.
No dramatist, however, in the "theatre of the absurd" can
claim to equal Jean Genet in force and flair. When he treats
authority in Church and State, he excels, and quite understandably. His constant themes are sin and evil, and so he
has fascinated Sartre enough to be the subject of a long,
existentialist biography. Another ardent champion and
defender was the author of <u>Bacchus</u>, the late Jean Cocteau.

The opening of Le <u>Balcon</u> features Irma, the madam;
The Woman, the recounter of false sins; and The Bishop, the
imaginary creation of an ordinary man. Speaking of the
House of Illusion, the False Bishop affirms:

> Je le sais bien. Ici il n'y a pas la possibilité
> de faire le mal. Vous vivez dans le mal. Dans
> l'absence de remords. Comment pourriez-vous faire
> le mal? Le Diable joue. C'ést à cela qu'on le
> reconnaît. C'est le grand Acteur. Et c'est pour-
> quoi l'Eglise a maudit les comédiens.[30]

Here is how he defines his own role: "Or, évêque, c'est
un mode d'être. C'est une charge. Un fardeau. Mitres,
dentelles, tissus d'or et de verroteries, génuflexions.
. . . Aux chiottes la fonction!" (pp. 19-20)

Another client of the bordello harps on the subject of
Good and Evil. He is the make-believe Judge, who ritual-
istically interrupts the Hangman's sadistic beating of The
Female Thief. With "<u>infinite sadness</u>," he relates:

> . . . J'allais emplir les Enfers de damnés, emplir
> les prisons. Prisons! Prisons! Prisons, cachots,
> lieux bénits où le mal est impossible, puisqu'ils
> sont le carrefour de toute la malédiction du monde.
> On ne peut pas commettre le mal dans le mal. Or
> ce n'est pas condamner que je désire surtout, c'est
> juger. . . . (pp. 38-39)

Good and Evil, Heaven and Hell constantly play antiphonally.
Irma's favorite employee, Carmen, longs for her illegitimate
daughter, while the madam laughs wryly: "Tu es la princesse
lointaine qui vient la voir avec des jouets et des parfums.
Elle te place au Ciel.   (Riant aux éclats.) Ah, ça c'est
trop fort, enfin, pour quelqu'un, mon bordel, c'est-à-dire
l'Enfer, est le Ciel!"   (p. 64)

The revolution in Le Balcon provides a political
counterpoint to the upheaval in the souls of the characters.
Likewise, Le Profanateur was framed against a backdrop of
the Crusades, while the Peasants' Revolt provided the setting for Bacchus and Le Diable et le Bon Dieu.

The unconventionality of Genet's attitudes on religion
clashes with his own basic desire for saintliness, a desire
paralleled by Carmen's longing for sanctification.   Irony
abounds in Genet's portrait, and a kind of humor pervades
Irma's gift to Carmen of the St. Theresa role.   She adds,
however, "Ah évidemment, de l'Immaculée-Conception à sainte
Thérèse, c'est une dégringolade, mais ce n'est pas mal non
plus . . . (Silence.)   Tu ne dis rien?   C'est pour un
banquier.   Très propre, tu sais.   Pas exigeant."   Carmen,
however, longs for her dress, veil, and rosary.   The latter,
as Irma assures Carmen, is an accoutrement of the St.
Theresa fabrication as well, and the false nun will even
wear the wedding ring that symbolizes a spiritual union with
God (p. 70).

Despite all the sham, illusion, and pretense, there is
a genuine kind of religiosity at the end of the twelfth
tableau (p. 157) as the Bishop apostrophizes his ecclesiastical ornaments: "C'est à partir de vous, c'est pour mieux
vous mettre en valeur, que je dessine mes gestes."   Later,
a crowd scene is marked by the same kind of Dionysian frenzy
that characterized Bacchus.   The chief of police claims that
"sont encore une fête, où le peuple s'en donne à coeur joie
de nous haïr" (p. 171).   This same official, Irma's special
lover, discusses with the Bishop, the Judge, and the General

the relative hierarchy of royalty, God, the Triumvirate, the
Police Chief. The people have been left far below, on their
knees before God.

Examinations of man's relation to other men, to the
supernatural, and to his own hidden, inner Self are myriad,
but even a glimpse of the recent French drama shows its
metaphysical bent that stems from Nietzsche. French dramatists continue to search for the meaning of human existence,
when religious answers prove personally inadequate. With
Adamov, the tone may be sarcastic, the heroes non-existent;
with Ionesco, the language brilliantly shaded and semanti-
cally challenging, the theatrical style completely daring;
with Genet, a sensitively developed and self-imposed bar-
barity may electrify the stage; and with Beckett, a wistful,
tender, nostalgic desperation may prove most pessimistic of
all. Atheism, antitheism, and a measure of anticlericalism
have singed the Parisian stage throughout the twentieth
century.

Notes

1. For a discussion of this play, see my article,
"Thierry Maulnier's Le Profanateur: A Nietzschean Tragedy,"
Symposium, 26, 3 (Fall 1972), 212-25.

2. In this sense, their debt is to the early Nietzsche,
who analyzed tragedy. Maulnier has concluded that, after
the dream of the Superman, Nietzsche's new myth of the
Eternal Return was willing to subjugate man "in order to
save him from despair" (see Thierry Maulnier, Nietzsche
[Paris, 1943], pp. 272-73 and passim). Overly eager for
cosmic unity, Nietzsche quite early replaces "the tragic
idea of life" by a Dionysian cult of living (p. 274).
Throughout this article, the translations from the French
are mine.

3. Jean Duché, "Jean-Paul Sartre répond à la critique
dramatique et offre un guide au spectateur pour suivre 'Le
Diable et le Bon Dieu,'" Le Figaro littéraire, 30 juin 1951,
p. 4.

4. Paul Ricoeur, "Réflexions sur 'Le Diable et le Bon
Dieu,'" Esprit, no. 184 (novembre 1951), p. 713.

5. Ibid., pp. 714-15.

6. Ibid., p. 715.

7. Ibid., pp. 717-18.

8. Wallace Fowlie, Dionysus in Paris (New York, 1960), p. 179.

9. Ibid., p. 144.

10. S. John, "Sacrilege and Metamorphosis: Two Aspects of Sartre's Imagery," MLQ, 20 (1959), 58.

11. Ibid., p. 60.

12. Fowlie, p. 179.

13. Ibid., p. 181.

14. Charles Moeller, Littérature du XXe siècle et le christianisme, 4 vols. (Tournai-Paris, 1953-60), II, 94-95.

15. Fowlie, p. 167.

16. Moeller, II, 40, Since 1968, Sartre's political pendulum seems again to have swung back towards Marxism, so that the critic is partially wrong now.

17. Philippe Sénart, Ionesco (Paris, 1964), p. 114.

18. Eugène Ionesco, Notes at contre-notes (Paris, 1962), p. 169.

19. Ibid., p. 216.

20. Tueur sans gages in Eugène Ionesco, Théâtre, 3e éd. (Paris, 1958), II, 79.

21. Ibid., p. 159.

22. Ibid., p. 169.

23. Ibid., p. 171.

24. Ionesco, Notes et contre-notes, p. 114.

25. Samuel Beckett, Fin de partie, suivi de Acte sans paroles I (Paris, 1957), p. 76.

26. Théâtre I (Paris, 1971), p. 60.

27. Ibid., p. 135.

28. Ibid., p. 136.

29. Arthur Adamov, Paolo Paoli, 4e éd. (Paris, 1957), p. 32. Further references to this play will appear parenthetically in the text itself.

30. Jean Genet, Le Balcon (Décines et Isère, 1956), p. 17. Further references to this play will appear parenthetically in the text itself.

IN SEARCH OF THE CRYSTAL: THE POETICS OF LITERARY ALCHEMY
Mary Ann Caws

> la voie d'où l'on ne revient jamais
>
> Michel Leiris

I. The Alchemical Work

Like the literary work, the true alchemical work proceeds
irreversibly toward a knowledge that is its own value, a
grail made one with the quest. Unalterably opposed to the
vulgar concentration on "dead gold" or ordinary material
representation, of appeal only to the more superficial
spirit, is the deeper search for a living gold to be identified with light, or with its intensity. Consider the
following distinction: "False alchemists seek only to make
gold; true philosophers desire only knowledge. The former
produce mere tinctures, sophistries, ineptitudes; the latter
enquire after the principles of things."[1] Or the famous
dictum: "Aurum nostrum non est aurum vulgi."[2] The object
of the quest separates the true seekers from the false, as
if the more difficult notion were to choose its own followers.

Antonin Artaud defines the alchemical undertaking as
"the passionate and decisive transfusion of matter by mind,"
in Le Théâtre et son double, itself in part a manifesto of
alchemical belief and a defense and illustration of the
Work. Mircea Eliade, for instance, considers it to be of a
wider scope than such traditions as Christianity, for whereas
the latter concentrates on the single human microcosm,
alchemy directs itself to the remaking and salvation of the
whole man and nature with him. It was at its origin a metal-
lurgical process; now the myth of metallurgy, with its
obsessive instruments of hammer, forge, and anvil, is a myth
of birth and rebirth: to confer life, to bring slowly into
existence, is a noble calling, and a difficult one.

For the poets, since Rimbaud's "alchemy of the word,"
the remaking of the world by language has been the definition
also of the poet's task and the justification of its passionate intensity, an operation to be carried on at a white-hot
level. Lest it be thought, however, that verbal alchemy is
merely another analogy, and therefore not serious, it should
be remembered that alchemy itself, as conceived of by the
greatest theoreticians and practitioners, was as much an
analogical process as a direct one. It is perhaps this
peculiar and abstruse language of analogy that best explains
the basically poetic appeal of the alchemical tradition for
those of us who are not given to the tracking down of
images, to the revelations of one-to-one allusions. This
essay could equally well be called "The Language of Alchemy
as Poetry."

The analogical or linking process perceives every
element in all elements, as in the vision of Paracelsus:
"All things are concealed in all."[3] It unites part to
part in a subtle and profound conception of the "oneness
of otherness," of a final coincidence of fragments into
a whole: "Un le Tout" or "One the All" is the motto of
the serpent biting its tail in a circular continuity.

                    o u r o b o r o s

Mallarmé's book (<u>Le Livre</u>), like Duchamp's major work, his
<u>Grand Verre</u>--whose importance lies partly in the fact that
it can be <u>seen through</u>, as a sort of self-destroying myth--
these conceptual constructions are, to an even greater
degree than most art, holistic and ideal summaries aimed at
a possible transcendence of the particular, where the
specific detail is subsumed under a larger heading, the
latter almost partaking of the miraculous.

But Surrealism is certainly the literary movement
nearest to the alchemical project (the word "project" taken
here in the sense of throwing oneself forward, a risk under-

taken absolutely, at whatever cost, or not at all). Before
considering four individual examples of different stages of
the literary perception of alchemy, we should examine very
briefly the theory of Surrealism as it intersects with the
philosophical statements of the alchemists. If the alchemist is seen as an operator of the world's becoming, the admirable characteristics of the alchemical endeavor have
been seen as a parallel to the ideal qualities of the writer:
sacrifice, probity, the use of scrupulous method, and the
resolute practice of unlimited patience in order to accom-
plish the final work.[4] Nonetheless, these latter qualities
have a slightly puritanical ring to them, particularly in
regard to the stress laid on the work. How are we to reconcile them with the principle, accepted by both the Dadaists
and the Surrealists, of poetry as the spontaneous marvelous?

Tristan Tzara, for example, states categorically that
work is a German thing and therefore to be eschewed at all
costs in favor of Latin spontaneity, the ease in writing that
he compares to a fountain endlessly spurting forth in a
crystalline perfection, like Duchamp's urinal entitled
"Fontaine." For Breton as for Tzara, the only acceptable
literary work is neither literary (a bourgeois product manufactured for bourgeois exchange) nor worked (hence the value
of automatic writing, in spite of the reservations we should
place on that term in certain cases). Writing is meant to
show, like the poet's life, the pure spontaneous contours
of the crystal, so often praised by Breton, representing
movement stopped at top speed--that is, of the salt cube or
the diamond whose facets capture and reflect light, accepting the exterior within the interior to send it out once
more, purified and multiplied. The point sublime of the
Surrealists and, under other names, of the Dadaists--the
meeting of high and low, life and death, the dream and the
real (or, for Tzara, the simple junction of the yes and the
no)--is, like the mystic point of one of the philosophical
alchemists, the "sum total of all subsequent mirrors"; it is
thus to be compared with the crystal as that state of trans-

parency in which the conjunction of opposites plays out its
most brilliant union, where matter exists but can be seen
through, where spirit and intellect overcome opacity in the
privileged place of luminous and transmuted vision, intensi-
fied because condensed into a center of the smallest conceivable magnitude. The crystal tends toward centrality, or,
as Bachelard puts it, the salt crystal is the form-giving
principle, source of the geometric contexture of things; it
represents, he says, "matter dreaming toward its center"
(ibid., p. 294). And in the collective myth of literature
as alchemical undertaking, the crystal in its complexity and
transparency is at once jewel and conductor of light, end
and passage, goal of the cosmic reverie and operator of
perfect understanding.

      Now for those who still believe, against heavy odds, in
the text as its own perfection, it is clear that this discussion has been focused so far not just on the crystal but on
the possibility of poetry. "It is the light only that can be
truly multiplied," says Thomas Vaughan, "for this ascends to,
and descends from the first fountain of multiplication and
generation."[5] The endless facets of the diamond as they fix
and then diffuse the light streaming through them are the
source of multiple understanding, collective illumination,
and universal transmutation.

      Only a dialectical apparatus can explore alchemy,
Bachelard reminds us. If we are attached above all to the
single, the simple, and the gentle interplay of nuance, to
unitary theories or ideologies and water-color landscapes,
then the violent initial clashes productive of energy, the
battle of double with double, fire with mercury, volatile
element with fixed, male with female, will seem needlessly
melodramatic, just as the deliberately provoked confrontations of verbal opposites, adjective against opposite adjective as recommended by the futurists, the Dadaists, and the
Surrealists will appear needlessly destructive of textual
calm, of intellectual tranquility and spiritual assurance.

      To follow the ambiguous way of language working itself
out as knowledge--a way corresponding to the ambivalent

processes of alchemy--we must not refuse at any point a full
participation in the stages of the road, even as it leads
over the chasm Breton deliberately seeks, toward which his
whole attitude is an _attente_, an impassioned waiting. The
most trivial fact can become a _fait-précipice_, he warns;
there are no railings to the bridge over the abyss, and the
most heroic among us will be tempted to turn back. Poetry
may lead--has often led--to madness and to self-destruction;
it may, on occasion, also lead to the crystalline center of
the labyrinth, but from there, the outward passage may be
invisible. The vessel of language, alchemical or literary,
is closed by a hermetic seal--as in the famous statement:
"Occultons le surréalisme" or in the title _Arcane 17_--but
in the same fashion as the athanor or the furnace was connected to the tower, the vessels are seen as communicating
(_Les Vases communicants_), at least at the beginning.

It is, of course, from the beginning that we must take
the path, as initiates, and from a specific point. The marvelous synthesis as it is worked by means of the furnace or
the egg (wherein the transmutation by fire and the fecundity
of mercury are joined, a process for which Paracelsus allows
exactly nine months) depends also on the concept of the humid
fire. Water most favors transformation, metaphorically suitable for the fluidity of vision that enables the metamorphosis of element into element: "All the operation takes
place in our water,"[6] Paracelsus reminds us. The alchemical
imagination brings about the mental transmutation of the
universe by a rearrangement of its categories. Here
Surrealism's muse is also the muse of alchemy. Melusina,
who is at once fairy and mermaid, woman and child, _soror_ to
the alchemists and mistress, virgin priestess, and principle
of fecundity, poses the irrational miracle against a world
petrified into a mold of rational stability. Over Melusina,
says Breton, time holds no sway; the real end of alchemy and
of the literary work we are identifying with it is the
freeing of the spirit from the bond of time. Melusina is
the magnesia of Paracelsus, stone and no stone, sperm and
secret water met as one, a middle nature and a meditation,

an aerial substance to be found everywhere and at all sea-
sons. Patron muse of the Surrealist imagination, she is also
the dreaming child of Surrealist texts, worker of magic, way
from thought to action of from the interior to the exterior,
giver of language and the only one who sings after the language of men dies out. She is the soul of the world as it
is written under the sign of anima, the dreaming principle
as opposed to the animus of male rationality: if Hermes,
messenger of the gods, is also the inspirer of the closed
doctrine, the Melusina, muse of poets, is the inspirer of
language.

II. Language and Enigma
Alchemical language, meant both to hide and to reveal, is
based on plurality and enigma, often a double image of a
double significance--alchemical books are written without
and within, and examples of Surrealist word play can be read
from both sides, for similar effect. An alchemical text is
at once a manual of practice, an allegory for the initiate,
and a complicated vessel covered in code; like the outer sarcophagus hiding the inner sarcophagus, its mystery is both
apparent and profound. Here the microcosm of the alchemical
text responds perfectly to the macrocosm of the world beyond,
and enigma flourishes into revelation, if only for some.
Paracelsus speaks for the latter: "According to this, each
person, by his own mental grasp, can choose out for himself
a better way and Art, and therein find truth, for the man
who follows up a thing intently does find the truth" (ibid.).
It is understood that those of inferior intelligence will
not be able to interpret the writing on the stone, and to
the impure or the undialectical in spirit, those to whom it
has not been given to see, the responses of the apprentice
or the adept may seem not only impenetrable but idle.
     The point is, of course, that within the characteristic
formulae apparently penetrable or translatable into actual
directions lies another more spiritual formula, which few of
us will ever be able to interpret, since the language is
closed off, and with it the way. Cyrano de Bergerac tells

us of a book without pages or characters, and it is this book that we would have to learn to read.

Two warnings should be heeded: the first, from Artephius, being a mild reprimand directed at those who would try to penetrate the text: "Poor idiot, could you be so simple-minded as to believe that we shall teach you clearly and openly the greatest and most important of secrets, and to take our words literally?"[7] The second warning, graver because it is directed at our whole quest for knowledge, reminds us that there is, after understanding, no way out. For Ethan Allen Hitchcock, a nineteenth-century philosopher of alchemy, the threat is interior: "Should man ever attain to the internal intuition of his whole being, he would be swallowed up and consumed in himself."[8] As in cabalistic writing, and as in the enigma of the cycle represented by the self-swallowing serpent, the end is devoured by its beginning, the text consumes itself in its saying, and code becomes knowledge so that the sign is the signified.

In the most frequent enigmas, the question is simply avoided or the elements are hidden within a formula so that the listener is derouted and the hermetic remains hermetic. René Alleau points out that the "initiable" reader confined himself to not understanding, whereas the profane reader, believing in his own understanding, interpreted the contradictions, arbitrary values, and useless passwords according to their surface meaning or their easiest interpretation and was therefore never able to understand. Two main principles should be followed in reading the enigmas: secret or sacred terms must not be confused with ordinary borrowings, and it must be recognized that any merely chemical interpretation is false from beginning to end. Endless examples could be given of enigmatic writing, for example, of texts written backward, of the confusion by supplementary letter and by code. But of more linguistic and even poetic interest are the formulas made to conceal by ellipsis, by randomness, by disguise.

Wonk llew ouy rettam taht ekat (Take that matter you well know)

M. the axothi aoefth epuhiloqosophersa lisati ptheiruri imeracurety (the axoth of the philosophers is their mercury)

VISITA INTERIORA TERRA, RECTIFICANDO INVENIES OCCULTUM LAPIDEM (Visit the Bowels of the Earth, in Order that You May Come Upon the Hidden Stone by Rectification)

Ongra netigilluk ende firseigli (through filtration after resolution in distilled vinegar).[9]

Often the deliberate vagueness verges on humor for those of us who look from without. For example, Rhazis says, "Take of some unknown thing any quantity that you wish."[10] Morienus is only slightly more helpful.

Scion of the true doctrine, I bid you congeal (crystallize) mercury. From several things make 2, 3 and 3, 1, 1 with 3 is 4, 3, 2, and 1. From 4 to 3 there is 1; from 3 to 4 there is 1, thus 1 and 1, 3, and 4; from 3 to 1, there is 2, from 2 to 3 there is 1, from 3 to 2, 1, 1, 1, 2 and 3. And 1, 2 from 2 and 1, 1 from 1 to 2, 1 thus 1. I have told you all.[11]

Of course I am not pretending that the numbers mean nothing, but simply trying to show, by means of that absurd and brilliant conclusion, "I have told you all," what there is about the style of alchemical language that fascinates students of literature. Little wonder that the enigmas produce such results as these: René Alleau tells of Ali ibn Abdan, who knew a madman given to raving all day long and praying all night long. "How long," he asked the madman, "have you been mad?" "Ever since I have known" [sic].[12] Clearly, this response, seemingly incomplete (known _what_?) has the same quality to it as the enigmas; it is, in short, a perfect answer, as the answers given in the Short Catechism of Alchemy of Paracelsus are perfect. They completely avoid the question.

Q.   What is the pass-word of Magnesia?
A.   You know whether I can or should answer: I
     reserve my speech.

Q.   Give me the greeting of the Philosopher.
A.   Begin; I will reply to you.
Q.   Are you an apprentice Philosopher?
A.   My friends, and the wise, know me.[13]

For a less sophisticated answer, we can consider the
reply made to the telling of a myth recounted by Arnauld
of Villanova. A mother, penitent and washed of sins, gives
birth to a sinning son. Signs appear in the sun and the
moon warning her to chastise this son, to put him in bed,
then in cold water, then in the bed once more until he comes
to his senses, and to give him then to the Jews to crucify.
Thereupon the sun is crucified and no moon is to be seen,
the curtain of the temple is torn, an earthquake leads to a
great fire, which in its turn delivers up a spirit "about
whom everyone had been wrong." To this the response of the
listener was, understandably: "Master, I do not understand."[14] (It might be of interest to compare that myth
with some of the myths that Lévi-Strauss analyzes for us.)

Here is part of another, in which the generation of the
myth by the code of color is at work: "Now, as I was going
on a trip, I saw with admiration a field laborer, grave and
modest, clothed in a grey coat, with a black ribbon on his
hat, a white scarf wound about his neck, wearing a yellow
belt and shod in red boots." (J. Hutin, loc. cit.)

                           *
                        *   *

Now the sublime point of the Surrealists and the
mystics is the enigma resolved and crystallized, "Solve et
coagula," wherein the alchemical motto joins with the
visionaries' creed of unity stated in The Emerald Table of
Hermes Trismegistus: "What is below is as what is above,
and what is above is as what is below; by these things are
brought about the miracle of one single thing."[15] The
closure of the poem from the outside intensifies the dialectical energy within, until the text opens the way to be
explored, itself key and path, expansion and endless unfold-
ing, the passage at whose conclusion the beginning recom-
mences. Meeting of text and doctrine, action and linguistic

enigma, this transparent and perpetual mirage where matter
is endlessly consumed and transmuted, the poem is a mandala
for our private meditation, the labyrinth leading to an
interior crystal.

III. The Poem as Mandala

The enigmatic remains so. The crystal corridors of Dada
and the glass dwelling of Surrealism are in no way to be
confused with a common openness, the separateness of this
lower heaven, as Paracelsus calls alchemy, maintains always
its difference. Moreover, most crucial and most difficult
dogma, the void remains void, no matter what paths, textual
or practical, are stretched across it. "To people space in
covering over emptiness is to find the path of emptiness."[16]
To the ancient Mexicans, says Artaud, the will to make emptiness mature was the supreme science of space (of which the
Code laid down the rules); the Mexicans saw the spirit placed
in the center of space so that a cross would grow around it.

The poem might be compared to that placing of the self
in the center of space so that emptiness may mature into a
mandala, a pattern at once recuperating the void and preserving it. The mandala is also a crystal, perfection in
complexity, transparent condensation and source fecund with
light, the stone become passage or the verbal vessel transformed into the grail, transcendent yet interior object of
contemplation. Melusina and Hermes, the alchemist of the
closed vessel and the poet of a closed or circular poetry,
clear and enigmatic representation, the path also the goal,
all these opposites meet on the ground of alchemy, which is
one of the privileged places of the poem. Paracelsus in his
definitions is one of the best of poets: to deny to the
following description of the philosopher's stone the name of
prose poem one would have to be insensitive to the language
and the deepest conceptions of the poetic attitude. Here he
speaks of the Stone of the Philosophers:

It is the one thing, proclaimed by veritable philosophers, which overcomes all, is itself overcome by

nothing, searches heart and body, penetrates everything
stony and solid, strengthens all things delicate, and
establishes its own power on the opposition of that
which is most hard. It is the way of truth . . .
rectifying and transmuting that which is no more into
that which it was before conception, even into something better, and that which is not into that which
it ought to be.[17]

Briefly the main attributes of the surrealist poem that might
justify its comparison with the alchemical understanding are
the following--and a case could be made for the application
of these to much contemporary poetry:

1.   The opposed elements struggle against each other
toward a final synthesis, described as crystalline in its
transparency, golden in its quality as a source of light,
unique in its power to multiply and to extend. So the poem
is based on tension and aimed at the final expanded perception of a luminous sensitivity.

2.   The simplicity and innocence of Melusina provoke
the complexity of the dialectical process of transmutation;
Grillot de Givry describes the vessel of the alchemical
work: "A single substance, a single vase!"[18] So the poem
is at once single and complex, tending toward its center.

3.   The enigmatic writing on the philosophical stone
is the agent of knowledge, as the book, written outside and
in, is open to believers, yet hermetically sealed. So
Bonnefoy's _Pierre écrite_ or written stone is the page of
signs, and the poem, which Artaud calls an agent of nervous
illumination, moves from interior to exterior while remaining in the same place.[19]

4.   The alchemical substance is consumed by itself,
acts and is acted upon, is the end as well as the passage.
Pierre de Touche explains, "The substance sought is the same
as that from which one must extract it."[20] So the poem is,
finally, a text turning about its own language and about
itself as subject.

5.   Alchemy, like poetry, depends on a synchronicity
of consciousness, a unity of vision through strife and an
enigmatic apartness: "Careful lest your eggshell break, be

cracked, let air pass through, for otherwise you will do
nothing of worth" (ibid., p. 199).

*
*   *

Finally, we might illustrate four attitudes toward the
alchemical work held by very different contemporary poets
all associated at one time with Surrealism, and marked by
its intimate relation to what Rimbaud called the "alchemy
of the word."

For Artaud, poetry is the knowledge of the dynamic
interior destiny of thought, as alchemy is a direct meta-
phor, a justification of a sort of metaphysical theatre of
the mind. The language here is deliberately theatrical, of
an analogical intensity on the brink of violence, where the
images conflict in chaos before the fiery purification,
destruction leading eventually to spiritual sublimation in
the strict sense--that is, an ascent. Artaud's <u>Alchemical</u>
<u>Theatre</u> is to be seen as the representational double of a
real operation, a mirror of the absent undertaking; it could
be called the Theatre of Alchemical Poetry.

> . . . Projections and precipitations of conflicts,
> indescribable battles of principles joined from
> that dizzying ane slippery perspective in which
> every truth is lost in the realization of the inex-
> tricable and unique fusion of the abstract and the
> concrete . . . to resolve by conjunctions unimagin-
> ably strange to our waking minds, to resolve or even
> annihilate every conflict produced by the antagonism
> of matter and mind, idea and form, concrete and
> abstract, and to dissolve all appearances into one
> unique expression which must have been the equivalent
> of spiritualized gold.[21]

Breton represents this point of view most clearly; such
poems as his "Union libre" (or the free union of opposites)
offer a serious object of alchemical study. The collection
"L'Air de l'eau," also to be read as a word play on the
"L'Ere de l'eau," the era of metamorphosis of which Aragon
speaks, since water is the privileged place of metamor-
phosis--or as The Era of Air of O, the circle in the latter
title alluding to the continuity we have examined, here,

with emptiness at its center. The collection exemplifies a
series of explicit and implicit allegories related to the
alchemy of the word, of which we take only two examples.
First, the poem beginning "Je rêve" recounts what may be
interpreted as an alchemical dream, where a crescent moon
is identified with the crescent diamond worn by the woman
who combs her hair with a wing of water. Like a Melusina
both fairy and child, she calls forth an imagery of transposition and understated possibilities:

> Je rêve je te vois superposée indéfiniment à toi-même
> Tu es assise sur le haut tabouret de corail
> Devant ton miroir toujours à son premier quartier
> Deux doigts sur l'aile d'eau du peigne
> Et en même temps
> Tu reviens de voyage tu t'attardes la dernière
>   dans la grotte
> Ruisselante d'éclairs
> . . .
> Et la même
> Enfant
> Prise dans un soufflet de paillettes
> . . .
> (I dream I see your image indefinitely superposed
>   upon yourself
> You are seated on the high coral stool
> Before your mirror always in its first quarter
> Two fingers on the water wing of the comb
> And at the same time
> You come back from a trip you linger last in the grotto
> Streaming with sparks
> . . .
> And still the same
> Child
> Caught in a bellows of spangles
> . . .)

Aerial and lunar images converge with the element of water,
while in the poet's vision, the grotto serves as the source
for the transformation, marked by the phosphorescent union
of water and brilliance, then shown to be a child's game at
its highest point, where the prisoner of the game is also
the magician: for the operation of rope-jumping brings
forth the apparition of the marvelous--the only green
butterfly frequenting Asian mountains. This unique marvel
responds to the infinite original superposition of the

vision of Melusina.

The second text begins as with a legend: "On me dit
que là-bas. . . ." In that far-off land, none the less
legendary for our knowing that is Ténérife, beaches black
from volcanic lava are transformed by a "second" and miraculous sunlight into a landscape of light where matter or
evil and original sin are burned out into a time of lumino-
sity, and of "afterwards" in which expansion of outline is
infinite, and images of land flower outward into the images
of sea. The last line shows the final result of the transmutation, from the "plages . . . noires" to the radiant
totality of a tripartite image:

> Tout le pommier en fleur de la mer.
> (All the flowering apple tree of the sea.)

This convergence of elements reminds us of another
of Breton's greatest poems, "Sur la route qui monte et qui
descend," which concerns a luminous fire, invoked by the
poet as a guide to the path of transmutation--of elements,
language, and the speaking voice. The route is the poem
itself, which ends by a final invocation to the operation
of supreme convergence, where the conjunctio oppositorum
is doubly realized:

> Flamme d'eau guide-moi jusqu'à la mer de feu.
> (Flame of water lead me to the sea of fire.)

This conclusion responds perfectly to the surrealist quest
of the "sublime point," a transmutation of vision realized
within the mind, like a golden center always sought: "Point
de l'esprit d'où la vie et la mort, le réel et l'imaginaire,
le passé et le futur, le communicable et l'incommunicable,
le haut et le bas cessent d'être perçus contradictoirement."
(A point in the mind from which life and death, the real and
the imaginary, the past and the future, the communicable and
the incommunicable, the high and the low are no longer per-
ceived as contradictory.) (Second manifeste.)

In Paul Eluard, the imagery of solar light, multiplication, and birth is clear but mingled. What basic alchemical impetus there might have been is absorbed into the general theme of this poetry, which is outward movement toward total light, from the cave of darkness and misunderstanding toward comprehension. It is a matter only of using certain reverberations of imagery, a certain vocabulary, the opposite, if one looks closely, of the complicated and extensive use of alchemical imagery made by such artists as Duchamp.

> Nous approchons
> Dans les forêts
> Prenez la rue du matin
> Montez les marches de la brume
>
> Nous approchons
> La terre en a le coeur crispé
> Encore un jour à mettre au monde.
>   . . .
>
> Le ciel s'élargira
> Nous en avions assez
> D'habiter dans les ruines du sommeil
> . . .
>
> Et je ne suis pas seul
> Mille images de moi multiplient ma lumière
> . . .
>
> L'or éclate de rire de se voir hors du gouffre
> L'eau le feu se dénudent pour une seule saison
> Il n'y a plus d'éclipse au front de l'univers
> . . .
>
> Le prisme respire avec nous
> Aube abondante
> . . .
>
> Des enfances persistantes
> Hors de toutes les cavernes
> Hors de nous-mêmes.
>   . . .
>
> (We draw nearer
> In the forests
> Take the street of morning
> Climb the steps of mist
> . . .
>
> We draw nearer
> The earth is impatient
> Once more a day to be born.
>   . . .

```
          The sky will open out
          We were tired
          Of living in the ruins of sleep
          . . .

          And I am not alone
          A thousand of my images multiply my light
          . . .

          The gold laughs to find itself outside the chasm
          Water fire bare themselves for a single season
          There is no more eclipse on the forehead of the
               universe.
          . . .

          The prism breathes with us
          Abundant dawn
          . . .

          Lasting childhoods
          Outside all caves
          Outside ourselves.)22
```

   The poetry of René Char, itself a closed vase to which
the scattered and hermetic references are only temporary
keys, best represents what is here called the alchemy of
the poem as mandala. (See, for instance, his series of complicated prose poems called Abondance viendra, whose alchemical meaning becomes clear upon multiple re-readings.)23
Furthermore, like a condensation leading toward an interior
unifying perception, his aphorisms can each be called a poem,
and each is a source of multiplication and luminous extension, retaining the definite ambiguity of poetic language in
its multilayered meaning as a convergence suddenly situated
on the brink of silence.

```
     "Sans doute, un poème se passant la nuit doit-il être
     lapidé de vers-luisants. Mais un autre allant le jour?
     Père amant, voyez-nous jouir, très éprises, le fleuret
     d'un miroir dans les doigts." (Doubtless a poem pass-
     ing by at night must be stoned with glow worms. But
     another, traveling in daylight? Father and lover, see
     us exulting and exalted, the fencing foil of a mirror
     in our hands.)24
```

   The alchemical path from which there is no returning
leads to the word, but in its turn that word opens on the
inside onto an empty space that is the true interior crystal.

In a brilliant confusion of presence and absence, the
junction of doubles and enigmas make a light, complicated,
and transparent construction, where the Idea is finally
identical with the void. Picabia's definition of the
infinite may be seen as describing the place and the trans-
cendency of poetry at the heart of the verbal labyrinth:
"Two mirrors placed across from each other, in emptiness."[25]

The mandala of the poem interchanges void and crystal
in a perpetual transmutation whose object is hidden within
the text, far removed from common gold and difficult of
access even for the true believers, or the truest readers.
But for them also, the long struggle which one of the
deepest of contemporary poets, Yves Bonnefoy, calls "Le
Dialogue d'angoisse et du désir" leads at last to a path
burned and lacerated, but lucid, towards a central light,
a path not of legendary time only but of here and now:

        Ici, nous allons,
        Où nous avons appris l'universel langage,

        Ouvre-toi, parle-nous, déchire-toi
        Couronne incendiée, battement clair,
        Ambre du coeur solaire.[26]

        (Here, we are moving,
        where we have learned the universal tongue,

        Open, speak to us, tear apart now
        Crown consumed, bright beating,
        Amber of the solar heart.)

Notes

1. Becher, "Physica Subterranea," in M. Caron and
S. Hutin, The Alchemists (New York: Grove), p. 79. (All
English translations of French texts are mine.)

2. "Our gold is not the common gold."

3. The Hermetic and Alchemical Writings of Paracelsus,
ed. A. E. Waite (New Hyde Park: University Books, 1967),
I, 5.

4. Gaston Bachelard, La Terre et les rêveries de la
volonté (Paris: Corti, 1948), p. 327.

5. Thomas Vaughan, Anima Magica Abscondita, in
Paracelsus, op. cit., p. 351.

6. Paracelsus, op. cit., I, 16.

7. Artephius (Al-Toghrâi), in The Alchemists, p. 133.

8. Ethan Allen Hitchcock, Remarks on Alchemy and the Alchemists, indicating a method of discovering the true nature of hermetic philosophy, and of showing that the search after the philosophers' sonte had not for its object the discovery of an agent for the transmutation of metals (Boston: Crosby, Nichols, and Co., 1857).

9. From The Alchemists, from Hutin, L'Alchimie, and from Grillot de Givry.

10. In Guillaume Louis Figuier, L'Alchimie et les alchimistes: Essai critique sur la philosophie hermétique (Paris: 1859), p. 58.

11. From La Tourbe des philosophes, quoted in Figuier, op. cit., p. 42.

12. René Alleau, Aspects de l'alchimie, p. 149.

13. Paracelsus, op. cit., "A Short Lexicon of Alchemy," II, 351-55.

14. In Figuier, op. cit., p. 42.

15. In Marguerite de Surany, L'Alchimie: Du visible à l'invisible (Paris: Presses de l'Echiquier, 1967), p. 195. (My translation.)

16. Antonin Artaud, Oeuvres complètes (Paris: Gallimard, 1970), VII, 164. (My translation.)

17. Paracelsus, op. cit., II, 381.

18. In Grillot de Givry and Emile Angelo, A Pictorial Anthology of Witchcraft, Magic, and Alchemy (New York: n.p., n.d.), p. 378.

19. Artaud, op. cit., VII, 164.

20. René Alleau, Aspects de l'alchimie traditionnelle (Paris: Minuit, 1953), p. 195.

21. Antonin Artaud, "The Alchemical Theatre," in The Theatre and its Double, trans. (New York: Grove Press, 1958), p. 46.

22. Paul Eluard, "Sans âge," in Cours naturel, 1937, Oeuvres complètes, Bibl. de la Pléiade (Paris: Gallimard, 1962), pp. 799-800. Discussed in my Poetry of Dada and Surrealism (Princeton, 1970), pp. 146-51.

23. Analyzed in my Presence of René Char (Princeton University Press, 1976) in the "Cycle of Alchemy," pp. 134-45.

24. René Char, Moulin premier, in Le Marteau sans maître, (Paris: Corti, 1970), p. 138. For another poem relating to alchemy, by a younger poet but in the same tone as many of Char's writings, compare Jacques Dupin's "Coagula solve," from Gravir (Gallimard, 1963):

Il enferme l'eau dans sa tour. Une roue d'ombre
tourne sur son front. Il gagne le point culminant du
regard. Il fortifie ses noces solitaires. Il se
dénude par le rire. Il affronte midi-en-armes.

. . .

Contre l'or intérieur est échangée l'eau rare.
Virant avec lenteur de l'orage au velours, il rentre
        dans le jeu.
L'harmonie alors, à jamais!

(He confines the water in his tower. A wheel
of shadow turns on his forehead. He wins the highest
summit of the outlook. He fortifies his solitary
nuptials. He bares himself by laughter. He faces
noontime at arms.

. . .

For the inner gold rare water is exchanged.
Slowly swerving from storm to velvet, he gets back in
        the game.
Then, forever, harmony.)

25. In the single issue of La Pomme de pin.

26. "Le Dialogue d'angoisse et du désir," in Hier
régnant désert (Paris: Mercure de France, 1958).

Herman BRAET. Chargé de cours, Séminaire de littérature médiévale (Romanica), Université de Louvain.

Glyn BURGESS. Lecturer, Department of French, University of Liverpool, England.

Mary Ann CAWS. Professor of Romance Languages and Comparative Literature, Hunter College and Graduate Center, C.U.N.Y.

Barbara M. CRAIG. Professor of French and Chairman, Department of French and Italian, University of Kansas, Lawrence.

Willa B. FOLCH-PI. Associate Academic Dean, Jackson College, and Lecturer, Department of Romance Languages, Tufts University.

Charlotte F. GERRARD. Associate Professor, Department of French and Italian, Indiana University, Bloomington.

James F. HAMILTON. Associate Professor of French, Department of Romance Languages and Literatures, University of Cincinnati.

William L. HENDRICKSON. Associate Professor of French, Arizona State University, Tempe.

Douglas KELLY. Professor of French, University of Wisconsin, Madison.

William W. KIBLER. Associate Professor of French, University of Texas, Austin.

Donald MADDOX. Andrew Mellon Assistant Professor of Medieval Studies, Brandeis University, Waltham, Mass.

Diana T. MERIZ. Associate Professor of French and Italian, University of Pittsburgh.

Daniel POIRION. Professeur de Civilisation Médiévale, Institut de Littérature Française, Université de Paris IV Sorbonne.

A. R. PRESS. Senior Lecturer, Department of French and Romance Philology, The Queen's University of Belfast, Northern Ireland.

Nathaniel B. SMITH. Assistant Professor of French and Provençal, University of Georgia, Athens.

Leo WEINSTEIN. Professor of French, Stanford University, California.

Friederike WIESEMANN-WIEDEMANN. Assistant Professor of
    Foreign Languages, Northeastern Illinois State Univer-
    sity, Chicago.

Harry F. WILLIAMS. Professor of Modern Languages, Florida
    State University, Tallahassee.